Remembering Glenn Gould

Remembering Glenn Gould:
Twenty Interviews With People Who Knew Him

Colin Eatock

PENUMBRA PRESS

Copyright © Colin Eatock 2012; except pp. 126-142 © copyright Colin Eatock and John Roberts 2012 (printed with permission).

Published by Penumbra Press
Printed and bound in Canada

No part of this publication may be reproduced, stored in a retrieval system or transmitted, in any form or by any means, without the prior written consent of the publisher or a licence from The Canadian Copyright Licensing Agency (Access Copyright). For an Access Copyright licence, call toll free to 1-800-893-5777 or visit www.accesscopyright.ca.

Cover and Frontispiece Photos by Don Hunstein, courtesy of Sony Classical and Glenn Gould Limited.

LIBRARY AND ARCHIVES CANADA CATALOGUING IN PUBLICATION

Eatock, Colin, 1958-
    Remembering Glenn Gould : twenty interviews with people who knew him / Colin Eatock, editor. -- 1st ed.

(Archives of Canadian arts, culture, and heritage)
Includes bibliographical references.
ISBN 978-1-897323-20-5

1. Gould, Glenn, 1932-1982.
2. Pianists--Canada--Biography.
3. Interviews--Canada.

I. Title.
II. Series: Archives of Canadian arts, culture & heritage

ML417.G69E14 2012   786.2092   C2012-903478-9

CONTENTS

Acknowledgements vii

Introduction
Would the Real Glenn Gould Please Stand Up?   ix

Chapter 1: Working for Mr. Gould
Introduction   1
Walter Homburger: the Discreet Manager   3
Verne Edquist: Gould's Piano Man   13
Stephen Posen: Gould's Lawyer   21
Ray Roberts: the Loyal Assistant   29

Chapter 2: The Musicians Speak
Introduction   37
Stuart Hamilton: a Portrait of the Young Artist   38
John Beckwith: Alberto Guerrero's Studio   46
Ezra Schabas: Gould in Stratford   53
Anton Kuerti: Pianist to Pianist   60
Jaime Laredo: an Artistic Partner   66
Timothy Maloney: Gould in Decline   72

Chapter 3: Microphone and Camera
Introduction   83
Andrew Kazdin: Behind the Microphone   85
John McGreevy: Documenting Gould's Toronto   93
Vincent Tovell: Gould on TV   101
Margaret Pacsu: a Kindred Spirit   111
Lorne Tulk: the Brother Gould Never Had   118
John P.L. Roberts: Gould on the Radio and in Life   126

Chapter 4: Two Personal Relationships
Introduction   143
Robert Fulford: the Boy Next Door   144
Cornelia Foss: a Woman in Gould's Life   153

Chapter 5: Writing about Gould
Introduction   161
William Littler: the Critic Downstairs   162
Tim Page: a Special Bond   171

Index   179
About the Author   189

Acknowledgements

First and foremost, I must thank the twenty fascinating people who shared their personal memories and insights with me. There's no need for me to name them here, or explain the nature of their contributions: they all appear on the Contents page, and their contributions form the substance of this book. All were generous with their time and with their memories, and I am in their debt for their helpfulness with this project.

Less obvious to the reader was the invaluable assistance I received from Faye Perkins of the Glenn Gould Estate, for her assistance with contacting and setting up meetings with many of my interview subjects.

CE

Introduction: Would the Real Glenn Gould Please Stand Up?

"Why another book about Glenn Gould?"

I was asked this question on several occasions in the last two years, as I prepared *Remembering Glenn Gould*. And it's a question I've asked often myself.

Certainly the abundance of Gouldiana in the world might suggest that the topic of Canada's most famous concert pianist has been dealt with exhaustively. There are several biographies, collections of essays, commentaries on his playing, inquiries into his philosophical views, books of photographs, scholarly dissertations, and countless magazine and newspaper articles.

Remembering Glenn Gould is as much a book about Gould's friends and associates as it is about Gould himself. Here, the people in Gould's circle are placed in the foreground, and their voices are heard in a direct and essentially unmediated way, in a collection of "Q&A" interviews. (I'll say more later about the way in which these interviews were conducted.) *Remembering Glenn Gould* isn't a biography: in fact, it assumes that the reader will already have some knowledge of Gould's life and achievements. Rather, it is an exploration Gould's life and art through the eyes and ears of those who knew him.

Like many others who have written about Gould, there were certain issues that I personally wanted to investigate. In what ways did Gould's Torontonian-ness and his Canadian-ness form him? How and why did he rise to fame so dramatically? What effect did he have on the musical life of Canada and the world? What was the makeup of his character and the state of his mental health? And why, thirty years after his death, are so many people still so fascinated with him? My inquiries have led me to some tentative conclusions.

One of the first things I learned was that Gould surrounded himself with some very interesting people. Without exception, they are all smart, engaging and open minded (to get along with Gould, they pretty much had to be). Some are prominent figures, musically or for other reasons, while others haven't led the kind of lives that attract public attention. But however their paths crossed with Gould's – and whatever they thought of him – he made a deep and vivid impression. (For this, I, who never met him or heard him perform, envy them.)

Like most other people, Gould harboured contradictions in his personality. In Walt Whitman's words, he was large and contained multitudes. But unlike most other people, these contradictions were extreme – and their extremity is revealed in the testimonies here. When presented as a list, the (apparent) inconsistencies in his character are bewildering.

Gould was friendly and charming, or he was an isolated misanthrope. He loved public attention, but he hated audiences. He was humble; he was egotistical. He was selfless; he was selfish. He was hard to work with; he was a good collaborator. He had a cool, rational mind; he was a bundle of superstitions and phobias. He was a profound thinker; his ideas were often naïve and sophomoric. He was clever and witty; his humour was forced and lame. He was unworldly and impractical; he was down-to-earth and businesslike. He was ingenuous and without guile in his dealings with the world; his public image was a deliberately contrived sham. He was a good and loyal friend; he used people and then discarded them. He was shy with women and shunned intimacy; he was an ardent heterosexual male. He was an austere Puritan; he was a sensualist and an ecstatic. He was a regular guy; he was as mad as a hatter.

Many of these views, and more still, may be found in these pages. Evidently, Gould was a chameleon, whose personality took on different "colours" with different people and in different contexts. (Think of the Woody Allen film *Zelig*.) As a result, there's no "one-stop shopping source" for explaining him. That a man with such a personality could have risen to such heights is perhaps surprising: not all eccentrics are successful people, and often they end up alienating others. Indeed, the indulgence he was granted by the musical world – to cancel engagements, program unfamiliar repertoire, and even to defy Leonard Bernstein's interpretive decisions – is simply astonishing.

Gould was lucky in other ways, as well. Of course, much of his "luck" was the sort that the Canadian humourist Stephen Leacock had in mind when he said, "I'm a great believer in luck, and I find that the harder I work the more I have of it." The young boy worked at the piano for so many hours a day that his mother had to *limit* the time he spent practising. But Gould was also fortunate enough to find himself in the right place at the right time – Toronto, Canada, in the middle of the twentieth century – and he was ready to take full advantage of it.

During the post-World War II era, Canada was buoyed up with a sense of national pride and optimism. And nowhere was this burgeoning confidence more strongly felt than in Toronto, the largest city in the English-speaking part of the country. When Gould was born, in 1931, Toronto was a provincial place, largely unknown beyond Canada's borders and still firmly attached to its British colonial roots. However, the city already had a good musical infrastructure in place: a professional orchestra, and a music conservatory that could provide instruction to the highest levels. Both institutions would recognize and foster Gould's talent.

By the late 1940s, when Gould began to emerge as a force to be reckoned with, Toronto had started to change. The city was rapidly expanding, immigrants were arriving from all over the world, and a "sky's-the-limit" mentality took hold. Toronto was wealthy, and its newfound self-esteem made bold ventures possible. Big ideas were in the air: should the city build a subway system, an elevated expressway or a large social housing project? Why not do it all?

Torontonians embraced Gould with the same "Why not do it all?" attitude. It mattered little, in this era of exciting new possibilities, that the city had never before produced a concert pianist of international stature. What did matter to Torontonians – very much to the young pianist's advantage – was that Gould was one of them. In a city used to concerts by visiting musicians with exotic accents and unpronounceable names, here was a native-born White Anglo-Saxon Protestant Canadian who was as good as any foreigner.

From Gould's earliest concert appearances, reviews in the local press glowed with high praise and hopeful predictions. "Glenn Gould, fifteen," reported *Globe and Mail* critic Colin Sabiston in 1947, "gave a recital at Eaton Auditorium last night which should qualify him for a place among ranking adult artists." Reviewing the same recital, Augustus Brindle of the *Toronto Star* declared, "This boy is on the road to pianistic fame." The critics, like so many other Torontonians, were unabashedly rooting for him.

Gould's favourable reception in the USA – beginning with his appearances at Washington's Phillips Gallery and New York's Town Hall, in 1955 – was glowingly reported in Toronto's newspapers. Similarly, Gould's 1957 tour of Russia was treated as a major news event. And by the end of the 1950s, scarcely a week went by without some Toronto paper publishing something about him. The press loved him – and he responded in kind, mastering the art of getting his picture in print.

Crucial to Gould's rising fame across Canada was the support he received from the Canadian Broadcasting Corporation. Gould made his first national broadcast on the CBC in 1950: he called the radio recital the beginning of his "love affair with the microphone," but it was also the beginning of Canada's love affair with him. As love affairs go, Gould's relationship with the CBC was impressively durable, continuing for the rest of his life – and sometimes taking directions that nobody would have predicted in 1950. And the feelings were mutual, with

Canada's state broadcaster giving Gould almost unlimited access to its staff and facilities.

The outpouring of civic and national support that Gould received made his hoped-for rise to international prominence into a civic and a national "cause." No other Canadian classical musician before or since Gould has enjoyed so much public support. Of course, Canadians always want a good return for their investments – so the nation that prepared and supported him expected impressive results. Yet the adoring nation had very little clout in the classical music world. When Gould stepped into the international arena, he had to rely on his own resources.

But what resources! Despite all the differing views of Gould found in the testimonials presented here, there's one thing everyone agrees on: Gould was not just absolutely brilliant but also strikingly original. As a pianist he had a distinctive style that is immediately recognizable. It was, of course, his interpretations of Bach that especially impressed listeners – poised midway between the delicate, precise pianism of Rosalyn Tureck and the rigours of the early music movement. Gould made Bach modern, infusing his keyboard music with an intensity that no pianist had yet achieved. Like a Canadian lake, his Bach was fresh, cool and crystal clear.

Gould recorded many other composers, as well. Mostly, he stuck to the Germanic "mainstream": starting from his beloved Bach, touching on Haydn, exploring his love-hate relationship with Mozart, delving into Beethoven, paying his respects to Brahms, and displaying a fascination with Wagner and Strauss (even though they produced little solo piano music). And at the modern end of his musical spectrum lay Arnold Schoenberg – a composer whose dissonant works are openly disdained by many listeners.

Occasionally Gould would deviate from his emphasis on Mittel-European music, to record Orlando Gibbons (testing the public's credulity by declaring him his favourite composer), or Domenico Scarlatti or the Canadian composer Jacques Hétu. However, prominent piano composers such as Chopin and Debussy are almost absent from his catalogue. Gould's tastes were broad – but he had his druthers, and generally stuck to them.

If all Glenn Gould had done with his life was to play the piano, he would still be remembered as a remarkable artist – by some people. Even the most celebrated musicians tend to fade from public consciousness after their deaths: today, yesteryear's piano giants, such as Alfred Cortot, Josef Hofmann and Benno

Moiseiwitsch, are of interest only to connoisseurs. But Gould's star remains high in the broader culture – and this, I'm convinced, is because he challenged orthodox thinking, both on stage and off.

From the outset, it was apparent that Gould was different, and had no qualms about being different. His stage mannerisms were unconventional and his technical approach to playing the piano – sitting low to the keys on his custom-built chair – was unique. In his interpretations he aspired to originality, and this became a kind of moral imperative for him. "I believe that the only excuse we have for being musicians," he observed, "and for making music in any fashion, is to make it differently – to perform it differently to establish the music's difference vis-à-vis our own difference."

His novel approach to concertizing was merely a harbinger of greater things to come. In 1964, when Gould made good on his promise to end his concert career and focus entirely on his recordings, he shook the music industry to its foundations. Gould changed forever the relationship between the musician and the recording, in ways that extended beyond classical music. (Two years later, the Beatles also stopped giving live performances.)

Rather than casting him into obscurity, Gould's withdrawal from the concert stage only added to his fame. He became the subject of a heated debate – a debate to which Gould himself was very much a party. As an essayist, his prose often fell victim to the over-reaching erudition of a high-school dropout trying to sound educated; yet he displayed a superior mind bursting with ideas in his articles and interviews. He went to great lengths to explain himself – more thoroughly and articulately than most artists could, or would.

His ongoing quest for new ways to express himself led to his radio "documentaries" for the CBC. Beginning in 1967 with *The Idea of North*, he pioneered a technique he called "contrapuntal radio": several speaking voices heard simultaneously, or fading in and out of each other. Broadcasters call this "cross talk," and consider it undesirable. Gould did it deliberately, and considered it a fine thing. His radio work was controversial, and some, like *Globe and Mail* critic John Kraglund, regarded his non-pianistic exploits as self-indulgent distractions from what he should have been doing with his talents. But his radio documentaries made the world see and hear Gould as more than "just" a pianist.

Moreover, there was an internal logic to his creative "digressions." Even if Gould the man was a jumble of contradictions, Gould the artist remained true and constant to his aesthetic ideals. As the philosopher Georges Leroux has eloquently argued, Gould's whole life was consumed by his own artistic values: whether playing the piano, writing polemical essays or hamming it up for the television cameras, his art claimed him entirely. In all that he did, he was unswervingly committed to the autonomy of the artist, and to spiritual and technical perfectionism as an artistic ideal.

Gould's untimely passing was the final cause of his enduring place in the world. While his unexpected death at the age of fifty could scarcely be called "fortunate," Gould was swept up in a "JFK syndrome": the sudden end to a great man's life at the height of his fame. The world decided then and there that it would not soon forget him, and thirty years later it stands by that decision.

Gould didn't succeed at everything he set out to do. His aspirations to be a composer never really got off the ground. And he turned to conducting too late in his life to establish a presence on the podium. But his was a life cut short – and we can only wonder what Gould would have done if he had lived for another twenty or thirty years. Would he have continued to push boundaries in music and other arts? Would he have abandoned the piano altogether? Would his fragile mental health have worsened to the point of breakdown? There's no way to answer these questions with certainty – but the questions themselves once again underscore the contradictions in Gould's character. Ask twenty people who knew him, and you'll get twenty different answers.

All of the people interviewed here knew Gould at some point in their lives: some for days and others for decades. Most were only too happy to participate in the creation of this book, a few needed to be persuaded for various reasons, and only one person I approached declined to be interviewed. Some looked upon the format I've adopted – Q&A transcriptions – as an opportunity to demythologize Gould and "set the record straight," with regard to their own opinions. I hope I have helped them to achieve this goal.

Almost all the interviews were done in person. (The one exception is my interview with Andrew Kazdin, which was, at his request, conducted via a Skype connection from Toronto to Long Island.) In all cases, I relied on recording devices to help me accurately transcribe our conversations. While I attempted to remain as faithful as possible to the words and intentions of my interviewees, some editing was inevitably necessary. For this reason, I showed drafts of the edited transcripts to all interviewees, inviting them to make any changes or corrections – just in case I'd unintentionally misrepresented their ideas. And although all my subjects expressed themselves clearly, I have added explanatory notes wherever they might be helpful.

One of the things I was worried about as I was conducting these interviews was the possibility that a "law of diminishing returns" might come into effect, and the responses to my questions would grow repetitive. To avoid this problem, I carefully customized each interview, with as many unique questions as possible. However, even when I did ask several different people the same question, I found their answers to be fascinatingly different. The law of diminishing returns never raised its ugly head.

In part, the variety of the responses I received (even when I did ask the same question several times) was due to the diversity of my interviewees. However, a complex, multi-faceted spirit hovered over the enterprise, ensuring that the results of my research would be rich and rewarding, if not always consistent. As I said earlier, there is no "one-stop shopping source" for understanding Glenn Gould.

Colin Eatock
January 2012

Chapter 1: Working for Mr. Gould

Introduction

In Toronto, Glenn Gould surrounded himself with a hand-picked support network: a group of people who attended to his various professional and personal needs – and without whom he wouldn't have been able to function. Four of them are interviewed here: Walter Homburger, his concert manager; Verne Edquist, his piano tuner; Stephen Posen, his lawyer; and Ray Roberts, his personal assistant.

They each share their memories and thoughts about what it was like to work for Gould, in their various capacities. And in all cases, their proximity to Gould – a man who could be hard to approach – gave them privileged insights into Gould's ways of dealing with the world. To be sure, they saw his many eccentricities, but also his brilliance, respectfulness and generosity.

The first to know and work with Gould was Walter Homberger, who began a successful career in concert management with the Wunderkind pianist of Toronto. Even though Gould had no further need of a concert manager by 1964 (because he ceased to give live concerts), the two men remained friends.

Gould and Verne Edquist got off to a rocky start in 1962, when the piano tuner refused to work on Gould's old and dilapidated Chickering piano. However, the two men gradually came to respect and understand each other: in Edquist, Gould found a technician willing and able to accommodate his unconventional ideas, and his penchant for experimentation.

Stephen Posen became Gould's lawyer almost by chance, around the year 1970. (He's uncertain of the exact date.) Through Posen's interview we see a side of Gould that few others have: a shrewd businessman who knew how to act in his best financial interests. Posen's association with Gould continues to this day, through his legal work for the Gould Estate, and his association with the Glenn Gould Foundation.

Finally, of these four men, Ray Roberts probably had the closest view of Gould. His professional association with Gould began in 1970. Beginning with odd jobs, his work for Gould expanded into a wide variety of services and duties. And it was to Roberts that the responsibility fell, in 1982, of taking Gould to the hospital when he suffered his fatal stroke.

It's clear from the testimonials here that these men held (and continue to hold) Gould in the highest esteem. All speak warmly of their time spent with Gould as a special time in their own professional lives. And although other people (including some others interviewed for this book) have given accounts of being suddenly shunned or shut out of Gould's life, none of these four men experienced any such unpleasantness.

CE

Walter Homburger: the Discreet Manager

Walter Homburger was born into a musical family in Karlsruhe, Germany, in 1924, and immigrated to Canada in 1940, via England. Six years after his arrival in this country, he decided to become a promoter of classical musicians and concerts – and his first undertaking in this line of work was to manage the career of Glenn Gould. The Wunderkind pianist was just fourteen years old when Homburger began to represent him.

Homburger also founded International Artists Concert Agency, and brought such distinguished artists as Vladimir Horowitz, Itzhak Perlman, Luciano Pavarotti and Louis Armstrong to Canada. In 1962 he became General Manager of the Toronto Symphony Orchestra, a position he held for twenty-five years. Today he is semi-retired, and lives with his wife on a quiet North Toronto street. This interview took place in his home on October 31, 2008.

CE: Why did you decide to become a manager of classical musicians?

WH: I was rather cheeky, I guess. I'm not a musician myself – I can't read music. I just react like anybody else in the public, but I seem to have a good sense about it.

CE: And how did you become Glenn Gould's manager?

WH: I first heard Glenn Gould at the Toronto Kiwanis Festival: he performed Beethoven's *Fourth Piano Concerto*, with Alberto Guerrero on the second piano. In those days I had a lot of time and I enjoyed going to these things. And when this kid came out and played the *Fourth Beethoven Concerto*, I said to myself, "This can't be possible."

I went backstage and met Glenn, and said I'd love to meet his parents. Soon afterwards, I went to the Goulds' home at 32 Southwood Drive, in the Beaches, and told his parents that I wanted to manage their son. This was in 1946, and at that time I was twenty-two years old. My theory was that if I was right and Glenn was as good as I thought he was, then he would get a great career going. People would find out who his manager was and send me a telegram or give me a phone call.

CE: How did Gould's parents react to this proposal?

WH: They were very kind, and said, "Sure, go ahead." His father was a furrier with a store on the second floor of the King Edward Hotel, and his mother was a piano teacher.

CE: *When you became his manager, did many people already know about Gould?*

WH: In Canada, a lot of people knew him, because he had already played in public several times.[1] I'm not sure that he had given concerts very far across Canada at that point, but he was well known in Toronto.

CE: *Initially, how did you work with Gould?*

WH: If I remember correctly, we wrote up a biography: we printed a leaflet, with a picture of him on front, and the bio on the back, and we mailed it out to concert presenters. We began to get some responses. Of course Canada was in the forefront of interest, because people already knew about him.

CE: *Gould's first international success was a recital at the Phillips Gallery in Washington, in 1955. How did you secure this engagement?*

WH: It was just by writing to the gallery, and following up with a phone call. They were interested in introducing young, up-and-coming artists, so Glenn fit in with their programing. Paul Hume, the critic, was there and wrote an absolutely rave review.[2]

CE: *What can you tell me about your management style in the early days? What was your role?*

WH: I told him that it wasn't going to be easy, in the beginning, to get engagements. And I advised him to take time to learn as much repertoire as possible – especially concertos. I told him that once he became well known, he might not have the time to study all the works that people would ask him to play.

CE: *Did he take your advice?*

WH: He certainly did.

CE: *What else did you do for him as his manager?*

WH: When he performed concerts, we had to arrange for hotel accommodation, and for planes or trains. I can remember that sometimes when we booked a flight, Glenn would call my secretary and say, "I've just dreamed that the plane is going to crash. Could you please change my flight?" I also introduced him to my lawyer, and to this day his firm is still the executor of Glenn's estate. And I introduced Glenn to my best friend, who was a stockbroker. Glenn did very well investing – or gambling – on the stock market, I don't know which!

CE: Did you travel with him?

WH: I did, on occasion. I wasn't in Washington, but I went to St Catharines, Kitchener, and other places near to Toronto.

CE: Gould was also famous for his unconventional appearance on stage: sitting on a low chair, and hunching over the keyboard. And, as you know, he also used to hum during performances and recordings. What did you think or say about his stage presence?

WH: Glenn had his own ideas about easing the pressure on the elbows. It was his technique – and I wasn't concerned about it. But I can tell you a story. Josef Krips was the music director of the Buffalo Philharmonic, and I met him when Glenn played with his orchestra. He said, "Now about this young man, don't let him do any funny things. Just let him play." And I said, "Don't worry." After the rehearsal, Krips came up to me and said, "If he plays like that, he can do anything he wants!"[3]

CE: And of course he would only sit on the special chair that his father built.[4]

WH: Once, in Berlin, the chair was really very shaky. I said to Glenn, "I think I'm going to build another chair here, because you can't use this one." He tried my chair out, but he never used it. I have no idea what happened to the chair I built.

CE: So you weren't very concerned about his stage-presence?

WH: Not at all. I have represented a lot of artists, and they all have different ways of performing. So what?

CE: What about the humming?

WH: I would tell Glenn when I could hear his humming. But I never said, "You can't do it." A genius will have certain idiosyncrasies that are part of his stage-presence, and that's fine. If you say, "You can't do it," it will only inhibit the artist. All geniuses have their own methods.

CE: *As his manager, how well did you know Gould personally? Did you become friends?*

WH: Oh, yes! He would call sometimes at midnight, and then he'd talk for an hour, or an hour and a half. We had a very good rapport. The other day, I found a letter that Glenn wrote to me in 1961, congratulating me on my marriage. He wrote it while he was having lunch at the Windsor Arms Hotel. He wrote, in brackets, "Main course just arrived," and then continued with the letter.

CE: *So how would you describe him, as a man, in his younger years?*

WH: He was an ordinary fellow. You didn't know he was a great pianist; he was just an ordinary guy, and that was it.

CE: *And what was he like as an artist?*

WH: He had an amazing capacity to learn. I remember one recital where he played a Haydn sonata, and I'd never heard him play Haydn before. I said, "Glenn, when did you learn that sonata?" And he said, "A week ago I was in Vancouver, and I learned it on the plane back to Toronto." He was also very fortunate in that he didn't have to practise continuously. He could be away from the piano for several days, and his technique would come back in no time at all.

CE: *Gould's repertoire was sometimes unusual. Did you have any influence over his programing choices for recitals?*

WH: None whatsoever. As I've said, I'm not a musician. For instance, I had never even heard of Sweelinck until Glenn played him.[5] When he said he was going to start a recital with Sweelinck, I said that would be fine – but I had no idea who he was!

CE: *But as a concert manager, you must have had a sense of what the public did and didn't want.*

WH: I always hoped that there would be something on the program that I'd understand and enjoy. And Glenn always included a Beethoven sonata, or something like that. By the time his reputation had reached its heights, he could have played anything.

CE: *When Glenn asked for your opinion about a concert, how did you respond?*

WH: He would ask, "How do you think the concert went?" And I would say this was wonderful, but that didn't grab me – or whatever. But it was just my own personal reaction. I would also say that he could tell from the audience how it went, because an audience is very knowledgeable, and also very honest.

CE: *What other early performances were significant to his early career?*

WH: The first recital he gave in New York was in Town Hall.[6] At the end of the concert, a man came up to me who introduced himself as David Oppenheim, from Columbia Records.[7] He said, "I'd like to sign Glenn up for some recordings." I asked Glenn what he thought – I always discussed anything like that with Glenn – and he said, "Great!" And Oppenheim asked him what he would like to record. Glenn said he wanted to record the *Goldberg Variations*. I said, "Glenn, are you sure? Because there is Wanda Landowska who has recorded the *Goldbergs* on the harpsichord; and there is Rosalyn Turek, who has recorded them on the piano." But that was what he wanted to do, and that was what he did.[8]

The contract that we signed with Columbia is basically still in effect. In later years, after he retired from performing, Glenn would call me to tell me that he'd just received a six-month statement from Columbia. He would ask me to guess the amount of the royalty. I would try to guess high, and usually he would say, "Wrong – you are too low."

CE: *Another milestone was Gould's tour to Russia in 1957. How did you arrange that tour?*

WH: I started by contacting Gosconcert, the Russian concert agency. We corresponded, and they said they were interested. Finally, they sent us a contract in Russian rubles.

CE: *Why did you want to send Gould to Russia?*

WH: I felt it would give Glenn some good publicity. As it turned out, he was the first Western artist to visit the Soviet Union after the war. But it was the McCarthy era, and I was very concerned about Glenn not being able to get into the United States, after visiting Russia. So I had some correspondence with the Canadian government – with Lester Pearson, who was at that time our External Affairs minister. The government was behind the idea, and they helped me with contacts in Russia. I asked them to please let their colleagues in the USA know that they are in favour of Glenn going to Russia, so that he wouldn't be banned from the United States.

We flew SAS to Copenhagen. In those days, the planes had berths – and Glenn said, "Let's flip a coin to see who sleeps up, and who sleeps down." He slept up. In Copenhagen we changed to a plane for Moscow, and were met by an interpreter, who was with us all the time we were in Russia.

Glenn's first concert in Moscow was a recital, in a hall that was about half full. The intermission was very long, and at the time I didn't know why. Finally, they asked Glenn to go out for the second half of the concert – and by then the place was jammed. We found out afterwards that they held the curtain because a lot of the people phoned their friends and said, "Come on down, you have to hear this." I understand that Oistrakh was there, and so were Gilels and Richter.[9]

Glenn was a huge success, and the news spread like wildfire – not only in Moscow, but also in Leningrad: by the time he played there every performance was sold out. Glenn was also asked to give lectures. He said, "I'm going to lecture on Schoenberg and Berg."[10] The lectures were full, and of course everybody wanted an autograph.

CE: *What effect did the tour to Russia have on his reputation?*

WH: By that time he already had a worldwide reputation, but the trip to Russia enhanced it.

CE: *Yet even as Gould's stature as a concert pianist was growing, so too was his dislike of playing in public.*

WH: He just wasn't comfortable with it. He hated the idea of 3,000 people watching him, rather than listening.

CE: *When did you first start to notice that he had this problem?*

WH: He may have first mentioned it in 1961, or 1962. He became more and more interested in recordings and radio productions, and things like that. And in the later part of his career he cancelled concerts more often.

CE: *Did this alarm you?*

WH: I was busy with other things. I had my recital series here in Toronto, and I was the manager of the National Ballet for four years. And in 1962 I joined the Toronto Symphony as manager.

CE: What can you say about the incident that led to him suing Steinway & Sons? Do you think he was really injured by a slap on the back?[11]

WH: I can't say much because I wasn't there. And I don't like to interfere with things that are – as far as I am concerned – personal. It was a problem between Glenn and Steinway's. I didn't interfere.

CE: But what did you think of Gould's way of handling the situation?

WH: I thought, "Why sue Steinway's, who have done so much for you?" But I didn't express these views to Glenn.

CE: Another controversial incident that occurred in New York was Leonard Bernstein's public statement just before Gould played Brahms's First Piano Concerto with the New York Philharmonic. Some people were shocked when Bernstein described Gould's ideas as "incompatible" with his own.[12]

WH: I liked his remarks very much. Sometimes a conductor has certain ideas, and a soloist will have different ideas. And often they make compromises. But in this case, perhaps the compromises were not so easy to make. I guess that's why Lenny made his statement – and I don't think Glenn was offended.

CE: There's been much speculation about Glenn Gould's romantic life.

WH: I knew nothing about it. I never asked. I never knew that he met with Lukas Foss's wife, or anything like that.[13] I only read about it recently.

CE: Some people would say that Gould was a hypochondriac.[14]

WH: I would say so, yes.

CE: Did you see signs of this?

WH: I'm sure that sometimes he thought he was sick, and maybe he wasn't. But again I say that geniuses have their own problems – and they live with them.

CE: How did your professional relationship with Gould come to an end?

WH: It came to an end when he stopped giving concerts. Over the last couple of years of his concert career, he indicated that he really didn't like to play in public, because he thought people were there to gawk at him. His last concert was in Los Angeles, in 1964 – and that was it.[15]

CE: *And you didn't try to dissuade him?*

WH: No.

CE: *Did you have much contact with him after he left the concert stage?*

WH: For a while he would call, and we would talk. But with me he couldn't really discuss music, and he was always very interested in talking about music. So we just socialized, so to speak.

CE: *What did you learn from managing Gould?*

WH: I learned how to manage artists. I've had only a few – but they were always musicians whom I liked as individuals and as artists.[16]

CE: *What impact did Gould have on the musical world?*

WH: Today, if someone wants to know what I've done, I say, "I was the manager of Glenn Gould." And they say, "Oh, really?" – no matter where they come from. His reputation is worldwide, and it's still right up there. Can you name another pianist today who is as well known around the world as Glenn Gould?

Postscript

This interview with Walter Homburger is the earliest of the interviews that appear here, and as such marked the beginning of my research for this book. In another sense, the interview was conducted before I began this book: my original intention was that this interview would appear as an article in the journal *Queen's Quarterly* (which it did, in the Winter of 2009). It was only after I conducted this interview that it occurred to me to expand upon my initial idea, and interview other people as well.

I was, frankly, somewhat surprised that Homburger granted me permission to interview him. He's well known for his discretion – a trait which is certainly a professional virtue in the concert management business – and has spoken "on the record" about Gould on only a few occasions. Perhaps it was my promise to him that he would be allowed to review and edit my transcription of our interview that made the idea appealing to him. However, he made very few alterations to the transcription.

During the interview, Homburger's discreet nature felt like a constant, palpable force in the room: I don't doubt that he could have said more about Gould than he did. But at the same time, he offered a valuable perspective on Gould's brief but stellar concert career.

CE

NOTES

1. As a child, Gould performed at numerous school and church events. Beginning in 1944, he performed in Toronto's Kiwanis Music Festivals, and in concerts at the Royal Conservatory.

2. This recital took place on January 2, 1955. The following day, the *Washington Post* published a review by critic Paul Hume which began, "January is early for predictions, but it is unlikely that the year 1955 will bring us a finer piano recital than that played yesterday afternoon in the Phillips Gallery." He continued: "Glenn Gould of Toronto, Canada, and barely into his twenties, was the pianist. Few pianists play the instrument so beautifully, so lovingly, so musicianly in manner, and with such regard for its real nature and its enormous literature."

3. Gould first performed under Krips's baton on February 7, 1958. Krips became a great admirer of Gould, and the two musicians collaborated in subsequent concerto performances in Buffalo and London.

4. Gould's chair was built for him by his father in 1953, and was designed so that the length of each leg could be individually adjusted. Gould used it all his life – even after it became decrepit and the stuffing fell out of the seat. Today the chair is preserved by Library and Archives Canada.

5. Jan Pieterszoon Sweelinck (1562-1621) was a Dutch composer and keyboard musician. Gould can be heard playing his *Fantasia Chromatica* on the CD *Glenn Gould Edition: Gibbons, Byrd, Sweelinck* (Sony Classical SMK 52589). The performance on this disc was originally recorded for broadcast by the CBC in 1964.

6. This recital took place on January 11, 1955.

7. From 1950 to 1959 David Oppenheim was director of Columbia Records's Masterworks division.

8. Gould made his first recording of Bach's *Goldberg Variations* in June 1955 at the CBS studios in New York. When the LP was released the following year, Harold C. Schonberg of the *New York Times* praised Gould's "clear sharp technique that enables him to toss off the contrapuntal intricacies of the writing with no apparent effort."

9. This recital took place on May 7, in the Great Hall of the Moscow Conservatory. It is unlikely that any of the famous musicians mentioned by Homburger – the violinist

David Oistrakh or the pianists Emil Gilels and Sviatoslav Richter – had ever heard of Gould before this event.

10 This lecture-recital took place on May 12, at the Moscow Conservatory. Entitled "Music of the West," Gould's lecture focused on the modernist composer Arnold Schoenberg and his disciples, even though these composers were officially frowned upon in the Soviet Union.

11 In 1960 Gould sued Steinway & Sons for $300,000, because of an incident that occurred in the piano manufacturer's New York showrooms in December 1959. Gould alleged that a piano technician named William Hupfer caused him an injury when the man greeted Gould with a friendly slap on the back. The dispute dragged on for more than a year and was eventually settled out of court.

12 This performance took place on April 6, 1962. Disagreements between Gould and Bernstein arose during rehearsal for this concert, as Gould wished to play the first movement of the concerto at a much slower tempo than Bernstein was used to. Before the performance, Bernstein made a public statement in which he carefully hedged his bets. On one hand, he gave full credit to Gould for the "unorthodox" musical interpretation that the audience was about to hear. On the other, he made it clear that he did not agree with Gould. Bernstein cryptically concluded, "I can assure you that it has been an adventure this week collaborating with Mr. Gould on this Brahms concerto."

13 According to an article that appeared in the *Toronto Star* on August 25, 2007, Gould carried on a love affair for five years with Cornelia Foss, a painter and the wife of the American composer, pianist and conductor Lukas Foss. The article claimed that the pair saw each other frequently between 1967 and 1972, when Foss ended the affair. For more information, see Chapter 4: Cornelia Foss.

14 Gould had an intense fear of germs, and sometimes refused to shake hands with people. He was also obsessed with measuring and recording his own vital signs, including his temperature, blood pressure and sleeping patterns. Moreover, he medicated himself with Valium, Librax, Placidyl, Dalmane, Nembutal, Luminal, Aldomet, Indoral and other prescription drugs. For more information see Kevin Bazzana, *Wondrous Strange: the Life and Art of Glenn Gould* (Toronto: McClelland & Stewart, 2003), p. 485.

15 Gould's withdrawal from the concert stage did not mean an end to his career. He remained active as a recording artist, releasing numerous solo discs, and collaborating in the recording studio with such artists as the violinist Yehudi Menuhin and the soprano Elisabeth Schwarzkopf. As well, he wrote about music, dabbled in composition and conducting, made several television appearances and created innovative radio documentaries for the CBC.

16 Homburger's small but prestigious roster of classical musicians has included the baritone Victor Braun, the bass Jan Rubes, the pianist Louis Lortie and the violinist James Ehnes.

Verne Edquist: Gould's Piano Man

Verne Edquist was born in 1931 in a rural part of the province of Saskatchewan, in western Canada. Due to his poor eyesight, at the age of eight he was sent to the Ontario School for the Blind in Brantford. There he learned the trade of piano tuning, and he moved to Toronto in 1950, to earn a living as a tuner. For several years he was employed in piano factories: at the Winter Company (owned by Mason & Risch), and later at Heintzman & Company. In 1961, he was hired as Chief Concert Tuner at Eaton's department store in Toronto; and in 1969 he left Eaton's to tune pianos on a freelance basis.

This interview took place in Edquist's home in northern Toronto on January 12, 2011.

CE: I understand that you first met Gould when you went to his home to tune his Chickering piano.

VE: Yes, I first met in him in 1962, when I was called to his home to look at his Chickering piano. I had seen him before, when I was working at Heintzman[1] – from a distance, peeking around a corner.

The Chickering had been at the Goulds' cottage at Lake Simcoe, where Glenn spent a lot of time. As long as it was up there, the moisture content in the wood was fine, and it stayed in tune. But it had been brought back to the city, where of course it had dried out. Other tuners had been there, and they had blocked off certain strings that wouldn't stay in tune: there were about twenty pieces of felt in the piano! So I said I didn't want to work on it. He said, "You mean you refuse to tune it?" I said, "Yes, I refuse to tune it." I took a taxi back to Eaton's, and I went to my boss and said, "If my job depends on saying yes to that guy, let me know right now – because I have my standards." Fortunately, my boss respected my judgement.

CE: Why was Gould so fond of that Chickering piano, if it was in such bad shape?

VE: It's like the way he was attached to that chair he used all his life.[2] It was like Linus and his blanket: he felt more secure if things didn't change. I've heard that Glenn may have suffered from some kind of arrested development. I'm not a psychiatrist, but I think that may be true.

CE: The first meeting with Gould didn't go well – yet you became Gould's favourite piano technician in Toronto. How did this happen?

VE: I was tuning at the old CBC studios on Parliament Street. I think Glenn was quite pleased with what I was doing with the piano there: the way I set the strings and the tension. I heard him say, "That's a pretty good tuning." And I remember there was one time when he came to a recording session and said that he'd lost the key for the piano. But I wasn't going to take a hacksaw to the piano to open it up. And then after a while he said he'd found the key. I don't know whether he did that on purpose – to see if I would panic – but I just sat there and waited. Then he boiled some water, soaked his hands, and got going with the recording.

After that, he wanted me to tune for him. In 1969 he asked me if I would mind if he called me whenever he needed a tuner. I said, "Okay, but my vision isn't very good." So he would phone up to set up appointments ahead of time. He trusted me to work with him, and I didn't push his trust. I suspect he had me investigated, he was so security conscious. I used to have reporters try to get to him through me, but I'd say, "No, you can't do that." There was a certain diplomatic responsibility that came with working for Glenn.

CE: *When word got out that you were Gould's preferred piano tuner, what effect did this have on your career?*

VE: At the same time as I was working for Glenn, I was working for others. I was doing the concert scene – that's what kept bread on my table. I tuned for players like Ben McPeek and Gary Williamson, and I worked for Liberace when he was in Toronto.[3] I had good work – but you can only do so much, and I didn't want to get too big. So Glenn was my main concert pianist.

I can remember that once Glenn phoned to say he wanted me at the CBC the next day. Another pianist who was going to play the *Emperor Concerto* had backed out, and Glenn was filling in.[4] I was able to do it because I could change my schedule. But if I'd had several artists at Glenn's level, I wouldn't have been able to do it. Glenn was my top priority.

CE: *I want to ask you about Gould's favourite piano, Steinway CD318. Why was this instrument so special to Gould?*

VE: There was a stable of Steinway concert grands at Eaton's.[5] Glenn liked number 400 – it was a good piano – but it was sold to the University of Toronto. He also liked number 50. When he stumbled on 318, in 1960, he really liked that one. I liked it too: everything was balanced, it stayed in tune, there were no buzzes or harmonic patterns in it, and the touch was very even. Number 318 was a very reliable piano.

CE: *You did some work on it, didn't you?*

VE: He wanted me to make the action faster. But there's a limit to how fast a piano's action can be: once you start shortening the blow-distance then you lose power.

CE: *Gould described the piano as having the "hiccups." What does that mean, exactly?*

VE: The hammer would very quickly strike the string twice. That's what happens when you shorten the blow-distance, and the check isn't checking the hammers as soon as it should. Glenn liked to deliberately make the piano do it – he thought it might be a useful special effect. But I didn't like it.

CE: *What did the Steinway people in New York think of your alterations to CD318?*

VE: They didn't care, as long as I was keeping Glenn happy!

CE: *Did Glenn have exclusive use of the piano? Did anyone else ever play it?*

VE: It was the property of Steinway, but only Glenn could play it. It was kept locked, at Eaton's, and it had a packing case that was built like a fortress. After his last recital in Los Angeles, in 1964, he had it shipped back to Toronto by airfreight.[6] After that, it didn't move around much – other than back and forth from the CBC studios, or up to Eaton Auditorium.

CE: *What can you tell me about Gould's fondness for Eaton Auditorium as a recording venue?*[7]

VE: It was secure, and it was acoustically perfect, with very little reverb. As a child he played the organ in there, so he was familiar with it, and attached to it.[8] We tried the St Lawrence Hall, and we considered the Leah Posluns Theatre and a few other places, but they didn't work out.[9] But when Eaton's was sold to a developer in the 1970s,[10] they didn't drain the water tanks on the roof, and the ceiling of the auditorium collapsed. It was an awful mess, and downright dangerous – we had to bring in special heaters to keep the place warm – but Glenn insisted on working there. Once again, it was like Linus with his blanket.

CE: *And what was it like working with Gould on his all-night recording sessions in Eaton Auditorium?*

VE: Glenn always wanted to wait till after nine o'clock to begin recording, after the elevators in the building had been shut down. I would get there perhaps two-and-a-half hours ahead, to make sure the piano was right. Andrew Kazdin[11] would get there to make sure the microphones were set up in exactly the correct position. Glenn would come bounding in with his music and a change of clothing, humming something by Bach. After chatting for a while, Glenn would go and soak his hands in hot water. While he was doing this, we'd put wooden blocks under each castor, to raise the piano two inches higher, and then we'd take the lid off. Glenn would come back in and dicker with Kazdin about what music he was going to record that night.

At the end of the session, I'd be worn out – they would go until three or four o'clock in the morning. When Glenn was finished recording, he'd be soaking wet with perspiration. He'd go off to change his clothes, and when he came back he'd play some music from a Broadway show, just for fun. Right there on the spot, Glenn would write me a cheque for my services, and sometimes he'd drive me home. If we had recording sessions three nights in a row, I'd be working on sheer nervous energy, and would need to take a day off just to recover.

To give you a specific example of how things could go, in September 1972 we started to record *Die Meistersinger*, and we did part of it. At the next session, Glenn said he wanted to do something else, and it wasn't until March of the following year that he wanted to go back to *Die Meistersinger*. In September, I had tuned the piano about two beats sharp of A440, because Glenn wanted it that way. I had to remember those two beats in March, so it would match on the tape. And it did.[12]

CE: *I understand that CD318 was damaged in 1971. How did this happen?*

VE: The piano was shipped to Cleveland for a recording session with the Cleveland Orchestra. I'd already bought myself a plane ticket to go down there, but then Glenn called me to say he was cancelling. The piano had to be brought back. When it arrived in Toronto, I went down to Eaton Auditorium and unlocked the piano for a recording session. I hit middle C it and sounded an octave higher. Then I saw that the casting had been broken in about four different places – it was really bad. It looked like the piano had somehow fallen on its top.

I sat around and waited for Glenn to show up. I thought he would be more upset than he was when he saw what had happened to the piano. But he quizzed me like a lawyer. What had happened to the piano? How could it have been dropped?

The piano was shipped to Steinway, in New York, for repairs. However, Steinway had stopped casting their own plates at their factory on Long Island, and they had a new plate cast somewhere else. And when the piano came back to Toronto, the new plate wasn't right. The bearings were not the same, and we were getting buzzing in the treble. I phoned Franz Mohr[13] at Steinway and said, "This is a mess." He said, "I know, but I can't do anything about it." So I laced some felt here and there, and moved wire around – that's when the whole exercise became like a dog chasing its tail.

CE: Do you have any theories of your own as to how CD318 was damaged, and who damaged it?

VE: It fell upside down, lid first, and it must have fallen from a height of about five feet. I think it was dropped at the loading dock at Eaton's, here in Toronto. But nobody would admit to being responsible for the accident, and the whole thing was hushed up.

CE: Did Gould continue to record on CD318?

VE: Oh yes, he kept on using it. Once, when I heard a new recording by Gould, I said to Kazdin, "You boosted the treble a bit, didn't you?" He said, "Yes, I had to." The treble on 318 was never as pure and clean as it had been.

CE: And that's when Gould decided to buy the piano?

VE: He never asked me whether he should buy it – he just went and did it. I never would have bought it! It got to a point where I was really fed up with the whole thing. Jokingly, I said to Glenn, "Why don't you try a Yamaha?", because anything would have been better than what he had.

CE: Evidently, he took you seriously. What did you think of the Yamaha he bought in 1981?[14]

VE: I didn't like it, but I did the best I could with it. The dampers weren't cut right, and I had to take them out and work on them. But Glenn said he only wanted to use the middle three octaves, to play Bach. Glenn managed to work with it.

CE: You also tuned a harpsichord for Gould. What was that like?

VE: I'll never forget it! When Glenn said he wanted to record on the harpsichord, I suggested he get one with piano-sized keys, and an iron frame, so it would stay in tune longer than most harpsichords.[15] But Glenn always wanted more sound from the instrument, and I was able to get a little more. Also, there were problems with some of the keys. With the harpsichord, the keys are supposed to be tight, but the keys on this instrument were getting loose. Some of the keys would "hang up" – the strings didn't dampen properly – and they had to be adjusted.

CE: *When Gould was recording Bach, or other baroque composers, did he ever propose using any tuning system other than equal temperament?*

VE: No, he didn't get into that kind of thing.

CE: *Because of your work with Gould, you have a unique perspective on his relationship to the piano. In your opinion, what made him so special as a pianist?*

VE: I think one of the main reasons why Glenn's music is so distinctive is because of his sense of meter. He puts an emphasis on the upbeat – there's a little skip to it. Nobody else does that. I once said to him that his fingers were so independent that each one seemed to have a mind of its own. Also, the shallowness of the touch that Glenn wanted from his keyboard gave him a more rapid response, which had an effect on his playing. He played with the soft pedal down a lot, so only two strings were sounding – which was a problem for me, because it's much harder to keep two strings in tune than three. And he had a special gift from his teacher, which was to keep his hands above the keys all the time, like a high-stepping pony. I think all of Guerrero's students played that way: whenever I tuned for any of them I would always notice how little wear-and-tear there was on their pianos.[16]

Postscript

Verne Edquist responded to my request for an interview about Glenn Gould with warmth and enthusiasm. Although he tuned pianos for many musicians during his long career – some quite eminent – it soon became apparent that Gould was a very special client. And despite their inauspicious first encounter, it also became apparent that the two men had a great deal of respect for each other. In his dealings with Gould, Edquist displayed a flexibility that allowed him to go along with Gould's unorthodox ideas about pianos, which couldn't have been easy for someone rigorously trained in the "right way" to do things.

And although Gould could have had any piano tuner in Toronto – or in the world – that he wanted, he relied on Edquist for two decades.

For those wishing to know more about Edquist's relationship with Gould, and Gould's relationship with pianos, I recommend Katie Hafner's book *A Romance on Three Legs*. I'm indebted to this well written book as a valuable source of background information for my interview with Edquist.

CE

NOTES

1. Heintzman & Co. was established in Toronto in 1866, and grew to become Canada's foremost piano manufacturer.

2. In 1953 Glenn Gould's father modified a chair so that the length of each leg could be individually adjusted. Gould insisted on using this chair for more than two decades, even after the stuffing fell out of the seat. See also Chapter 1: Walter Homburger (p.5).

3. Ben McPeek was a Canadian pianist and composer who often played with dance bands; and Gary Williamson is a Toronto-based jazz pianist. The popular American pianist Wladziu Valentino Liberace frequently performed in Toronto.

4. CBC Television broadcast Gould's recording of Beethoven's *Piano Concerto No. 5 "The Emperor"* with the Toronto Symphony Orchestra conducted by Karel Ancerl on December 9, 1970. The pianist originally scheduled to make this recording was Arturo Benedetti Michelangeli.

5. The T. Eaton Company (commonly called "Eaton's") was a chain of Canadian department stores. In Toronto, Eaton's was the official dealer for the sale and rental of Steinway pianos.

6. Gould's last public performance took place on April 10, 1964, at the Wilshire Ebell Theatre in Los Angeles.

7. Eaton Auditorium was located on the seventh floor of Eaton's College Street store in Toronto. The 1,300-seat auditorium was a popular concert venue for local and visiting musicians. Gould first recorded in Eaton Auditorium in 1970, and continued to use it for recordings until 1981.

8. Gould gave his first public concert as an organist at Eaton Auditorium on December 12, 1945.

9. St Lawrence Hall, located at 92-95 King St. E., is a National Historic Site, built in 1850 and containing a 1,000-seat theatre. The Leah Posluns Theatre is located within the Bathurst Jewish Community Centre at 4588 Bathurst St.

10 Eaton's College Street department store was sold to Toronto College Park Centre Ltd. in 1976.

11 Andrew Kadzin was Gould's recording producer for Columbia Records.

12 Gould's recording *Piano Transcriptions of Orchestral Showpieces* (CBS Masterworks MP 39764) consisted of his own transcriptions of Wagner's *Prelude to Die Meistersinger*, "Dawn" and "Siegrfried's Journey" from *Götterdämmerung*, and the *Siegfried Idyll*.

13 Franz Mohr was the Chief Concert Technician for Steinway & Sons, in New York.

14 After several years spent searching for a suitable new Steinway piano, Gould purchased a Yamaha CF Concert Grand in 1981, and used it for subsequent recordings.

15 In 1972, Gould recorded works by Handel and Bach for CBS Masterworks (on a Wittmayer harpsichord).

16 For more information on Gould's piano teacher, Alberto Guerrero, see Chapter 2: Stuart Hamilton (pp. 38-40) and John Beckwith (pp. 46-49).

Stephen Posen: Gould's Lawyer

Stephen Posen was born in Toronto in 1938, and attended law school at the University of Toronto. He joined the prominent Toronto law firm Minden Gross in 1967 and a few years later was assigned to look after the legal affairs of Glenn Gould. Although he initially viewed the Gould account as a relatively minor task, his work with the pianist blossomed into an ongoing and multifaceted involvement that has continued to this day.

This interview took place in the offices of Minden Gross LLP in downtown Toronto on May 12, 2011.

CE: How did you come to be Glenn Gould's lawyer?

SP: Glenn was already a client of Minden Gross before I joined the firm: he had been introduced by Walter Homburger to my late senior partner, Morris Gross. Gould's legal work was generally done by the most junior lawyer in the firm because it was so straightforward, and he did most of the work himself. So around 1970 I was handed the file. When I started to work with Glenn, he was one of the most engaging and brilliant of people – and on top of that I was enchanted by his reputation as a performing artist. I didn't pass him on to the next juniors. I kept him as a client until he passed away.

CE: Did you have any kind of musical education or training?

SP: I took private piano lessons when I was a kid. I still love playing the piano, but I only do it privately – I'm not a serious musician. And I also played a wind instrument in high school and university.

CE: Is it fair to say that your interest in music is what made Gould so interesting to you?

SP: That may be partly true. But what I found most interesting about him is that he was one of the few geniuses I've known in my life. He was so brilliant and such an engaging personality that I found it wonderful to have exposure to him on an ongoing basis.

CE: Did you listen to his recordings?

SP: The one I recall best is the 1955 *Goldbergs*. And I used to listen to *The Well-Tempered Clavier* all the time. It's a shocking thing for the executor of Glenn

Gould's estate to say, but Bach's music is not my favourite. However, I can tell you that if I turned on the radio in the middle of someone playing something on the piano, I knew it was either Glenn or it was someone else in the universe. The way he played was unique and immediately recognizable.

Further, my favourite Gould recordings are his recordings of Brahms's compositions. I believe there were three: *Intermezzi*, *Ballades* and *Rhapsodies* (my absolute favourite) and the *D Minor Piano Concerto* conducted by Leonard Bernstein. Sony released the piano concerto together with a completely charming, as well as informative, "disclaimer" by Leonard Bernstein.

CE: *Was Gould a demanding client?*

SP: He wasn't demanding, actually. He was a very forgiving kind of client, from the point of view of what he expected from me, and he was very respectful of what I could do for him. But it was not very complex – and, as I said, he did a lot of the work himself. I remember, for example, discussing various contracts with him, for movies or television. When I said I didn't like a certain paragraph because it posed a liability, he would know better than I did that several pages later in another paragraph there was something which – although not directly – addressed to his satisfaction what I was concerned about. He understood the concepts and the form of a contract very well. And when I sent him notes, he sometimes said he didn't like my sentence-structure. He would comment on what he would call the "musical phrasing" of my sentences.

CE: *You say he did a lot of his own work himself. What exactly did he do?*

SP: If he had a contract to negotiate, he himself would usually do the negotiation of the terms. It was only rarely that I became involved in negotiations with the parties on the other side of the contract.

CE: *Who was he contracting with, when you were representing him?*

SP: I didn't deal with CBS Records because his contracts with CBS were all done prior to my involvement with Glenn. There was the film *Slaughterhouse Five*,[1] and various TV producers who were doing things with him. There were contracts with the CBC. And I remember there was a contract for the acquisition of a high-quality tape recorder.

CE: *Did Gould have a strong grasp of the music business? Was he a good businessman?*

SP: Oh, was he ever! I don't act for a lot of people in the artistic world, but from what I know he was remarkable for his strong grasp of the business elements of music. He was very clear in his understanding, and in what his desires were.

CE: *I've also heard that he did very well on the stock market. Did you have anything to do with that?*

SP: No I didn't. But after he passed away, when I was looking into the organization of his assets, I realized he had a stock portfolio and that he had been dealing with a certain stockbroker. I contacted the broker and asked him to sell the stocks. His reply really impressed me. "Steve," he said, "I have exactly one client who has made money in the stock market in the last two years, and that was Glenn." It's pretty impressive that a recording artist and writer was the only client to make money with a broker during the recessionary period of the early 1980s. To me, that was just another indication of his overwhelmingly brilliant mind.

CE: *He also got a lot of traffic citations. Did you have anything to do with them?*

SP: Yes, with some of them. I recall one in particular that really amused me: at the intersection of Mount Pleasant and St Clair, the stoplights going east-west were green. When they turned red, he made his left turn on to St Clair, not realizing that there was a delayed green going north. In effect, he made a left turn against a red light. He objected on moral grounds: that it was inappropriate that there should be a delayed green light without some kind of forewarning sign. He felt he should be able to contest the ticket on that basis. Indignant though he was, I advised him that I felt he was legally incorrect.

CE: *I understand you drew up his will. What can you tell me about that?*

SP: I had mentioned to him a number of times that he should draft a will. In 1979, when he decided what he wanted to do, he contacted me and gave me instructions for the preparation of his will. I asked, "Who will be your executor?" He said, "You will." I said that I might not be the perfect executor, and he replied, "Even you, sir, can buy a GIC." He explained that he was only drawing up a will for family reasons, and in case some truck driver with bad karma ran him down. He said that we would make a "perfect will when we were in our eighties."

Glenn felt it was bad luck to make a will. I thought of this when I visited him at the hospital after he had his stroke, and was in a coma, which turned out to be terminal. I thought to myself that maybe it was bad luck to make a will, and how sorry I was.

The will is a public document. He divided his estate in half: one half for the Salvation Army, and the other half for the Toronto Humane Society. He also left a $50,000 fund for his father, which became part of the residue of Glenn's estate when his father passed away.

CE: *Is there anything else you did for him as his lawyer?*

SP: I don't think I did anything else for him, professionally. I do recall his asking me to join him on a tour of a condominium unit he was considering as an investment. That was when I first met Ray Roberts. Also, I was the beneficiary of some of his lengthy phone calls – about things that had nothing to do with legal matters. When we were on the phone, his conversations tended to be one-sided, and he spoke in the most baroque sentences: you had to carefully follow all the clauses and parentheses.

Because of Glenn's sleep-patterns, these conversations usually happened in the afternoon. If one of my colleagues came by to speak with me and saw I was on the phone, he would make a motion with his hands like he was playing the piano, as a way of asking me if I was talking to Glenn. I'd nod yes, and he would know that I'd be unavailable for a couple of hours.

And there were some occasions when he would call me at home in the evenings. I recall one such Saturday evening, when I had guests for dinner. I excused myself from dinner because I didn't want to lose the opportunity to talk to him. I would listen to him go on about his editing, and his scripts, and so on.

CE: *Did he ever do anything for you in any way?*

SP: I was a very small player in his world. But I remember when I was looking at a condominium apartment, he told me I wasn't permitted to buy it until he inspected it. He came and sniffed around to make sure there was no bad air, and then approved my purchase.

And when I was buying a piano for my apartment, he arranged for me to go to a dealer, and get a certain type of piano. It was a Yamaha upright. And when I'd chosen it, he said I wasn't allowed to buy it until he had tested it. So he went to the store, and played the piano for all of a minute or so, just to make sure that it was okay. He liked it, and so I bought it. I've had that piano for forty years.

The biggest thing that Glenn did for me was actually after he passed away: I've been so privileged to be Glenn's executor. Over the past almost thirty years I have learned so much more about Glenn and his recordings, writings, radio and TV documentaries through reading and speaking to many other relatives and associates of his, and numerous others who have studied Glenn and written or produced documentaries about him. That's what he did most for me – and that is, to me, the real Gould legacy.

CE: I know that you were involved in the establishment of the Glenn Gould Foundation. What did you do?

SP: Yes, I was involved. I didn't consider myself qualified to establish a foundation, but people kept asking me when I was going to do it. So I ended up going to a few people with the idea. John Roberts was the one who picked up the challenge to establish the Glenn Gould Foundation, and the Glenn Gould Prize.[2]

He arranged for a meeting with Joan Chalmers, and he told her of his plans. She had a positive reaction and said we should go and ask her father, Floyd Chalmers, who was a major arts patron.[3] So we went to his apartment, on a miserable day in December of 1983. Joan said she liked the idea, and Floyd said, "How's about $150,000?" I was awestruck: they were talking about numbers that were beyond my experience for charitable donations. That was the cornerstone donation that established the foundation. Other donations were obtained from three levels of government: Toronto, Ontario and Canada, which, combined with the Chalmers donation and the donation from the 1985 International Piano Competition – I'll say more about that in a minute – made up the original funding of about $600,000.

John Roberts arranged for me to meet with a lawyer friend of his, John Lawson, and we discussed some of the terms by which the Glenn Gould name would be licensed by the foundation. John Lawson did the incorporation.

John Roberts was the one who attracted a number of people to join the original board of the foundation. He also arranged to get other donations from the 1985 International Bach Piano Competition: Nikki Goldschmidt, who was running it, said he would give the proceeds to the foundation.

Nikki was a great guy, but he was a little bit of a loveable scoundrel.[4] He asked me if he could call it the "1985 International Glenn Gould Bach Piano Competition."
I said no, you can't, because you can't use Glenn's name in conjunction with a

competition.
CE: Was this because of Gould's abhorrence of competitions?

SP: Yes. Then Nikki invited me to come to a press conference to announce his competition, and he announced it as the "Glenn Gould Piano Competition."[5] I laughed to myself! In the end, the Gould name wasn't used – but when he asked if he could say that proceeds would go to the Glenn Gould Foundation, I of course said yes.

CE: You remain the executor of Gould's estate, and royalties are still coming in. Is Glenn Gould still a very profitable client?

SP: When we were doing the probate for the will we needed some concept as to the value of the estate. So we got advice from knowledgeable people about what happens to the royalty stream for deceased artists. We were told that the royalties could be expected to decline to zero over a period of about ten years. But the truth is that Glenn Gould earned more after he died than before. There have been years when he earned a great deal more than when he was alive. And he's still earning very respectable numbers, almost thirty years later, relative to what was anticipated. It's an ongoing source of revenue for the two beneficiaries.

My own view is that because there was nobody who played the piano the way he did – and because new people are being born all the time, and there are new territories in the world that haven't been much exposed to Gould – he has the capability of being a perpetually successful recording artist. And I keep driving this home to the recording companies.

Of course, the foundation has contributed to keeping his name alive. There are also books, films and plays, and the like – and the Glenn Gould Studio is named on CBC Radio daily. I feel very proud of the work we have done in maintaining the revenue stream. Over time I've learned how to run the affairs of the estate in what has thus far been a successful way.

CE: Looking back on your association with Gould, how would you describe his personality?

SP: As I've already said, he was absolutely brilliant, he was courteous, and a lot of fun. I enjoyed him tremendously. He was an independent thinker, and was able to foresee the future in many ways. Not only was he one of the greatest pianists of the twentieth century, but he was also a prolific thinker and writer, a creative radio producer, and a maker of in-depth TV documentaries. The breadth and scope of his activities is unbelievable.

And I don't think it's been fully articulated just how heroic he was. He overcame physical and psychological impediments to doing what he wanted to do in a brilliant way, because, I believe, of his super brain-power as well as determination.

Despite the feeling of some that Glenn had hypochondriac tendencies, I have no doubt that he had physical ailments. There's a neurologist named Frank Wilson who worked at UC Berkeley with whom I once appeared on a panel, in San Francisco. Afterwards, over dinner, he talked about having watched Gould on television. He picked up the phone and called his friend Peter Ostwald, a psychiatrist who knew Glenn, and said, "Quick, turn on the television. What do you see?" Together they diagnosed Gould as having focal dystonia.[6] Frank told me that for anyone else it was a career-ending ailment. According to Dr. Wilson, Glenn Gould was the only artist able to overcome it to any significant degree.

Frank also explained to me that his disability might have had an effect on Glenn's repertoire. He would play baroque and classical music, and also modern music, but he shied away from much of the big the romantic repertoire. Despite his physical ailments and his psychological problems – I'm not qualified to say if he had Asperger's or not – Glenn lived an amazingly creative and productive life.[7]

Postscript

Like many others who knew Gould, Stephen Posen admired him as an artist, thinker and human being. But as a lawyer immersed in the business world, Posen also thought highly of Gould as a businessman. His words of praise for Gould's business acumen run contrary to the common impression that Gould didn't have a worldly or pragmatic bone in his body. As well, Posen's suggestion – based on the opinions of two medical doctors – that Gould may have suffered from focal dystonia adds an extra facet to Gould's achievements as a pianist.

CE

NOTES

1 Gould's recorded performances of Bach's *Goldberg Variations* and *Keyboard Concerto No. 3 in D* were used in Universal Studios' 1972 film *Slaughterhouse Five*, based on a novel of the same title by Kurt Vonnegut Jr.

2 For more information, see Chapter 3: John Roberts (p. 140).

3 Floyd Chalmers (1898-1993) was the head of the Canadian publishing firm Maclean-Hunter, and a prominent philanthropist.

4 Nicholas Goldschmidt (1908-2004) was born in Moravia and emigrated to the USA in 1937. Seven years later, he moved to Canada. In Toronto he helped to found the Canadian Opera Company, and became a prominent impresario.

5 For more information, see Chapter 2: John Beckwith (p. 50).

6 Focal dystonia is a neurological disorder that affects muscle co-ordination, often in the hands. The pianist Leon Fleisher has struggled with the condition throughout his career.

7 For more information on the theory that Gould suffered from Asperger's syndrome (a form of autism), see Chapter 2: Timothy Maloney (pp. 76-78).

Ray Roberts: the Loyal Assistant

Ray Roberts was born in Toronto, in 1939. As a boy he attended Lord Dufferin Public School, where he befriended Lorne Tulk, who later became the recording technician for Gould's radio documentaries at the CBC. It was through Tulk that Roberts was introduced to Gould, for whom he began to work. At first he did odd jobs – but he gradually became Gould's man-of-all-work, helping him with many practical aspects of his life and career.

Today, Roberts works as a financial consultant. This interview took place in his business office in Toronto on January 24, 2011.

CE: When and where did you first meet Gould?

RR: It was in 1970, and I was working for Coca-Cola, as a salesman, at the time. I met Glenn through Lorne Tulk, who was working with Glenn.[1] He had gone out and purchased some recording equipment to use at Eaton Auditorium. Lorne and I had gone to school together, and he asked me to help him move the equipment. For the first couple of sessions I helped them set up, and then Glenn would come in and I'd disappear.

But Glenn was constantly having car problems, and I'd offer to help. My father was a mechanic, so I had some knowledge of cars. The whole thing grew like Topsy: he'd start to call me about various things. It got more and more intense, until by the end of our relationship he was calling me three times a day: seven o'clock in the morning, four o'clock in the afternoon and eleven o'clock at night.

Having a part-time job to make some money on the side seemed like a good idea to me. Glenn could be demanding, but he was good to work for: he did realize that I had other work, and a family.

CE: What was your impression of Gould, when you first met him?

RR: There was a kind of mystical quality surrounding the man, as if he walked on water. But I found him quite approachable. He liked to be on a first-name basis with people he worked with. But the one area I didn't lay a paw on was music, or artistic interpretation, or anything like that. That was a no-no.

But we did talk about politics. In our eleven o'clock phone calls, we would get into great debates, usually about a news story. He'd get on one side of the story, and I'd get on the other. Generally, I tended to be slightly leftish in my views. He would often be further to the left than I was – but at times he would go to the other extreme, and take a far-right position. There were some things he felt strongly about. But it was all in good fun, and never taken too seriously.

CE: *What sort of things did he have you doing for him?*

RR: You could call me a personal assistant – or a glorified "gofer." It started small: what I started doing was making arrangements to try out halls and pianos, making calls to New York, and doing some banking for him. And always there were car problems to attend to: I arranged to have work done on his vehicles.

For recording sessions in Eaton Auditorium[2] during the winter, I'd rent great, huge propane burners called salamanders. I'd bring the propane tanks in and set them up. They made a horrendous racket – but we'd get these things going to get the temperature up. Then we'd shut them down and Glenn would do some recording.

Also, when he was having problems with his muscles, I would go to his apartment and heat up a tub of wax, and he'd put his arm in it. And he had his own ultrasound machines, and I applied them. He wanted to me to assist him, and so I did. But when I look back on it, I wonder if it was safe. Those machines were powerful – you could have killed a rabbit with them.

CE: *There are stories about Gould leading a nocturnal existence: working all night and sleeping all day. Is this really how he lived?*

RR: Yes, it was. When he phoned me at seven o'clock in the morning, it was just before he went to bed, and he would wake up at about 3:30 in the afternoon. It was his choice: he liked to work all night, when things were quieter and more peaceful. When we travelled together, I'd have to live on his schedule – but ordinarily I didn't.

CE: *What particular moments stand out in your memory?*

RR: I remember that we had a couple of naked females show up at Glenn's apartment, on St Clair Avenue![3] And there was an obsessed woman in Texas who wrote to him every day. It got kind of scary when she said she was going to come to Toronto and start shooting people until he agreed to marry her! But she never showed up in Toronto. When Glenn died, I phoned the police in Texas, and told them to keep an eye on her, because she might do something crazy.

And I remember our car trips to New York.[4] There was a time when Eaton's had noisy transformers installed in their College Park building, and you couldn't use Eaton Auditorium for recording. So we were driving to New York more often.

Glenn drove a big Lincoln, which he called Longfellow. It was notoriously unreliable. We drove in tandem: I used to drive another one of his cars, a Chevrolet Monte Carlo, which Roxy Roslak had named Lance. We would make the trip from Toronto to New York in one day, straight down the New York Thruway, and staying in a Holiday Inn in New Jersey. The next morning we'd take the Palisades Parkway into New York.

In New York State, if you get nailed three times for speeding, you're not allowed to drive there any more. Glenn got caught twice, and I got caught once. Glenn decided that if he were ever caught again, we'd switch identities: he'd be Ray Roberts, and I'd be Glenn Gould! If we were in the same car, he'd turn the radio on and we'd play Name That Tune with whatever was playing. When we stopped for a break, we'd play a game called Swiss Navy, which was much like the game Battleship.

Most of the time, my relations with Glenn were very good – but he did fire me on one occasion, right in the middle of the New York Thruway. Glenn was always sort of estranged from his father, Bert. And after Glenn's mother died, Bert decided he was going to get married again.[5] Glenn was horrified, but I defended Bert. We had an argument about it, and he fired me in the car. But by the time we got to New York City I was basically rehired.

CE: Did Gould ever fly anywhere, in the years you knew him?

RR: No place. But there are stories of him being sighted in Sweden, England and Germany, months before he died! Flying was out of the question. Of course, in the early days of his career, when he was flying around on piston-propeller aircraft, there were a lot of accidents. His fear of flying was well founded.[6]

CE: Gould had a reputation for going to great lengths to preserve his privacy.

RR: At the Inn on the Park, where he kept a room, all of the front-desk staff were instructed to say "Glenn who?" if people came snooping around. He had a telephone answering service – and anyone who phoned to talk to Glenn Gould got a return call from me. Sometimes we'd get calls from people wanting to hire Glenn to play at a birthday party, or something like that. We had a code for that kind of request: I'd say, "Someone wants you to push a pink piano down Yonge Street naked, playing Chopin." That meant that it was something Glenn wouldn't want to bother with.

CE: Was it common-sense prudence that made him guard his privacy, or did it go beyond that?

RR: It was a bit of everything. He had a certain kind of paranoia about strange people coming at him unexpectedly. But when he was dealing with an average person in a controlled environment, it was a very comfortable thing.

CE: How would you describe Gould's personality in the ten years you knew him?

RR: He could be a lot of fun, and he was remarkably understanding. Also, he was a generous man: one of my jobs was to try to get money back from some people who were indebted to him. I suggested we might take stronger measures to recover his money, but he would have none of it. And he loved animals: he said to me, one time, that animals wouldn't disappoint you, but people always did. To a point, I agreed with that.

CE: Were there two Glenn Goulds – the public and the private man?

RR: Absolutely. Very early on, I saw that he talked about "Glenn Gould" as though he was someone else. He would say and do things that were provocative to get his name in the paper. And then there was the whole thing about giving up live concerts: he chose to disappear for a while, and that generated a lot of publicity. If you're famous, you have to have a front that you put on – a certain way that people see you – and you have to maintain it. But when you're away from that, you can be a totally different human being.

CE: Did you know about Gould's relationship with Cornelia Foss?[7]

RR: I've never really met her, but I spoke to her on the phone on one occasion. And I met one of her sons, Christopher, when he lived in Toronto. I knew about the relationship, but it was none of my business, and I didn't broadcast it. It wasn't exactly a secret – Glenn never told me it was – but talking about Glenn's personal life wasn't something I was inclined to do.

CE: I believe you were the one who took Glenn Gould to the hospital on the day he had his stroke. How do you remember that?

RR: I was at my office on St Clair, at about 3:30.[8] He phoned me from the Inn on the Park, and immediately I knew that something was wrong. He asked me to come over, and I dropped everything and went straight there. When I got there, at about four o'clock, he got up and unlocked the door, so I could come in. He'd obviously had a stroke.

CE: So you knew the symptoms of a stroke?

RR: Yes. I immediately said we should go to a hospital, but he didn't want to go. So I got on the phone to call all kinds of doctors, but most of the time I couldn't get them on the phone. It was getting worse – his mobility was decreasing – and he finally agreed that he had to go to the hospital. I called the front desk of the hotel, and the manager and assistant manager brought a wheelchair to the room. They helped me get Glenn into the wheelchair and down to my car. And I took Glenn to Toronto General Hospital.

There's always been a question about this: if Glenn had received treatment sooner, would things have been any different? But he didn't want an ambulance. Today, the way stroke victims are treated is different. The paramedics would come in right away, and they can modify the effects if it's caught early. Of course, you have to look at the family history: his mother died of a stroke, and his father had had a stroke, as well. Glenn's lifestyle and diet were not helping: he ate scrambled eggs every day for breakfast, and he was not athletic at all. We all hoped he would make a recovery, but the swelling in his brain only got worse.

Somehow I could never see Glenn as an eighty-year-old, or as a man who was half paralyzed by a stroke. If he had survived, there would have been some kind of career for him: writing about music, or something like that. But I could never imagine him as immobile, or not able to do things he wanted to do. Glenn enjoyed his freedom, and his ability to be in control. And if he couldn't be in control of his life, he would have been very frustrated.

CE: I understand you were involved with clearing out Gould's apartment, after he died.

RR: It was like taking a pickaxe to Gibraltar! He had literally thousands of tapes, many of them unlabeled, lying all over the apartment. Basically, what I did was get two people – Chris Wilson and Ruth Pincoe[9] – to help get things into some sort of order.

They did a marvelous job. We set up Chris with a tape machine, in the apartment, and he went through literally all of the tapes. It took a year. Meanwhile, Ruth was busy cataloguing all the papers and personal effects. Then we shipped the stuff up to the National Archives, in Ottawa.

CE: There are stories about jars full of prescription drugs that were also found in his apartment. Is this true?[10]

RR: He had a lot of medication, but there was probably more in his room at the Inn on the Park than in his apartment. It wasn't a huge quantity – but it was more than he should have had. That was one point of disagreement between us. I don't think he should have taken so much medication.

CE: You've said that Glenn had his life planned for ten years when he died.

RR: He once predicted that he would die at fifty – and that's how it turned out. But at the same time, he had some plans about retiring: he wanted to retire to Manitoulin Island and start the Glenn Gould Puppy Farm.[11] He wanted me to run it, but as a city-boy I wasn't exactly thrilled with the idea.

CE: What about his artistic intentions?

RR: He didn't discuss that much with me. He was supposed to do something with Oscar Peterson, but that never happened. And he wanted to work with Neville Marriner, in England, but that never got off the ground. And there was an idea to do a recording with von Karajan and the Berlin Phil – Glenn was going to record his own part separately from the orchestra – but that never happened, either.

CE: Are there any misconceptions in the world today about Gould that you would like to see corrected?

RR: Some people think he was very dry and humourless, and didn't laugh or joke around. That was his public image, but it was far from the truth. He was dead serious about music, of course, but he was also a good sport. We could discuss just about anything. And he had his eccentricities, but he could laugh at them. I remember he once jokingly said to someone, "You're crazier than I am!" He understood that he wasn't exactly a middle-of-the-road type.

Postscript

I intend no disrespect at all in saying that Ray Roberts is a typical native-born Torontonian of his generation: uncomplicated and unpretentious. He grew up in a city that was prosperous and rapidly expanding – but was as yet untouched by musical greatness. And in my conversation with Roberts, the sense of astonishment he felt, four decades ago, at coming face to face with a full-blown genius was never far beneath the surface of his comments.

Although endowed with a sunny disposition and an impish sense of humour, a shadow of sadness fell across Roberts when I asked about the circumstances surrounding Gould's death. The loss he experienced at Gould's passing is a wound that time has done little to heal.

CE

NOTES

1 For more information, see Chapter 3: Lorne Tulk.

2 For more information on Eaton Auditorium and Gould's recording work there, see Chapter 1: Verne Edquist (p. 15) and Chapter 3: Andrew Kazdin (p. 87).

3 Gould maintained an apartment at 110 St Clair Ave. W. He also rented a room at the Inn on the Park, at 1075 Leslie St.

4 By road, Toronto is 490 miles from New York City. Gould and Roberts would drive on the Queen Elizabeth Way from Toronto to Fort Erie, Ontario, cross over the Niagara River on the Peace Bridge to Buffalo, New York, and continue the journey on the New York State Thruway.

5 Bert Gould married his second wife, Vera Dobson, in 1980. Glenn Gould did not attend the wedding.

6 Gould stopped flying in 1962.

7 Gould carried on a relationship for five years with Cornelia Foss, a painter and the wife of American composer, conductor and pianist Lukas Foss. In 1967 she left her husband and moved with her two children to Toronto, to be near Gould. However, in 1972 she ended the relationship with Gould and returned to her husband.

8 Gould suffered a stroke on September 27, 1982, two days after his fiftieth birthday.

9 Chris Wilson was a script-writer for classical-music programs on Toronto's CJRT radio station; Ruth Pincoe is a book editor, with a knowledge of classical music.

10 According to biographer Kevin Bazzana, Gould took Placidyl, Dalamene, Nembutal and Luminal, among other prescription drugs. Kevin Bazzana, *Wondrous Strange: The Life and Art of Glenn Gould* (Toronto: McClelland & Stewart, 2003), p. 355.

11 Manitoulin is a large island located in Lake Huron, about 350 miles north of Toronto.

Chapter 2: The Musicians Speak

Introduction

Musicians have ways of sizing each other up that can be fundamentally different from the way the rest of the world assesses them. The fact that they share the same profession endows them with special insights into their peers' strengths and weaknesses. As well, rivalry and jealousy can sometimes colour perceptions. So perhaps it isn't surprising that in this chapter, devoted to musicians who knew and in some cases worked with Gould, a complex picture emerges.

The violinist Jaime Laredo, who collaborated with Gould on a recording of Bach sonatas, stands out here for his words of unqualified praise. For him, working with Gould was "like heaven." Although he wasn't blind to the pianist's eccentricities, his artistic collaboration with Gould was smooth and successful. Today, Laredo remembers it as one of the high points of his career.

However, the remaining five – while not denying Gould's brilliance as a pianist – offer caveats. For them, Gould could be problematic, both professionally and personally. Several have sad stories to tell about being cut out of Gould's life, perhaps due to some incident, or simply because Gould was no longer interested in them.

Ezra Schabas, a clarinetist and administrator who knew Gould in the 1950s and 60s, recalls that Gould could be quarrelsome, and notes that he was capable of doing harm to a fellow musician's career. And the clarinetist-librarian Timothy Maloney, who played in Gould's *Siegfried Idyll* orchestra in 1982, found Gould a conductor of uneven ability – and was shocked by his physical and mental condition. This initial impression led Maloney to pursue the theory that Gould suffered from Asperger's syndrome.

Two musicians who knew Gould in his younger days – the composer John Beckwith and the pianist Stuart Hamilton – both studied with Gould's piano teacher in Toronto, Alberto Guerrero. While they have fond memories of Gould, they take strong exception to his claim that he learned little from his teacher.

The pianist Anton Kuerti takes Gould to task for what he sees as his willful and contrarian approach to interpretation. And both Kuerti and Beckwith make clear their opinion that Gould's achievements have been blown out of proportion by a posthumous "industry" that has grown up around him.

CE

Stuart Hamilton: a Portrait of the Young Artist

Stuart Hamilton was born in Regina, Saskatchewan, in 1929, and moved to Toronto to study piano with Alberto Guerrero – who was also Glenn Gould's teacher. From 1967 to 1971 he appeared in recitals as a solo pianist, in New York, London and throughout Canada. Subsequently, he rose to musical prominence in Toronto as a vocal coach and accompanist, working with many of Canada's leading singers. He was also the founder of Toronto's Opera in Concert company, which he directed from 1974 to 1994. As well, his voice became known across Canada for his work on the CBC *Saturday Afternoon at the Opera* radio broadcasts.

This interview took place in Hamilton's downtown Toronto apartment on March 31, 2011.

CE: Please tell me how you came to Toronto.

SH: I was eighteen at the time, and had won the top scholarship at the Saskatchewan music festival, in 1948. My sister was already in Toronto, studying singing from Dr. Vinci.[1] She had a coach who studied with Alberto Guerrero,[2] and her coach said I should study with him. I had already met Guerrero in Regina, when he was doing examinations for the Conservatory. I knew a lot about opera, but I had a very limited repertoire at the time. At our first lesson, he said, "Play something for me," and I played Debussy's *Claire de Lune*. He said, "That was very beautiful, now play some Beethoven." I said, "I don't have any Beethoven." Then he asked about Bach, and I said I didn't have any Bach, either. So I had lots of work to do on my repertoire!

CE: When did you first meet Gould?

SH: It was shortly after I arrived in Toronto. Guerrero would have musical soirees on Tuesday evenings at his studio, where people played. I wasn't advanced enough to play at these soirees, but many other pupils were quite advanced. The first one I attended was in October – and everyone was talking about a young man who was going to play at the next one. At the next one, Glenn turned up. He would have been fifteen years old at the time. I remember he played a Czerny sonata – and I couldn't believe how beautifully he played it, with fabulous technique. People often think of Czerny's music as dry and mechanical, but this was lovely.

Glenn was charming. He was a modest kid – although aware of his powers – and he was very outgoing. He wasn't the spiky person he became later. We were introduced, and he wanted to know who I was and what I did, and who was my favourite composer. I said, "Debussy," and he said, "I hate Debussy." So we got off to a rocky start! But after that, he was always genuinely interested in what I was doing. There was no question that he thought very little of my abilities as a pianist, but we liked each other. For about three years we had a very nice friendship.

CE: Did you view each other as competitors?

SH: Technically, Glenn was worlds ahead of me, so there was no question of rivalry. And I always wanted to play for singers. But there was another Guerrero student, Ray Dudley,[3] who developed something of a rivalry with Glenn.

CE: What did Gould learn from Guerrero?

SH: On one occasion I said something to Glenn about how much I admired Guerrero. Glenn's response was, "I learned nothing from Guerrero." And I said, "Glenn, that's the dumbest thing you've ever said in your whole life! Watching you play the piano is like having a lesson with Guerrero, because all that you do – all your technique, and even the way you sit at the piano – was influenced by Guerrero. You do everything that Guerrero asked us to do, only you do it better." Glenn said, "Is that so?" He wasn't about to get into a fight about it. But he often said that he learned nothing from Guerrero – and it was as stupid the last time he said it as it was the first time.

I also think Guerrero was something of a father-figure for Glenn. But temperamentally, Glenn and Guerrero were very different. Glenn was a Northerner, and his musical orientation was German. He didn't play French or Russian music, or anything like that. And he was dogmatic: he didn't want opinions, he wanted answers. Guerrero was from a Mediterranean culture, and had a broad worldview. He looked at things from all angles.

He didn't want to take Glenn on as a student when Glenn first approached him: he said that he knew nothing about teaching children. But even at the age of twelve, Glenn wouldn't take no for an answer. Guerrero was the only teacher in Toronto at the time whom Glenn had any respect for. Yet as time went on, Glenn became more and more obsessed with proving to the world that he was essentially self-taught.

CE: *Did you visit the Gould family home?*[4]

SH: I was invited there for supper several times. There was nothing distinguished about the house: it was a typical middle-class WASP Toronto home. One time, after supper, Glenn played a Bach suite. And then he asked, "What are you working on these days?" I said, "I'm looking through a lot of scores by Massenet." I played a few things, such as the "Saint-Suplice" scene from *Manon*. After I finished, he said, "What a bunch of garbage!" He was never interested in the same music I was. He was interested in Bach, Beethoven and Schoenberg.

CE: *And did you visit the family's cottage at Uptergrove?*[5]

SH: It was a wonderful place on Lake Simcoe – it would be worth a fortune today. I would go up for a week at a time in the summer, and listen to Glenn play Bach sinfonias. It was big property, and they had a croquet court. They loved to play, and Glenn and his father were intensely competitive. Once we arranged a quartet: Glenn and his father against Guerrero and me. I was never much of a sports person, but for some reason I got into a groove, and I couldn't do anything wrong. And when I hit Glenn's ball way over to the other side of the lawn, he was outraged! But finally I missed a shot. Glenn and his father went on to win the game.

CE: *What was your impression of Glenn's parents?*[6]

SH: Glenn's father was a nice man, but he didn't have an artistic bone in his body. He was a furrier, and a very successful businessman. Mr. Gould was a big man, very masculine, and also a generous, loving man. But having a son like Glenn was difficult for him: when Glenn showed all the signs of his genius, he became alienated from his father. His father wanted to do normal things with his son, like playing baseball.

The last time I saw Mr. Gould was at the inauguration of the Glenn Gould Studio at the CBC. He had remarried, and he introduced me to his new wife. At the time I said to him, "You must be very proud." His eyes filled with tears, but he didn't say anything.

Glenn and his father fought for Mrs. Gould's attention all the time. She was rather like a Southern Belle: she was very watery, without any backbone, and of average intellect. Yet she knew how to work the "tyranny of the weak," and she got what she wanted. I think Mr. Gould adored her. And I think it was a very happy marriage, except that Glenn was something of a disruptive influence.

CE: And she was also an amateur pianist.

SH: "Amateur" is the right word. But she was the musical parent in the family.

CE: What other events in your friendship with Gould stand out in your memory?

SH: You'll remember the famous time he played the Brahms concerto with Bernstein and the New York Philharmonic.[7] A few days beforehand he phoned me, and said, "I hear you're doing a recital, and I want to hear it." I said I'd be happy to play it for him. So this was arranged for the following week. And in the meantime he played the Brahms in New York.

When I visited Glenn the next week, he was just blazing mad, because of Harold Schonberg's review in the *New York Times*, which said that he didn't have the technique to play the concerto up to the correct tempo.[8] That's all we talked about for a while: Glenn was upset because he was very proud of his technical abilities.

Finally, Glenn said, "You're here to play, aren't you?" I replied, "I'll just play my Chopin for you." I played the *F Minor Ballade*. I was very careful with it, and it was sort of okay. Glenn said, "I can see that you've improved – but you still play like an accompanist." Then he looked through the volume of ballades that I had with me, and he sight-read the *A-Flat Ballade*. It was so beautiful I couldn't believe it! I said, "You must be practising that piece." But he said, "Oh no, I've heard the piece often – but I'm not interested in this music. It's so boring."

CE: It's interesting that Gould would make a disparaging remark about accompanists, because he himself sometimes accompanied singers.

SH: He did – but he wasn't very good at it. There's a recording of Lois Marshall singing Strauss with Glenn.[9] Lois knew exactly what she was doing, but Glenn played the piano part like it was a concerto, and Lois was sort of imposed on top of it. It wasn't really ensemble playing. He wasn't really an ensemble artist – he dominated everything he did. I remember he did a series of programs at the old Conservatory.[10] There was a lot of Bach, but on one of the concerts, they did Schoenberg's *Ode to Napoleon*. I helped prepare Barbara Franklin[11] for it, because she was the narrator, and I attended several rehearsals. Glenn absolutely dominated the ensemble: everybody did what he wanted, because he was so knowledgeable and on top of the whole thing.

CE: As a teenager, did Glenn talk to you about his professional ambitions?

SH: There was never any doubt that Glenn was going to have a big career. Everyone knew that.

CE: *Including Gould himself?*

SH: Oh yes. And he was creative and ambitious about his career.

CE: *Yet there was no real role-model for an aspiring concert pianist in Toronto at the time. There was no concert pianist with a full-blown international career living in the city.*

SH: Before the 1950s, Toronto was a musical backwater – as all of Canada was. Ernest MacMillan, the Toronto Symphony's conductor, was called Lord Largo by some, because of his broad tempi. But he was a very profound musician, and a much better conductor than many people realized. The Toronto Symphony wasn't a bad orchestra.

As for pianists, Reginald Godden[12] was active locally and nationally. And I remember the year after I arrived, a man named Béla Böszörményi-Nagy[13] came from Hungary. He was in Toronto for a few years before he went to teach at Indiana University. As well, there was Weldon Kilburn[14] – later the husband of Lois Marshall – who was well known for his work accompanying singers. Also, there was Boris Berlin,[15] who was a great pal of Guerrero.

But even if there weren't many professional concert pianists in Toronto, just about everyone had a piano in the home, and most people studied the piano, at least for a little while. So Toronto's conservatories were very busy places in those days. If you wanted to study with Guerrero, you had to audition for the privilege – especially once Glenn became famous.

CE: *Did you attend Gould's recitals?*

SH: Certainly – I always wanted to hear what he was doing. I remember a recital at Massey Hall that included Beethoven's *Op. 109 Sonata*, which has that wonderful "Theme and Variations" for the last movement. I've never heard anything so beautiful! That was one of the great musical experiences of my life. But then of course he stopped giving recitals.

CE: *Did you continue to follow his career through his recordings?*

SH: Sure. And occasionally he would phone me, and talk and talk. By that time he was doing his documentaries with the CBC about the North and all that. I didn't know what the hell he was talking about, so all I said was "Yes, Glenn," and "No, Glenn."[16] He fancied himself a great raconteur, but his jokes weren't funny. It was sometimes tiresome to be his friend, on that level.

CE: Did being Canadian help Gould in any way?

SH: It was novel that he was from Canada – but it was incidental, because it was his pianism that made everyone sit up and take notice, not the fact that he was from Canada. More than that, it was his eccentricities that captured popular interest.

CE: So why did he become so very famous?

SH: What made him famous was his first recording of the *Goldbergs*, for Columbia.[17] You could hear every voice with perfect clarity – and nobody else could do that. You could say he rode the crest of the growing interest in pre-classical music – particularly Bach, but he also admired composers like Sweelink and Gibbons.

CE: But he didn't formally align himself with the early music movement.

SH: No, that movement came later. But he was sincerely in love with baroque music, and the nineteenth century meant much less to him. Before Gould emerged, pianists mostly played Chopin, Liszt and Rachmaninoff – and Beethoven was considered "interesting." Glenn turned people's minds around. He was a unique musician.

Postscript

When I first proposed an interview about Glenn Gould to Stuart Hamilton, he responded with enthusiasm. However, the interview with Hamilton almost didn't happen: a week before our scheduled appointment, he suffered a heart attack, and underwent emergency bypass surgery. Happily, he came through the operation in good health – and with his youthful *joie de vivre* intact.

Hamilton has been a musical man-about-town in Toronto for decades, and is well known as a raconteur. Yet beneath his ingenuous exterior lies a keen, analytical mind. He remembers events that transpired half a century ago as if they happened yesterday, chooses his words with precision, and uncannily grasps the motivations that lie beneath human behaviour. CE

NOTES

1. Ernesto Vinci was born in Berlin in 1898 and died in Moncton, New Brunswick, in 1983. He moved to Canada in 1938, establishing himself as a voice instructor in Halifax. In 1945 he moved to Toronto, where he taught at the Royal Conservatory of Music and University of Toronto, until 1979.

2. Alberto Guerrero was born in 1886 in La Serena, Chile, and moved to Toronto in 1918. He taught at Toronto's Hambourg Conservatory until 1922 and at the Toronto (later Royal) Conservatory of Music until his death in Toronto in 1959. For more on Guerrero, see Chapter 2: John Beckwith (pp. 46-49).

3. Raymond Dudley was born in Bowmanville, Ontario, in 1931, and died in Columbia, South Carolina, in 2004. He first appeared with the Toronto Symphony Orchestra in 1951, and subsequently debuted at London's Wigmore Hall (1953) and New York's Town Hall (1955). Throughout his career, he toured extensively in Canada, the USA and Europe. Dudley cultivated an interest in historical keyboard instruments, and also took up conducting.

4. The Goulds lived at 32 Southwood Dr., in a Toronto neighbourhood known as "the Beach" (or "the Beaches"). For more information, see Chapter 4: Robert Fulford (p. 144).

5. Uptergrove is a hamlet near the town of Orillia, Ontario, on the shore of Lake Simcoe. The area, about sixty miles north of Toronto, is popular with Torontonians who enjoy summer cottages, and the Goulds owned a lakefront property there. The Goulds' cottage was winterized (heated and insulated against the cold Canadian winter) and Gould often went there when he wished to escape from Toronto.

6. Glenn Gould's parents were Florence Emma Greig and Russell Herbert Gould. For more information, see Chapter 4: Robert Fulford (pp. 145-146)

7. Gould performed Brahms's *Piano Concerto No. 1* with the New York Philharmonic on April 6, 1962. For more information see Chapter 1: Walter Homburger (p. 9), Chapter 2: Anton Kuerti (p. 61) and Chapter 3: John Roberts (pp. 132-133).

8. On April 7, 1962, a review entitled "Inner Voices of Glenn Gould," by Harold C. Schonberg, appeared in the *New York Times*. In it, Schonberg criticized Gould's tempos, suggesting, "maybe his technique is not so good." For more information, see Chapter 5: Wiliam Littler (p. 165).

9. This recording was made by Gould and Marshall for the Canadian Broadcasting Corporation, and was broadcast by CBC Television on October 15, 1962. The all-Strauss program included "Cäcilie" from *Op. 27*, "Beim Schlafengehen" from *Four Last Songs*, and the *Ophelia-Lieder*.

10. The Toronto (later Royal) Conservatory of Music was located at the corner of University Ave. and College St. until 1963, when it moved to 273 Bloor St. W.

11. The soprano and actress Barbara Franklin was born in Regina, Saskatchewan, in 1929, and died in Toronto in 2009.

12 Reginald Godden was born in Tunbridge Wells, England, in 1905, and died in Burlington, Ontario, in 1987. Beginning in 1928, he taught for twenty-one years at the Toronto (later Royal) Conservatory of Music. Touring as a pianist in Canada, he gave Canadian premiere performances of works by Prokofiev, Shostakovich and Copland.

13 Béla Böszörményi-Nagy was born in Satoraljaujhely, Hungary, in 1919. He studied music in Budapest, where his teachers included Ernö von Dohnányi and Zoltán Kodály. He died in 1990 in Boston.

14 Weldon Kilburn was born in Lloydminster, Alberta, in 1906, and died in Toronto in 1986. He began to teach at the Toronto Conservatory of Music in 1930, and became soprano Lois Marshall's vocal coach and accompanist in 1936, serving in this capacity until 1971. The two were married in 1968.

15 Boris Berlin was born in Kharkov, Russia, in 1907, and died in Toronto in 2001. Following studies in Sebastopol, Geneva and Berlin, he toured Europe as a concert pianist until he moved to Canada in 1925. After three years at Toronto's Hambourg Conservatory, he accepted a teaching position at the Toronto Conservatory in 1928. He also taught at the University of Toronto.

16 Gould's radio documentary *The Idea of North* was first broadcast by the CBC on December 27, 1967. For more information see Chapter 3: Vincent Tovell (p. 106) and Lorne Tulk (pp. 118-119).

17 Gould's first recording for Columbia Records of Bach's *Goldberg Variations* (ML 6022) was issued in 1955.

John Beckwith: Alberto Guerrero's Studio

John Beckwith is a prominent Canadian composer, pedagogue and writer on music. He moved to Toronto in 1945, and studied piano at the Toronto (later Royal) Conservatory of Music with Alberto Guerrero, who was also Glenn Gould's teacher. It was at this time that he first came to know Gould.

Subsequently, Beckwith taught at the University of Toronto for many years, and served as Dean of the U of T's Faculty of Music from 1970 to 1977. Throughout his career he maintained an interest in Gould's creative work, and he wrote reviews and articles about Gould on several occasions. Beckwith is also the author of *In Search of Alberto Guerrero*, a biography of his and Gould's teacher.

This interview took place at Beckwith's home in Toronto, on August 10, 2010.

CE: When did you first meet Glenn Gould? And when did you first hear him play the piano?

JB: It was in 1945, in the first year I came to Toronto. I was a student of Alberto Guerrero, and I met him at Guerrero's studio, I expect.[1] I used to have my lesson just before or just after Glenn's. We were all part of a group of students, including Malcolm Troup, Ray Dudley, Stuart Hamilton, and others. We saw each other frequently, and played for each other. Once or twice Glenn invited me to the Gould family cottage, on Lake Simcoe.

I heard him play on at least one Conservatory concert – and on one occasion we played on the same program: I was on a concert with Lois Marshall and Gould in 1946. And in the spring of 1946 I competed against Gould in the Kiwanis Festival. He came first, and I came third, out of twenty-five competitors. At the end of the school year, I heard him play Beethoven's *Fourth Piano Concerto* with the student orchestra, conducted by Mazzoleni.[2] Everyone who was there said that was a transfixing experience. I agreed. We couldn't believe that this thirteen-year-old could give such a luminous performance.

CE: What did you think of him at that time, as a person and as a pianist?

JB: I reacted with astonishment to how quickly he developed, and how powerful his ability to communicate was. His technique seemed effortless, although I know he worked very hard at it. In later years he always said he didn't practise – but in those days he practised like a demon. He was working very hard, and Guerrero was working hard to coach him.

CE: You've written about Guerrero's influence on Gould's technique.³ Did he also learn from Guerrero the business of being a professional concert pianist?

JB: Guerrero was great friends with Claudio Arrau, and if you talked to Guerrero about Arrau's international career, he would say "I wouldn't like that kind of life – to be always getting on and off a plane, and never to see your family for half a year." And I don't think Gould really wanted that kind of life, either. I recall that in the early 1950s he went through a kind of crisis – a kind of withdrawal – and he thought about how much concertizing he could take. When he went to Washington and New York, in 1955, it was the result of a decision to push his career. But I don't think it was the result of any discussion with Guerrero.

CE: Then perhaps Guerrero was, in some indirect way, an influence on Gould's decision to later withdraw from the concert stage?

JB: That's possible – but I wouldn't say so in exactly those terms.

CE: Gould was never inclined to credit Guerrero as much of an influence. Why do you think this was?

I don't know, because I never discussed that with Glenn. But the image of Gould as essentially self-taught made for a better story – and perhaps by the time Gould was an international celebrity he had become somewhat hard-nosed about that kind of thing. Yet Guerrero was Gould's principal music teacher for ten years. They were very close, and he influenced Gould from the ground up. It's no exaggeration to call him a "father figure."

To be sure, they had different temperaments. Gould liked to say that he was Nordic and Guerrero was Latin. I don't like that sort of racist way of expressing the idea – but they were quite different. And they did have disagreements: I remember Guerrero once said that if you wanted to get Glenn to do something, you should tell him to do the opposite!

At some point, Glenn started to take his differences with Guerrero more seriously. He found it difficult to agree to disagree. In an argument, he couldn't just say, "You see it one way and I see it another." That wasn't Glenn's way: either you agreed with him or you were cast out into the great beyond.

CE: What about Gould's keyboard mannerisms – leaning into the piano, and humming while he sang?

JB: Guerrero called them "antics," and he tried to get Gould to control them. I think that was a point of contention between them. However, Guerrero had his own characteristic way of playing: he sat quite low at the piano, and he had a flat-fingered way of playing. When I first saw Glenn play, I thought he was copying Guerrero. But the more eccentric things, like conducting with the left hand while he played with the right, were not Guerrero's style at all.

CE: *Did you attend many performances by Gould? Are there any, in particular, that stand out in your memory?*

JB: I was at a lot of his performances – before he went to the States, and afterwards. And I reviewed some of them for the *Canadian Music Journal* and the *Toronto Star*.[4] I remember an outstanding Toronto Symphony concert, where he did the Schoenberg *Concerto* and the Mozart *C Minor Concerto* on the same program, with Walter Susskind conducting. Also, I attended two concerts he organized with Robert Fulford at the Royal Conservatory in the 1950s.[5] They were revelatory, because the repertoire was entirely new: nobody had played any Webern in Toronto. And his performance of the Berg *Sonata* was amazing!

CE: *What was the source of Gould's affinity for the Second Viennese School?*

JB: One day, in a lesson, Guerrero played the *Op. 19* pieces by Schoenberg to Gould. Guerrero had played them in concerts, and he knew them quite well. Gould had never heard them, and he thought they were terrible. But it planted a seed: about three weeks later, he wrote some pieces of his own, in imitation of Schoenberg. Shortly after that, he learned Schoenberg's *Op. 25*.

I can also remember when the first recording of Berg's *Lulu* came out. Glenn and I got the score out of the library, and we sat down together at his house and listened to the recording. It wasn't a very good recording, but hearing it and discussing it with Glenn was tremendously stimulating.

CE: *Of course, Gould is most famous today for his recordings of J.S. Bach. Why was Gould so simpatico with Bach?*

JB: I first heard him play Bach in the Kiwanis Festival in 1946. He played the *B-Flat Minor Prelude and Fugue* from Book I of the *WTC*: the performance was incredibly beautiful, and as clear as a bell. I don't know anyone who could play contrapuntal parts so beautifully and expressively. He liked to say, "Music isn't expressive – it's just notes." But you wouldn't think so if you watched him play, intensely crouched over the keyboard, consumed in the music as though his life depended on it!

It's almost as if he felt if it has counterpoint in it, it must be good. What appealed to him in music was the impact of several things sounding against each other simultaneously. The only parts of Haydn and Mozart he liked were the development passages, where there was a little bit of fugato. And his love of counterpoint was a source of his later documentaries, which he called "contrapuntal radio."[6]

Gould's interest in Bach came from Guerrero.[7] When I studied with Guerrero, he was very insistent that his students do Bach: I performed all the inventions and sinfonias, as well as the *Goldbergs*. Guerrero got Gould to listen voice by voice, and to hear the interplay of the voices.

CE: Did you have much to do with Gould as he became increasingly famous?

JB: I didn't see him as much after his New York debut. He was standoffish towards a lot of people after the New York experience – he gradually became a different person. Until the late 1950s I would get a warm Christmas greeting from him every year. But at some point it became a printed card from his manager's office. And one time, in the early 1970s, I called him on the phone and asked if he would come to the University of Toronto to speak to the students. "I don't do that kind of thing anymore," he replied.

CE: Do you think that your reviews of Gould's performances led to a cooling of your friendship?

JB: That was certainly a cause – and I don't blame him, because I said some nasty things![8]

CE: In your 1961 Canadian Forum article you mention Gould's stated intention to give up live performance. What was your reaction when Gould stopped playing in public three years later?

JB: His manager, Walter Homburger, tried to dissuade him.[9] But I believed it was what Gould really wanted to do, and I thought that interesting things would come of it. "What will Glenn do next?" was always an open question, because you couldn't predict him. Sometimes what he did was marvelous and sometimes it was outrageous.

CE: One of the reasons Gould expressed for ending his concert career was to allow himself more time to compose. Yet he never wrote much music. Why do you think Gould composed so little?

JB: He found it hard. I remember when he was working on his string quartet, he would say he had made it up to bar 302, or bar 428, or something like that. Composing was a bar-by-bar struggle for him. When I first heard the piano miniatures he wrote in imitation of Schoenberg, I thought they were ingenious.[10] Now I think they're not very good. They're strained.

He had lots of ideas: one of his "retirement projects" was to compose an opera.[11] But he never got anywhere with it. *So You Want to Write a Fugue?* is a clever party-piece.[12] It has nice quotations in it, and the text is quite funny. But it's one thing to do something like that and another to do a twenty-minute string quartet.[13] Gould's string quartet is a labourious piece: it was performed at a Schoenberg conference in Ottawa a couple of years ago, and it's a hard thing to sit through. I admired the players for performing it because they hardly put their bows down from beginning to end. But because it's by Gould, it gets performances.

For Gould, the compositional spark just wasn't there. He understood music as a performer, but he couldn't really compose it. It's a different way of thinking – and it's not any professional antagonism that makes me say this.

CE: What do you think of Gould's posthumous reputation, as it has evolved?

JB: I'm glad that the recordings are still available, but I wish they were written about more. And I wish Glenn hadn't been turned into a cult, and an industry – I think turning Glenn Gould into James Dean was unfortunate. There's a lot of misinformation, and a lot of junk, and I think the production of books has become excessive. Let's have an end to the trivia and the gossip. Some of what's happened is the fault of people who were devoted to him, and were well meaning. But much of his reputation today also has to do with Gould's desire to control his own public image. I think a lot of the posthumous things that have happened are a result of that.

When the first Glenn Gould piano competition was going to take place, I wrote a letter to the *Globe and Mail* saying that it was a contradiction in terms to hold a competition in honour of Gould.[14] Nikki Goldschmidt, who was organizing the event, didn't like that. Of course, to have a concert hall and a park in Toronto named after Gould are ways of signifying that his achievements were extraordinary.[15] But is that the best way to do it, in his case? That's the question.

Postscript

It was not without some reluctance that John Beckwith consented to be interviewed here. The problem wasn't that Beckwith is not interested in Gould: he'd previously written about him on several occasions. But our interview left me with the impression he has come to feel, at this point in time, that he has already said all that he cares to say about Gould.

Did other motives underlie Beckwith's reluctance? He does not display the unalloyed joy in Gould's posthumous celebrity that some other interviewees in this book do. On the contrary, he speaks disparagingly of the "industry" and "cult" that have sprung up around Gould – and he does not wish to feed the beast. As well, a few of Beckwith's comments suggest that he thinks Gould is over-rated in some ways. Compared to Beckwith's own lifelong commitment to composition (he has written over 130 works), Gould's compositional efforts look dilettantish – and there is a touch of indignation in Beckwith's reaction to the musical world's interest in Gould's modest *oeuvre*.

CE

NOTES

1 Alberto Guerrero was born in 1886 in La Serena, Chile, and moved to Toronto in 1918. He taught at the Hambourg Conservatory until 1922 and at the Toronto (later Royal) Conservatory until his death in 1959.

2 On May 8, 1946, Gould performed the first movement of Beethoven's *Piano Concerto No. 4* at Massey Hall, with the Toronto Conservatory Orchestra under the baton of Ettore Mazzoleni.

3 Concerning Guerrero's influence on Gould's technique, Beckwith has written: "Gould studied to sit low at the keyboard, address the keys with a low wrist and flat fingers, and support his arms from the shoulder blades – all attitudes for which Guerrero's playing provided the model. Many [Guerrero] students remarked that Gould's playing always reminded them of Guerrero's." John Beckwith, *In Search of Alberto Guerrero* (Waterloo: Wilfrid Laurier University Press, 2006), p. 100. See also John Beckwith, "Shattering a Few Myths," *The Music Papers: Talks and Articles by a Canadian Composer, 1961-1994* (Ottawa: Golden Dog Press, 1997), pp. 166-175.

4 Among Beckwith's reviews for the *Toronto Star* are a discussion of Gould's recordings (published October 15, 1960), and a review of Gould's Toronto Symphony Orchestra engagement of December 7, 1960 (published the following day). In the *Canadian Music Journal* Beckwith wrote about Gould's recording of the last three Beethoven sonatas (Spring 1957) and performances at the Stratford Festival (Fall 1961). Beckwith also reviewed Gould's recordings for *Canadian Forum* magazine (January 1961).

5   Three concerts were presented by Gould, with the assistance of his friend Robert Fulford, under the rubric New Music Associates. The first, on October 4, 1952, was a program of music by Schoenberg; the second, on January 9, 1954, featured works by Schoenberg, Webern and Berg; and the third was entirely devoted to Bach. For more information see Chapter 4: Robert Fulford (p. 148).

6   Gould's radio documentaries include *The Idea of North*, *The Latecomers* and *Quiet in the Land*. For more information see Chapter 3: Vincent Tovell (p. 106) and Chapter 3: Lorne Tulk (pp. 118-119).

7   In *In Search of Alberto Guerrero*, Beckwith notes Guerrero's strong interest in Bach's music, mentioning performances of Bach by Guerrero in Toronto in 1918 and 1922 (pp. 49 and 54, respectively). Beckwith also lists repertoire for several all-Bach recitals by Guerrero between 1933 and 1935 (pp. 72-73): *Preludes and Fugues Nos. 1-11* from *WTC Volume I*, *Partita No. 1 in B Flat* and the *Chromatic Fantasia and Fugue*, performed on October 2, 1933; *Partita No. 4 in D*, the *Italian Concerto* and an *English Suite*, performed on November 3, 1934; and the *Inventions* and *Sinfonias*, performed on November 23, 1935.

8   Beckwith's judgements of Gould varied. For example, in his December 7, 1960, *Toronto Star* review of Gould's appearance with the TSO the previous evening, Beckwith praised Gould for "superb, deeply thoughtful performances of piano concertos by Schoenberg and Mozart." However, in his review of Gould's recording of the last three Beethoven sonatas (Columbia ML 5130) for *Canadian Forum* (January 1961), Beckwith accused Gould of "irrational decisions," "misconceptions of tempo or structure," "outright insensitivities" and "mugging."

9   Beckwith's recollection of Homburger's efforts to dissuade Gould from retiring from the concert stage differs substantially from Homburger's own testimonial on this subject. See Chapter 1: Walter Homburger (p. 10).

10 Gould's first serial piano compositions were written in 1950, and premiered by Gould in 1951. They were published under the title *Five Pieces for Piano* by Schott in 1995.

11 As early as 1956, Gould expressed interest in writing an opera based on Franz Kafka's *Metamorphosis*.

12 *So You Want to Write a Fugue?*, with music and text by Gould, is scored for SATB chorus with piano or string quartet. It was premiered on CBC Television in 1963 and published by Schirmer in 1964.

13 Gould's *String Quartet No. 1* was completed in 1955 and premiered by the Montreal String Quartet the following year. It was first recorded in 1960 by the Symphonia Quartet (Columbia MS 6178) and published by Schott in 1999.

14 The Toronto-based 1985 International Bach Piano Competition was intended by organizers (Toronto impresario Nicholas Goldschmidt and others) as a tribute to Gould. Beckwith's letter to Toronto's *Globe and Mail* newspaper appeared in print on March 21, 1984. It began: "There could hardly be a less appropriate memorial to Glenn Gould than the recently announced International Bach Piano Competition."

15 The Glenn Gould Studio is a recital hall and recording studio within the Canadian Broadcasting Centre, 250 Front St. W. in Toronto. Glenn Gould Park is located at the intersection of Avenue Rd. and St Clair Ave. W. in Toronto.

Ezra Schabas: Gould in Stratford

Ezra Schabas was born in New York in 1924, where he studied at the Juilliard School and Columbia University. In 1952 he moved to Toronto, where he became deeply involved in Canada's music culture, as a performing musician, teacher, journalist and administrator. Between 1978 and 1983 he was the Principal of Toronto's Royal Conservatory of Music.

Schabas is the author of several books, including *Theodore Thomas: America's Conductor and Builder of Orchestras, 1835-1905*; *Sir Ernest MacMillan: the Importance of Being Canadian*; and *There's Music in These Walls* (a history of the Royal Conservatory of Music).

This interview took place on June 17, 2011, at Schabas's apartment in mid-town Toronto.

CE: When did you first meet Glenn Gould?

ES: I came to Toronto in 1952 because there were a lot of playing possibilities, especially with the CBC. At that time I was, I can honestly say, a very good clarinetist – and this was borne out in the next eight years, when I was doing all the top work in town, except for the Toronto Symphony Orchestra.

And soon after I arrived, a job fell into my lap, as Director of the Concert Bureau and Publicity at the Royal Conservatory of Music. This position had been run by two different people, and the Conservatory decided to amalgamate the two jobs. I took the position, and I loved it. I didn't know much about the concert world, but I learned fast.

I'd certainly heard of Gould, as one of the outstanding artists in Toronto. And one day he walked into my office, and wanted to chat with me. Basically, he wanted to find out how much I knew about music, because he was looking for people to talk to and exchange ideas with. So we became quite friendly. In the first or second year of our acquaintance, he came to my house, and we played through the Brahms clarinet sonatas together. I found his approach eccentric – but in the best sense of the word. And I performed in one of his New Music Associates[1] concerts: I was the clarinetist in the Webern *Saxophone Quartet*. We had great fun rehearsing, because Gould couldn't get the triplets right. He was then in the midst of his twelve-tone period, and told me that he was interested in studying with Edward Steuermann,[2] in New York, but he didn't do it.

CE: I understand you were involved in one of Gould's European tours.

ES: Yes. In 1957 the conductor Boyd Neel[3] called the Canada Council, which had just been formed, and pointed out that Canada had no representation at the forthcoming World's Fair in Belgium.[4] Then he made inquiries with the authorities in Belgium, and they said, yes, they'd like to have a Canadian orchestra – but they'd like to have Gould, too. We got in touch with Gould, and he said he would be in Europe at the time, and could do it.

The long and short of it was that we flew a pick-up orchestra to London, where we rehearsed. A couple of days later, we got on a small plane and flew to Ostend. Gould was already there, waiting at the airport, in a big American Plymouth. We played there to a very modest crowd.

He drove off in his Plymouth, and I travelled with the orchestra to Scheveningen, near The Hague. In Scheveningen, we met him at the hall where we were going to play. When Gould went in to try out the piano, he complained that the hall was too cold, and an attendant brought in a heater, which made him happier. In fact, Gould tried to buy the heater from the man, but he wouldn't sell it. Unfortunately, the concert was a box office flop: there might have been fifty people in a hall that seated 1,500.

Then we travelled to Brussels, for the World's Fair, where Gould was very well received by a sophisticated audience. After the concerts in Brussels, Gould went off to his other European engagements. It was a very pleasant experience, and we had a lot of laughs.

CE: Let's talk about your connection with Gould at the Stratford Festival.[5] First of all, how did you come to be connected with Stratford?

ES: I played in Stratford from 1956 to 1960, whenever they needed a clarinetist. I performed in the orchestra for Britten's *Rape of Lucretia* in 1956 – and I was the contractor for the orchestra and a player in *The Turn of the Screw*, when Britten brought his English Opera Group to Stratford in 1957. And I also served as the concert manager for *The Beggar's Opera*, the following year. I was Lou Applebaum's[6] sidekick, and I helped him with management details. In some ways, I *was* the manager, although there were several other people who also helped.

In 1960, Lou said, "Why can't we have something like Marlboro[7] in Stratford?" His idea was to have some chamber music played by top artists. He said, "We could build it around Gould, if he's interested." And he was. Then Lou asked the violinist Oscar Shumsky and the cellist Leonard Rose, so we had a trio.[8] And I was appointed to manage the group in 1961.

CE: What was the summer of 1961 like for you at Stratford?

ES: I rented a house, and brought my family to Stratford. Glenn liked my children – I had five of them – and he came around constantly. He gave them all signed records, which they coveted. So generally it was a very warm relationship.

The intentions of the trio were high-minded – but I remember constant arguments about programing. Shumsky would say one thing, and Gould would say another. There was always a tension between Gould and Shumsky about programing, but they had great respect for each other as musicians. Rose just said, "Tell me what to play, and I'll play it."

CE: Did you sit in on the trio's rehearsals? What were they like?

ES: The rehearsals were very civilized. Gould and Shumsky talked a lot: I think Gould was learning as much from Shumsky as Shumsky was from Gould. And Rose would say, "Enough talking – let's play some more."

CE: And I understand that the summer of 1961 marked an end in your dealings with Gould.

ES: That summer, I spent a lot of time with Glenn preparing the concerts. And I recall getting into a slight tussle with him at a rehearsal. He spoke rather rudely to me, which was not in his character, but it happened. So I decided that even though I was being paid very well, it was a job I could do without. I resigned at the end of 1961 – and that was the end of my connection with the Stratford Festival, and with Glenn Gould.

CE: Did you part on frosty terms with Gould?

ES: Sort of. I never spoke to him again, until 1981. When he found out that I'd resigned, he never spoke to me about it, and I never spoke to him about it. Perhaps I took umbrage too easily: I hated to give up the association with three great musicians.

CE: As you know, three years later, Gould withdrew from the concert stage. Did you have any sense, in the summer of 1961, that he didn't enjoy playing in public?

55

ES: No, not at all. I think he enjoyed it very much – and he attracted a lot of attention, of course. I had no real inkling that he would give up public performance.

CE: *Gould frequently appeared at the Stratford Festival in the 1950s and 1960s. Why did Gould like Stratford so much?*

ES: For Gould, Stratford was the ideal setting for summer work. And he may have taken a kind of Canadian pride in the Stratford Festival, as many Canadians did, because Gould always felt very Canadian. Also, he fit in well there because his needs were small: the things Gould wanted to do didn't cost Stratford a lot of money. And he was quite a figure around town, with his overcoats in the summer.

CE: *Perhaps it was the right place for him to explore new repertoire.*

ES: Sure – absolutely. At Stratford, Gould was given free reign to do what he liked. Because he was fond of Richard Strauss he did a Strauss program with soprano Ellen Faull, from New York. Her husband was a psychiatrist, and he had great fun analyzing Gould with all kinds of Freudian theories. And on another concert, Gould had his string quartet played. I said that it sounded like Strauss, which I intended as a criticism. He agreed, and said, "People may not appreciate it now, but in fifty years they will." It's been fifty years, and the piece isn't exactly popular – so it looks like he was a little off the mark in his estimation of his own compositions.

CE: *You said that he contacted you again in 1981. What was that about?*

ES: He said he was going to conduct a recording the *Siegfried Idyll*, in the original orchestration.[9] The reason he called me was to go through a list of players he was thinking of hiring. He had respect for my knowledge of musicians. I'd say, "Yes, this one is fine," or "No, that one would be too difficult to deal with." And I put forward some ideas of my own. He said he was very pleased with my suggestions, and told me that the rehearsals were going well. But it was all done over the telephone: I never saw him in person at that time.

CE: *How would you describe Gould's personality in the years you knew him?*

ES: Basically, he was very well adjusted. He liked people very much, and he liked dropping in on friends in Toronto. He would drop in on me just because he felt like it, and I was just one of many friends he had. He had a great sense of humour – I think everyone who knew him at that time would say pretty much the same thing.

CE: Did you make much of his eccentricities?

ES: No. If a guy can play the piano like that, I'm not going to bother with personal eccentricities! I have the greatest respect for great artists. And as a great artist, he didn't have some of the quirks that other great artists might have. I can think of one pianist I know who totally lacks a sense of humour: he takes everything so seriously that it's very hard to talk to him. In the years that I knew Gould, he never had any of those manifestations.

However, there was one very disturbing situation that arose, with a string player in Toronto, in about 1960.[10] Glenn and this musician had done a lot of playing together – he was a first-class player. And then something happened: one day, when Gould had an orchestra concert coming up, he said, "I don't want to play this concert if this man is in the orchestra." So the man had to leave the orchestra – and after that he couldn't get hired for orchestras. And in 1961, Gould said he didn't want this man at Stratford, and was prepared to put this in his contract, if necessary.

Eventually, the player left Toronto and got work elsewhere – and came back in the 1970s, but avoided Gould like the plague. By this point, Gould was no longer playing in public, so he didn't have to worry about Gould telling people not to hire him. I once asked him – and again recently – if he knew why Gould shunned him, and he said, "I've racked my brains all these years, and I don't know why." He begged Gould to give him some idea as to what he did wrong, but Gould refused to say. And to this day, he doesn't know what happened. It was a very cruel thing to do.

CE: Why do you think the world remains so very interested in Gould, three decades after his death?

ES: He had a kind of personality that the concert world doesn't see very often. He had his crazy personal style – I think of that dispute with Bernstein over tempos – and he was a radio producer, and a writer, as well. There are so many aspects of Gould's life – and they're often so contradictory – that there's been nobody else like him. Who else do you know in the concert world who gives biographers so much to work on? That's why there's no end to all the Gouldiana.

Postscript

Ezra Schabas was certainly not the only person to suddenly find himself shut out of Gould's circle. In this interview, Schabas graciously accepts partial responsibility, for "taking umbrage too easily." But Gould was also capable of taking umbrage – and his tendency to turn his back on friends and associates wasn't one of the more admirable aspects of his character.

On the other hand, Gould did sometimes develop enduring relationships with people, places and things. His association with the Stratford Festival lasted a decade: from 1953, when he played two recitals in the festival's inaugural season, to his last appearance there in 1963, as his concert career was drawing to a close. Except for Gould's home city of Toronto, there's no place where he gave more public performances than Stratford, Ontario.

CE

NOTES

1. This concert took place on January 9, 1954. For more information, see Chapter 4: Robert Fulford (p. 151 [n. 8]).

2. Edward (or Eduard) Steuermann (1892-1964) was an Austrian-American pianist, composer and pedagogue. He was a student of Arnold Schoenberg, and a champion of his music in Toronto.

3. (Louis) Boyd Neel (1905-1981) was born in England, where he established the Boyd Neel Orchestra in 1933. In 1953 he was appointed Dean of the Royal Conservatory of Music.

4. The 1958 Brussels World's Fair (Expo 58) took place from April 17 to October 19. Other musical events at the fair included performances by the Prague Philharmonic and the world premiere of Edgard Varèse's *Poème électronique*.

5. Canada's Stratford Festival was founded in the town of Stratford, Ontario (eighty miles west of Toronto) in 1952. The annual event quickly grew to become one of the largest summer festivals in North America. While primarily a theatre festival, in the early years music was also presented at Stratford.

6. Louis Applebaum (1918-2000) was a Canadian composer of concert and film music. He was also an arts administrator, and served as the Stratford Festival's first music director, from 1953 to 1960. Subsequently, he was the first Executive Director of the Ontario Arts Council, and co-author of the *Report of the Federal Cultural Policy Review Committee* (commonly known as the "Applebaum-Hébert Report") in 1982, which greatly influenced Canada's cultural policies.

7. The Marlboro Music School and Festival was founded in Marlboro, Vermont, in 1951.

8   The violinist Oscar Shumsky was born in Philadelphia in 1917, and died in Rye, New York, in 2000. He studied with Leopold Auer, played in the Primrose Quartet, and was active as a concert soloist and pedagogue. The cellist Leonard Rose was born in 1918 in Washington, and passed away in White Plains, New York, in 1984. He served as principal cellist of the Cleveland Orchestra and the New York Philharmonic, before embarking on his solo career.

9   This recording was made in Toronto in the summer of 1982. For more information, see Chapter 2: Timothy Maloney (pp. 72-75).

10 This musician, whom Schabas discreetly declined to name, is the violinist Morry Kernerman. According to Gould biographer Kevin Bazzana, Gould and Kernerman "parted in a strange and bitter way," adding that "Kernerman could get no answer as to why he severed the relationship." *Wondrous Strange: the Life and Art of Glenn Gould* (Toronto: McClelland & Stewart, 2003), p. 376.

Anton Kuerti: Pianist to Pianist

Toronto-based concert pianist Anton Kuerti was born in Vienna in 1938. His family immigrated to the USA shortly thereafter, and he made his professional debut with the Boston Pops Orchestra at the age of eleven.

Kuerti moved to Toronto in 1965, and soon established himself as one of Canada's foremost pianists, with a worldwide career. A prolific recording artist, he has recorded the complete Beethoven sonatas and concertos for piano, as well as the Schubert sonatas and the Brahms concertos, among other works.

Kuerti is also an essayist on political and cultural issues, and in 1994 published an article in Toronto's *Globe and Mail* newspaper entitled "All That Glitters Is Not Gould."[1] In it, he questioned many aspects of Gould's interpretations – and also the posthumous admiration for Gould that shows no sign of abating. "Even in Gould's homeland," Kuerti asked rhetorically, "isn't this getting a bit out of proportion?"

This interview took place on November 5, 2011, at Kuerti's home in downtown Toronto.

CE: When did you become aware of Gould?

AK: It was in the 1950s, through John Roberts, who was a producer with the CBC in Winnipeg.[2] I played a concert with the Winnipeg CBC Orchestra, and we became friends. He told me about Glenn, and suggested I introduce myself to him.

At that time, I was still a student at the Curtis Institute of Music in Philadelphia. So I went to a concert that he gave at the Academy of Music – a recital, towards the end of the 1950s. I went backstage, and introduced myself. He seemed quite friendly, and we kept in touch.

I spent some time with him in various places: in Cleveland and in Salzburg, whenever we happened to be in the same place. One day in Salzburg we went to a restaurant together. This was before I became a vegetarian – and I don't know if I was trying to be a little bit mean, but I ordered scrambled brains with eggs, an Austrian specialty. It horrified him! He had to leave the table and retreat to his room.

CE: Where else did you hear him play?

AK: I was at that famous performance of Brahms's *First Piano Concerto*, with Bernstein, in New York.³ It was a pretty silly interpretation, in my opinion. But at the time I didn't realize – as I later came to realize – that it wasn't a joke for Glenn. And I think he was quite hurt and offended by Bernstein's remarks beforehand. He was feeling dejected after the performance: he wasn't seeing anyone afterwards.

But I went backstage and said, "Glenn, don't you want to see a friend? He said, "Oh yes, Anton, come in." I wasn't going to tell him that I liked the performance, because I absolutely didn't. So I said, "Hi Glenn, how are you feeling?" He said, "Now that I'm retiring from playing concerts, I'm feeling pretty good." And so I replied, "After what we've just heard, Glenn, maybe it's time."

I guess I was just trying to be funny – but perhaps it was a rather hollow joke. His reaction was "Et tu, Brute" – and he never spoke to me again. Glenn loved making fun of people, but he didn't take it very well when someone did it to him.

CE: In 1964, Gould fulfilled his dream, and stopped playing in public. What did you think of this decision?

AK: What you have to picture is that I was a younger pianist – and I would have loved to have some of the concerts he was giving up. His position struck me as a bit of one-upmanship, as if he were above playing for the public. It seemed like he was saying, "You might be thirsty for some engagements, but I don't want them anymore." That created a touch of resentment on my part.

CE: And the following year, 1965, you moved to Toronto. Did you make any attempt to communicate with Gould once you and he were living in the same city?

AK: I made one attempt. Quite a few years after I came to Canada, I sent him a Christmas card, which pretended to be from the Swiss ambassador, asking whether there was a possibility of discussions that might lead to negotiations that might lead to a resumption of relations between the Kuerti People's Republic and the Gould Kingdom.

I put it this way because I'm known for my left-wing views, and Glenn was a monarchist, and rather conservative. And I know he received the card, because it's in the Gould archives today. But he never replied.

CE: Did you listen to his recordings and broadcasts after Gould had withdrawn from the concert stage?

AK: I heard, by chance, the Beethoven *Sonata Op. 78* on the radio. And I thought it was so perverse: everywhere that Beethoven marks legato he played staccato, everywhere Beethoven marked staccato he played legato. Beethoven couldn't have been wrong all the time! Certainly, that's not my own approach. As I sometimes jokingly say, "Brendel should play Beethoven Brendel's way, and Ashkenazy should play Beethoven Ashkenazy's way – and I'll play Beethoven Beethoven's way."

I don't like to be too academic about doing everything exactly as a composer specified it. I change a few notes in the Beethoven sonatas – not very many, but a few that I think are simply wrong. Of course, we all want to have our own way of playing, and our own interpretations. And I think a fair amount of flexibility is needed to play music with excellent character and spirit. But Gould's approach seemed calculated. To turn everything upside down the way Gould did, as a trademark – I find that improper.

The interesting thing is that with some music one doesn't closely associate with Gould – like Scriabin, for example – his performances could be perfectly normal. You wouldn't immediately recognize these performances as Glenn Gould at all.

CE: *What about Gould's Bach?*

AK: There's a wonderful rhythmic intensity and propulsion, and wonderful control. But it seems as though, rather than following Bach, he's following his own method. Again, there are perverse things: in the *D Major Fugue* from the *Well-Tempered Clavier*, one can debate whether it should be played as a double dot, or a single dot. But Mr. Gould has to do it differently from everyone else, by playing the first as a double dot, and the next as a single dot. I do believe that the dot originally meant make the note longer – not necessarily fifty percent longer. But it can't be both ways, I don't think.

CE: *What did you think of Gould's performance technique?*

AK: It was amazing: his control, strength, speed, voicing – it was all very admirable.

CE: *I'm thinking of other things, like the way he sat so very low at the keyboard.*

AK: I'm sure he sat at the level that was comfortable to him. I sit fairly low, too. But I'm also convinced he was knowledgeable about how his "antics," as they might be called – his singing, his chair, his whole appearance – gave him huge publicity. I think he exploited that.

There's a story of Gould playing with George Szell in Cleveland: I don't know if it's true, but "si non è vero è ben trovato." Szell was thought of as a very serious person, but he had quite a wit. And once, before a rehearsal, Gould was adjusting his chair up and down, trying to get it just right. Apparently Szell said, "Mr. Gould, if you could shave a millimeter off your derriere perhaps we could get started with the rehearsal."

CE: Which pianists were influences on Gould?

AK: I would compare him with the composer Olivier Messiaen, who wrote as though he never heard any other music, ever. Gould was a unicum – and I don't see him as having been influenced very much. Certainly, he claimed that he didn't learn very much from his teacher.[4]

CE: One pianist whom Gould came to view as almost a personal nemesis was Vladimir Horowitz.[5] Do you have any thoughts on why Gould would have such an antipathy towards Horowitz?

AK: Gould was, first and foremost, an intellectual musician. But Horowitz was more instinctive. He did strange things, for no apparent reason, but they sound good, and beautiful. Gould had a similar way of doing strange things, but they were more intellectually based. If Gould was self-critical at all – and I'm not sure he was – maybe he heard some of the same mannerisms in Horowitz as he heard in his own playing.

CE: As an adult, Gould claimed that he didn't practise much. Is that possible?

AK: What Gould was able to do was amazing – and even more amazing if he didn't have to work at it. Obviously he was endowed with an extraordinary talent: he could play a Strauss opera score from memory. So who's to say that it was impossible for him to play without practising much? Of course, there are a number of musicians who pretend they don't have to practise much, and perhaps he was one of them. I know it would be impossible for me – I couldn't play without practising.

CE: Three decades after his death, do you think that the musical world's adulation of Glenn Gould is appropriate?

AK: He was extraordinary, of course, and he left much evidence of that. But when I went to the Toronto Public Library, I found twenty-three books on Gould. And I could only find one on Arthur Rubinstein, and two or three on Pablo Casals.[6] Is all this attention on Gould not a bit exaggerated?

CE: *So you think too much has been made of Gould?*

AK: Some of the radio shows, like *The Idea of North*,[7] are very pretentious. And some of his writings were rather hard to understand. His way of writing was complex and rarified: he could sound like he was talking down to people – assuming that anyone who didn't understand him was not worth addressing.

CE: *What impact do you think Gould has had on the musical world?*

AK: Gould had a huge influence. He was able to make lots of people appreciate Bach who hadn't really appreciated him before. And now, many pianists play the *Goldberg Variations*, which was relatively rare, until he recorded them. That's certainly a valuable contribution. You could disagree with his interpretations – but he made Bach something that you had to listen to. If you're listening to a recording by Glenn Gould, you have to concentrate, and follow the music.

Postscript

This interview with Anton Kuerti was the last of the twenty interviews I conducted for *Remembering Glenn Gould*. And when I arrived at Kuerti's downtown Toronto townhouse for my interview, he greeted me with the question, "Why another book on Glenn Gould?" I explained that my book would be different from most others: a collection of Q&A interviews with people who knew Gould. And I also told him that the opinions expressed in it ranged from profound admiration to views that were more critical, and perhaps even skeptical, in some ways. I summarized my work as an attempt to "de-mythologize Gould."

I'm not sure if I succeeded in convincing Kuerti that my efforts would be entirely worthwhile. But he graciously agreed to talk to me about his friendship with Gould (which, as with some other Gould friendships, was abruptly truncated), and to offer his frank opinions of Gould's achievements.

CE

NOTES

1 Anton Kuerti, "All That Glitters Is Not Gould," *Globe and Mail*, February 12, 1994, p. C9.

2 For more information on John Roberts's friendship with Gould, see Chapter 3: John Roberts.

3 Gould performed Brahms's *Piano Concerto No. 1* with the New York Philharmonic on April 6, 1962. For more information see Chapter 1: Walter Homburger (p. 9), and Chapter 3: John Roberts (pp. 132-133).

4 For more information on Gould and his teacher, Alberto Guerrero, see Chapter 2: Stuart Hamilton (pp. 38-39) and John Beckwith (pp. 46-49).

5 According to Andrew Kazdin, Gould's recording engineer at CBS Masterworks, shortly after Horowitz's return to the concert stage in 1974 (following a five-year hiatus) Gould proposed the release of an LP intended to poke fun at Horowitz. However, Columbia Records was cool to the idea. Andrew Kazdin, *Glenn Gould at Work* (New York: E.P. Dutton, 1989), p. 157.

6 At this time, three books on the pianist Arthur Rubinstein have been published, and seven books on the cellist Pablo Casals have appeared. Books on Glenn Gould now total more than thirty.

7 For more information on *The Idea of North*, see Chapter 3: Vincent Tovell (p. 106) and Lorne Tulk (pp. 118-119).

Jaime Laredo: an Artistic Partner

Violinist Jaime Laredo was born in 1941 in Cochabamba, Bolivia, and arrived in the USA at the age of six. Following his 1959 victory at the Queen Elisabeth Competition in Belgium, he debuted at Carnegie Hall in 1960, and subsequently toured all over the world. Today he is active as a soloist and member of the Kalichstein-Laredo-Robinson piano trio, and also conducts the Vermont Symphony Orchestra.

In 1975 and 1976, Laredo recorded all of J.S. Bach's violin sonatas (BWV 1014-1019) with Glenn Gould.[1] The recording was released by CBS Records in 1976 as an LP entitled *Bach: The Six Sonatas for Violin and Harpsichord* (CBS SM3K 52615).

This interview took place on April 25, 2011, in a hotel in downtown Toronto.

CE: How did you come to collaborate with Gould on a recording? Was it your idea, or his idea, or someone else's idea?

JL: It was someone else's idea. In those days, I had a contract with CBS Records to do a certain number of projects, and among them were the Bach violin sonatas. They weren't in the CBS catalogue, and they wanted a recording of them. One day, in 1973 or 1974,[2] I was speaking with Tom Shepard[3] about the various projects. When we came to the Bach, he asked if I'd decided on someone to record them with. I said I hadn't made a decision.

Tom said, "How's about Glenn Gould?" And I facetiously said, "Sure – why not?" I had never met Glenn, and as far as I knew he didn't even know who I was. Tom said, "I'm serious – can I approach him?" It was around five-thirty in the afternoon at this point. He looked at his watch and said, "Glenn should be just getting up now." To my surprise, Gould turned out to be well acquainted with my recordings. And when Tom asked him about working with me on the Bach sonatas, he said, "Yes, that's something I'd like to do." It was all decided within half an hour.

CE: At that point in your career, was Bach an important part of your repertoire?

JL: Bach was certainly an important part of my life. I played the solo sonatas and partitas in recital, and I had recorded the *E Major Partita* for RCA. But I didn't play the sonatas much, and I can't say these particular pieces were an important part of my repertoire.

CE: Gould is sometimes viewed as the kind of pianist who would be temperamentally unsuited to collaboration with other artists.[4] *How did you find working with Gould?*

JL: I found it to be very easy. I was a tremendous fan of his work – but I'd heard all these stories about this crazy man, so I didn't know what to expect. I can't tell you the trepidation I felt on my first trip to Toronto!

The first time I met him was just three days before our first recording session. The plan was to just play together for three evenings before the recording sessions began. I walked into his apartment – I knew better than to try to shake his hand – and we talked for about half an hour. And then I took out my violin and we started to play. It was like heaven, it really was. I never felt that he dictated anything: I don't remember him ever saying it must be like this or like that. It was a complete give-and-take.

CE: I understand that you'd already talked to Gould at some length on the telephone about the sonatas before you met him.

JL: We actually "rehearsed" over the phone. One particular night, I remember he called me in New York at about one-thirty in the morning. I was fast asleep. His first words were, "I didn't wake you, did I?" I replied, "Yes, but it's okay." He said, "I won't keep you long: I just have a couple of questions about tempos." He started singing the piano part, and he asked me to hum along with the violin part, to see if the tempo was right. Before long, we'd sung through the whole movement. And this happened more and more, as the recording sessions approached. There was something funny about it, yet at the same time it made perfect sense.

CE: So it was a productive thing to do?

JL: Absolutely, because when I got to Toronto, many of the tempos were already set.

CE: What were the recording sessions at Eaton Auditorium like?

JL: While I'd always thought of Glenn as a great musician, I'd never really thought of him as a great virtuoso pianist. But I found out in the recording sessions that he was every bit of a virtuoso. I've never, ever, in my life worked with anyone who played the piano better than he did. I've never heard anyone who played with his sonority – it was beguiling.

We started around 10:30 or eleven o'clock at night. And when Andy Kazdin[5] had to change reels on the tape machine, Glenn would play Liszt transcriptions of Wagner operas. I couldn't believe what I was hearing! It was astounding – I'd never even heard Horowitz play like that. That was really fascinating, to me.

CE: *Did the recording sessions go well?*

JL: We had a strange set-up for the recording sessions. I stood on the stage, close to the edge, and the piano was below me, on the floor. But it worked. Apparently he had already recorded Bach's gamba sonatas with Leonard Rose that way.[6]

But the sessions were very efficient. Glenn wasn't dogmatic about musical things, but he had his belief that in one fifteen-minute segment you should do fifteen minutes of music – no more, no less. So if things were going great, and we could have gone on for twenty-five minutes, he said no, and stopped. Another thing I found interesting is that sometimes we would record a movement, and we'd listen to it, and there was not a thing that was wrong with it. But he couldn't accept it – he had to say let's insert another bar from another take. He needed to edit everything, in some way.

CE: *And what did you think of Eaton Auditorium?*

JL: Honestly, I didn't think it was all that great. It had a good sound – but I don't know why he had such a love for that place. He wouldn't dream of recording anywhere else.

CE: *On the recordings, you can just barely hear Glenn humming, in some of the slow movements. Did this bother you?*

JL: Andy Kazdin was good at hiding Glenn's humming, and I don't ever recall having to redo something because of it. When we rehearsed at Glenn's apartment, he was singing in full voice!

CE: *Which of the two of you was fussier? And did you disagree much?*

JL: I'd have to say he was a little fussier. We were both very self-critical, but there were no real points of disagreement between us.

CE: *Not everyone he recorded with could make that claim.*[7]

JL: I know. I can remember when I heard the recording of the gamba sonatas that Leonard Rose recorded with Glenn. Leonard was not only a friend of mine, but someone I respected very much. And when I heard the recording, I thought that Lenny was trying to fit into Glenn's mold. There was something stilted about it: it didn't sound like Lenny, and I felt it wasn't the way he would have played if he were playing with someone else. When I heard it I said to myself, "When I record with Gould, I'm not going to try to do that." I was myself, and Glenn was himself – and somehow it all worked out okay.

CE: Did you have an equal voice in the final version?

JL: Yes. The only movement where I didn't have a voice was the solo piano movement in the *G Major Sonata*. I never even heard it until the record was released.

CE: The labelling on the record very clearly refers to Bach's Sonatas for Violin and Harpsichord, but Gould played the piano throughout the recordings. Was there ever any thought of using a harpsichord?

JL: No. I know that he experimented with the harpsichord a bit, at a time when his piano was being worked on.[8] But I don't think he really liked the instrument.

CE: Was recording with Gould a "learning experience"?

JL: It was one of the great learning experiences of my life. But it's very hard to put into words exactly what I learned. He had extraordinary lines in his playing. They were big lines, not just four or eight bars, but much bigger. I found myself incorporating that into what I was doing. I felt my playing had improved because I played with him – like I had a much better idea about phrasing.

And Glenn made me feel much more free and liberal about Bach. People had all kinds of restrictive ideas about playing this music: you can't do this or that, because it wasn't done in Bach's time. But he didn't care about things like that. He made me realize how wonderful it is to forget about those ideas, and just play the music.

CE: How would you describe Gould's personality?

JL: I found him a wonderful person to be with. He was as funny as hell, on a very intellectual level, and he had great stories to tell. I loved being around him.

But he had the most horrible eating habits of anyone I knew. The first time I went into his kitchen to get a glass of water, I opened the cupboards to find a glass and I saw about fifty boxes of Ritz crackers. It looked like he was living on crackers!

CE: *Did you plan any further projects with Gould?*

JL: The next thing we were going to do was the Strauss *Violin Sonata*: he wanted to include it on an LP with Leonard Rose playing Strauss's *Cello Sonata*. Another thing he was very interested in was making a recording of the three Grieg violin sonatas. And there was one other work that I had mentioned to him: Busoni's *Violin Sonata No. 2*. He didn't really know the piece, so on one of my trips to Toronto I gave him a recording of it. He said he'd love to do it with me.

CE: *Was it Gould's early death that prevented these recordings from being made?*

JL: Yes – we thought we were going to have a continuing relationship. We had an agreement with CBS to proceed with the Strauss and the Grieg, but we hadn't actually scheduled any recording sessions.

CE: *When was the last time you talked to him?*

JL: The last time I talked to him was on a visit to Toronto, when I was doing a concert at the St Lawrence Hall.9 I called him up to tell him I was in town. After the concert I went back to my hotel and we spoke for some time on the phone.

CE: *Looking over the course of your own long career, where do you place your recordings with Gould?*

JL: I think working with Glenn was one of the great highlights of my life. I still remember it vividly. And other people remember it, too: today, when I do interviews, one of the first questions I can expect to be asked is "What was it like working with Glenn Gould?" And if I'm doing a masterclass somewhere, and the students find out that I played with Gould, they think I'm some kind of God!

Postscript

When I interviewed Jaime Laredo, he was in Toronto with his piano trio (the

Kalichstein-Laredo-Robinson Trio) for a concert at the Royal Conservatory of Music. I'd never met him before – but he turned out to be an affable, down-to-earth sort of man. And he was very happy to talk about his work with Glenn Gould.

Like many people who crossed paths with Gould, his encounter with the pianist became more than just a professional matter. He was clearly impressed with Gould's unconventional ways of doing things (such as rehearsing over the phone), and found them artistically refreshing and personally endearing. Not all classical musicians are so flexible. It's more than a small shame that Laredo and Gould didn't have the opportunity to build on their artistic collaboration and friendship.

CE

NOTES

1. The recording sessions took place in Toronto's Eaton Auditorium on February 1-3, 1975, November 23-24, 1975, and January 9-11, 1976.

2. In a letter to the cellist Leonard Rose, dated September 22, 1974, Gould writes, "I have agreed to do the Bach violin sonatas with Laredo." *Glenn Gould: Selected Letters*, John P.L. Roberts and Ghyslaine Guertin, eds. (Oxford: Oxford University Press, 1992), p. 215.

3. Thomas Shepard was co-director of CBS Masterworks.

4. In a 1954 review in Toronto's *Globe and Mail* newspaper, John Kraglund had little praise for Gould as a collaborative pianist: "Superb though Mr. Gould was as a soloist, he was less than satisfactory as an accompanist." John Kraglund, "Music in Toronto," *Globe and Mail*, October 18, 1954, p. 28.

5. Andrew Kazdin was a recording engineer at CBS Records who worked with Gould from 1964 to 1979. For more information see Chapter 3: Andrew Kazdin.

6. Gould recorded Bach's *Sonatas for Viola da Gamba and Harpsichord*, BWV 1027-1029, with cellist Leonard Rose for CBS Masterworks (SM3K 52615).

7. In 1966 the soprano Elisabeth Schwarzkopf undertook to record Strauss's *Ophelia-Lieder* with Gould in New York – but withdrew from the project after just one session due to artistic differences.

8. For more information on Gould's interest in the harpsichord, see Chapter 1: Verne Edquist (pp. 17-18).

9. Laredo appeared with his piano trio on Toronto's "Music at the Centre" concert series on November 26, 1980. It is likely that his final conversation with Gould occurred at this time.

Timothy Maloney: Gould in Decline

Musician, educator and librarian Timothy Maloney was born in Toronto in 1947. He attended the University of Toronto and Catholic University in Washington, DC, and earned a doctorate in music performance and literature at the Eastman School in Rochester. From 1988 to 2002 he served as Director of the Music Division, and custodian of the Glenn Gould Archive, at the National Library of Canada. He currently lives in Minneapolis, where he is Head of the Music Library and an Adjunct Professor of Music at the University of Minnesota.

Maloney's first and last meetings with Glenn Gould were in 1982. In July of that year, he played first clarinet in a small orchestra led by Gould at Toronto's St Lawrence Hall, in a private recording of Wagner's *Siegfried Idyll*. The recording was issued on the Sony Classical label (SK 46279) in 1990. And for Maloney the experience formed the basis of a lifelong interest in Gould.

This interview took place in a hotel in Montreal on May 13, 2011.

CE: How did you come to play the clarinet in an orchestra conducted by Glenn Gould?

TM: I was back in Toronto that summer, doing research for my dissertation at Eastman. I got a phone call from Victor Di Bello.[1] I had worked for Victor at the Stratford Festival in the late 1960s. He was putting together a chamber orchestra for Glenn Gould's recording session, and asked if I was interested. Gould had left the hiring of the orchestra to Victor, who was using his old "Stratford mafia," and some musicians he worked with in Toronto. It just so happened that I was available, in the right place at the right time.

The idea of working with Gould sounded like fun. I owned many of his recordings, and I knew enough about him to expect it would an unusual experience. I said, "Count me in." I had no hesitation whatever.

The original recording sessions were in late July 1982 – but Gould called another session in early September to clean up a few spots. I wasn't available in September, so he hired Joaquin Valdepeñas[3] to play first clarinet for that session. As a result, there are a few notes on the recording that aren't mine. But it's basically my playing throughout.

CE: Did Gould know many of the players in his orchestra?

TM: No. Maybe a few of the older players from the Toronto Symphony had worked with him previously, but most of us hadn't.

CE: *What kind of impression did Gould make on you when you first met him?*

TM: I got there early, and warmed up well in advance of the appointed hour. It was a warm night, and we were all in shorts and tee-shirts and sandals. As I looked out the window at one point, I saw Glenn emerging from one of his big cars.

He was wearing a beat-up old tweed jacket – and when he came upstairs we could see he was also wearing two flannel shirts, and two pairs of baggy pants, held up with frayed cord. During the evening he'd have to pull up first one pair and then the other, because they fitted him so loosely. His socks were unmatched, and his shoes were old black Oxfords that were scuffed up beyond redemption. He carried his scores and other paraphernalia in a big green garbage bag. It was quite a shock: he looked for all the world like a homeless street-person.

The next thing that struck me was how pale he was. I've never seen a paler human being who was alive. His skin was almost translucent. He was stooped and paunchy and bloated looking, and his hair was thinning. He looked much older than forty-nine. I thought to myself, "My God, this man does not look well." And of course a few months later he was gone.

CE: *What was it like playing under Gould?*

TM: He certainly had a conception of the piece, and he was trying his best to be as true to his ideas about Wagner as possible. But he was not a trained conductor. He had a hard time looking us in the eye – he didn't make eye-contact very easily at all. As a corollary to that, he didn't give us a lot of direction as to details in our own parts, and he didn't cue us much. His conducting patterns were very flowery, and his beat didn't change with the dictates of the music. To compensate for these shortcomings, we had to go into "chamber music mode": listening intently to each other to match volume and articulations, communicating amongst ourselves with body language, as if there were no conductor. But it was compelling, all the same, and a wonderful thing to be part of.

CE: *Was it difficult to play the Siegfried Idyll at such a slow tempo?*

TM: He announced to the group before we began that this would be the slowest recording of it ever – and he was probably right.[4] It was a strain for the strings to keep their bows moving, and the wind players had to find new places to breathe. So there were some adjustments to be made. And because he conducted with his left hand, his patterns were opposite to those of right-handed conductors. That required some mental adjustments. He also used no baton; had there been one, it might have been a little easier.

It took me a long time to get my head around the slow tempo. Some years later, when Sony released the recording, I purchased a copy, and I've listened to it repeatedly. I eventually reconciled myself to Gould's tempo, to the point where other recordings of it now sound quick to me.

CE: Was there a lot of stopping and starting in the session?

TM: Gould took things in big chunks. He would do each chunk several times, trying to get things to gel. And then we would move on to the next one. There wasn't a lot of attention to detail, and he didn't give us a lot of direction on how he wanted solos played. There were lots of personal initiatives by the musicians in the recording, which he did nothing to change – and we appreciated that. We felt he was a "musician's musician" – he was implicitly inviting us to take care of our own nuances and interpretations.

I myself took a lot of liberties that he neither asked for nor commented on. There's a solo trill that I started very deliberately, and slowly sped up until it resolved. It was totally my initiative – but I later learned that on Gould's piano recording of the *Idyll* he does exactly the same thing.[5] And in another place, for expressive purposes, I started a slowdown one bar earlier than is marked in the score, and he allowed me to do it.

CE: How do you think Gould would have felt about the commercial release of this recording? Was this ever his intention?

TM: I think some loose ends remain on the disc: a few things he obviously didn't clean up in the September session. The American composer Gunther Schuller trashed the recording in a book he wrote called *The Compleat Conductor*.[6] But Tim Page and Peter Ostwald said some very generous things about it.[7] My own feeling is that the estate probably made a mistake in releasing it to the public.

For example, towards the very end of the recording there's an overlay of artificial reverb. That was anathema to Gould – he never used reverb. I've talked to the recording engineer, Kevin Doyle, about it, and he said that he put in the reverb because there were some changes of personnel in the group that recorded in September, and when he spliced in some tape from the later session, the tone quality or intonation didn't match up with the sound from the original sessions at that spot. So he added reverb to mask the discrepancy. My sense is that Gould might have chosen to park that recording in his drawer.

CE: *How seriously did he seem to take conducting?*

TM: At the time we knew only what Victor Di Bello was telling us. He said that Gould was following through with his longtime intention to quit playing the piano at the age of fifty, and turn to new projects. With that in mind, the orchestra had been engaged to begin a new recording project in October. It was going to be the *Fingal's Cave* overture by Mendelssohn. Obviously, that never happened.

I've seen some of the pages from his notepads. He had made lists of repertoire he intended to study and work on, week by week, in September and October. He was planning to carry on with more material after *Fingal's Cave*. So I think he was very serious about pursuing a whole series of recordings. However, what he was going to do with them is anyone's guess.

Physically, he was not the most coordinated person in the world, and coordination is everything in conducting. There was no great elegance in his beat. On the other hand, he had a fabulous musical mind. He focused heavily on the structure of music, heard structural elements in pieces that other people didn't, and made them the basis for his interpretations. So he might have produced some very interesting musical statements with his conducting that would have made people sit up and take notice.

CE: *Did you and Gould have time to become friends?*

TM: I didn't spend a lot of time with Gould. But I was impressed that he had taken the time to learn everybody's name, so we were all on a first-name basis from the beginning. He came across as very warm and interested in us. There was no prima donna act at all. He treated us all very well.

CE: *I believe your next encounter with Gould came after he had died: at the National Library of Canada.*[8] *How did you come to be in charge of the Gould Archive at the National Library?*

TM: I was teaching in Florida, but I was back in Toronto doing research on

Canadian music. At the Canadian Music Centre I happened to see the announcement that Helmut Kallmann, who had created the Music Division at the National Library, was retiring. I went back to Florida, and thought about it. I decided I could do the job: I had teaching and research skills, and I'm a historian as well as a performer. So at the last minute I decided to submit my application. I got the job, and started in May of 1988.

CE: *And by then the Gould Archive had already made its way to Ottawa?*

TM: It got there in 1983.[9] Stephen Willis, the archivist who began working on it when it arrived, was still working on it in 1988. But he had lots of other duties.

CE: *So what did you do when you got there?*

TM: I soon realized that the library had given researchers access to documents before they were properly organized. They had allowed whole boxes of Gould documents to go into private study rooms – and behind closed doors, people could do whatever they wanted. There were some shenanigans, and some items went missing.[10] So we tightened up the procedures.

CE: *What was it like being Gould's archivist?*

TM: There was enormous interest, and we had researchers coming from all over the world. To be able to play a role in facilitating research and publications was very enjoyable. I became a Gould specialist myself: I've taken exhibitions from his archives as far as China, Japan and Australia. I've spoken about him all over the world. It's not what I expected when I first went to the library, but it's what unfolded.

CE: *How long were you at the National Library?*

TM: I left in 2002. The amalgamation of the National Library and National Archives was underway. There were changes already starting to happen, and I saw the handwriting on the wall. Today, there is no Music Division any more, and the job I had no longer exists.

CE: *Let's talk about Asperger's. You weren't the first to suggest that Gould may have had Asperger's syndrome. Did it occur to you that Gould might have had Asperger's before Peter Ostwald presented the idea in his 1997 biography?*[11]

TM: I got to know Peter because he came to the National Library to do research.

And in his book, very much in passing, he describes Asperger's as a mild form of autism, and suggests that Gould might have had it.

But I didn't get the idea from him, because it had already crossed my mind. When I was playing in Gould's chamber orchestra, it occurred to me that some of his behaviours were like a pair of autistic brothers I had met many years ago. They couldn't make eye-contact, they were awkward in their gestures – there were many parallels. If you ever watch a video of Gould at the piano and speed it up, you'll notice much more clearly his constant rocking back and forth, and that's a classic autistic trait.

So the idea had occurred to me back when I met Gould in 1982 – but I didn't feel that I had the authority or licence to put it into print, because I'm not a medical doctor or specialist, and it could be inflammatory. However, once Ostwald, a psychiatrist, put the theory in print, I felt I had the licence to look further into it. While Ostwald talked about Gould's behaviours as a child and adolescent, I was interested in Gould as an adult. All of the traits he exhibited seemed to me like an open-and-shut case of some kind of autism.

CE: In your article, you go through various criteria the medical profession uses to diagnose autism and Asperger's, and you discuss how those indicators could be seen, in varying degrees, in Gould.[12] *But is there any evidence to the contrary? Did you uncover anything about him that would suggest he didn't have Asperger's?*

TM: Actually I didn't, although I tried very hard to find some evidence to the contrary – what the medical people call a "differential diagnosis." I still haven't found anything to dissuade me. I didn't necessarily want to arrive at a conclusion of autism when I started out. I just went where my research took me.

CE: And aren't there plausible explanations for all of Gould's "symptoms" that could be proposed that have nothing to do with Asperger's?

TM: Yes, there are. But the totality of the picture, and the degree to which he exhibited most of the autistic hallmarks, leads me in that direction. To me, it's incontrovertible. You know the old saying: "If it walks like a duck and swims like a duck and quacks like a duck, you don't have to be an ornithologist to call it a duck." Certainly, other people have reached other conclusions – but I think the autism theory at least offers a unified explanation. It encompasses both his extraordinary musical abilities and his behavioural oddities as part of a continuum, as a cohesive whole, rather than as a lot of separate things going on inside him, which is the approach taken by one psychiatrist.[13]

Gould's personality, lifestyle, behaviour and abilities were all so out of the ordinary that I find it impossible to accept the notion that a single, over-riding condition or syndrome was not at the root of it all. That's missing the forest for the trees – the equivalent of treating simultaneous coughing, sneezing, sinus congestion, runny nose, watery eyes, body aches, and fever as separate issues rather than seeing them as what they really are: the flu.

CE: *When did you first present this idea to the world?*

TM: It was at a Gould conference in Toronto in 1999.

CE: *And how did people react to this idea when you presented your theory?*

TM: It was probably a shock to some people to hear that their hero may not have been perfect. But, interestingly, people who spoke to me afterwards were supportive – including Ray Roberts,[14] who came up to me and said, "This is the first theory I've ever heard about Glenn that makes any sense at all. You've got to publish it."

CE: *What kind of artist and man do you think Gould would have been, if he had lived for another twenty or thirty years?*

TM: He would have done great things – but would have been increasingly out of touch with the world we consider "normal." At the end of his life, it was apparent in the Wagner recording sessions that his external appearance mattered not a hill of beans to him. He was so focused on what was going on in his head that he didn't care about anything else. I think that if he had lived longer, his lifestyle would have been seen as increasingly bizarre.

Gould's well-known wish to be able to issue a kit of variant performances and let the listener mix and match them to build a composite recording[15] is now possible with today's technology. He would undoubtedly have exploited such possibilities and continued to "push the envelope" to create some very intriguing results. They wouldn't necessarily have been everyone's cup of tea, but thinking "outside the box" – another Asperger's trait, by the way – was just the sort of thing he relished. To the end, he would have been a brilliant, if uneven, *agent provocateur* in the arts, and would have continued to attract attention and criticism.

CE: *How do you account for the world's enduring interest in Gould?*

TM: There were so many mysteries around him, because he didn't live long enough for them to be answered. His withdrawal from concert life made him look like a kind of recluse, like Bobby Fischer.[16] And his interpretations are deeply personal: only Glenn Gould could have come up with them. He was so personally invested in his music-making that his recordings remain compelling almost thirty years after his death. I think they will be listened to a century from now, when the Horowitzes and Ashkenazys may not be.

Postscript

Of all the people interviewed here, Timothy Maloney had the least personal contact with Gould: just two recording sessions. Yet the fact that such a brief encounter could lead to a lifelong interest speaks volumes about Gould's capacity to impress and fascinate people.

Some people who knew Gould much better than Maloney – Walter Homburger, Lorne Tulk or Cornelia Foss, for example – saw little evidence of any serious mental illness behind Gould's eccentricities. However, Maloney makes a strong case for his theory that Gould was afflicted with Asperger's syndrome. As well, Maloney's assessment that, had Gould lived longer, he would have become "increasingly out of touch with the world we consider 'normal'," is plausibly consistent with both Asperger's and the trajectory of Gould's personal and artistic life. It's possible that if Gould had not suddenly succumbed to a stroke at the age of fifty, he would soon have faced some other kind of crisis. What the consequences of such a thing would have been are beyond imagining.

CE

NOTES

1 Victor Di Bello (1933-1997) organized and conducted the Toronto-based Pro Arte Orchestra. From 1960 to 1972 he also oversaw the musical administration of the Stratford Festival, in Stratford, Ontario.

2 The *Siegfried Idyll* recording sessions took place from July 27 to 29. July 27 was for strings only; the full ensemble met July 28 and 29. The additional session was on September 8.

3 Joaquin Valdepeñas is a Mexican clarinetist who joined the Toronto Symphony Orchestra in 1979.

4 Gould's conducted performance of the *Siegfried Idyll* is over twenty-four minutes in duration – quite likely the slowest recording ever made of this work.

5 Gould recorded his own piano transcription of the *Siegfried Idyll* in 1973, for Columbia Masterworks (M 32351).

6 The American composer and conductor Gunther Schuller criticized Gould's recording of the *Siegfried Idyll* as "probably the most inept, amateurish, wrong-headed rendition of a major classic ever put to vinyl." *The Compleat Conductor* (New York and Oxford: Oxford University Press, 1997), p. 6 (n. 2).

7 Peter Ostwald described Gould's recording of the *Siegfried Idyll* as "an elegant, slow-paced performance that emphasized the contrapuntal structure of Wagner's composition." Peter Ostwald, *Glenn Gould: The Ecstasy and Tragedy of Genius* (New York and London: W.W. Norton and Co., 1997), p. 323. Tim Page called it "a reading of melting and surpassing tenderness," in *Tim Page on Music: Views and Reviews*, 68-73: "Glenn Gould in Retrospect" (Portland, Oregon: Amadeus Press, 2002), p. 71.

8 The National Library of Canada was founded in 1953, in Ottawa. In 2004 it joined with the National Archives of Canada to form one institution: Library and Archives Canada.

9 For more information on the donation of the Glenn Gould Archive to the National Library of Canada, see Chapter 1: Ray Roberts (pp. 33-34).

10 In 2006, a New York State court convicted Texas college professor Barbara Moore with criminal possession of stolen property. Several items in her possession had been removed from the Glenn Gould Archive.

11 The psychiatrist and Gould biographer Peter Ostwald writes: "… some of the behaviour he [Gould] manifested later in childhood and during his adolescence – a marked fear of certain physical objects, disturbances in empathy, social withdrawal, self-isolation, and obsessive attention to ritualized behaviour – does resemble a condition called Asperger disease, which is a variant of autism." Peter F. Ostwald, *Glenn Gould: The Ecstasy and Tragedy of Genius* (New York: W.W. Norton, 1977), p. 42.

12 The ten manifestations of Asperger's syndrome that Maloney connected to Gould are: 1] impairment of reciprocal social interaction; 2] non-verbal communication problems; 3] unchanging routines and rituals; 4] fixations and obsessive interests; 5] speech and language idiosyncrasies; 6] abnormal reactions to sensory stimuli; 7] motor abnormalities; 8] mental imaging and feats of memory; 9] savant gifts; 10] late onset and chronic health problems. S. Timothy Maloney, "Glenn Gould, Autistic Savant," in *Sounding Off: Theorizing Disability in Music*, Neil Lerner and Joseph N. Straus, eds. (New York and London: Routledge, 2006), p. 126.

13 In a medical journal in the year 2000, the psychiatrist Helen Mesaros wrote, "As an author of a forthcoming psychobiography of Gould, I gathered a substantial body of material pertaining to his early developmental years – especially his infancy and childhood…. Nowhere in my ten-year-long research did Asperger's disorder come even close to being considered as a differential diagnosis among Gould's complex diagnostic formulation." "Did Glenn Gould Have a Form of Autism?" *Medical Post*, 36/18 (May 9, 2000), p.24. Ten years later, in her book on Gould, she attributed his strange behaviours to a combination of problems, including narcissism, hypochondria, anxiety, depression, mood swings, obsessive-compulsive disorder, various pho-

bias, and parent-separation issues. In summary, she argued that he suffered from "obstinate and multiple mental health problems." Helen Mesaros, *Bravo Fortissimo Glenn Gould* (Baltimore, Maryland: Heritage Special Edition American Literary Press, 2010), p. 366.

14 Ray Roberts was Glenn Gould's personal assistant from 1970 to the end of Gould's life. For more information, see Chapter 1: Ray Roberts.

15 See *Glenn Gould by Himself and his Friends*, John McGreevy, ed. (Toronto: Doubleday, 1983), p. 134.

16 Robert James "Bobby" Fischer (1943-2008) was an American chess grandmaster who won the World Chess Championship in 1972, defeating Boris Spassky of the USSR. His later life was marked by reclusiveness and arguably paranoid political outbursts.

Chapter 3: Microphone and Camera

Introduction

Glenn Gould loved electronic media as much as he loved the piano. The microphone and the camera were tools that allowed him to reach out to the world while at the same time carefully controlling the content of his message.

Following his early successes in the recording studio – he was just twenty-four years old when Columbia released his first *Goldberg Variations* – his "love-affair with the microphone" soon began to take on new dimensions. He actively courted the worlds of radio, television and film, and his love was very much returned. And as Gould's aversion to live performance grew, his successes in electronic media encouraged him to abandon concertizing altogether. In 1964, it was an unprecedented thing for a concert pianist to do, and it remains a unique phenomenon in the classical music world.

Would Gould have left the concert platform if there were not other "electronic platforms" available to him? We'll never know – but there can be little doubt that, armed with a McLuhanesque faith in technology, Gould had no intention of letting his exit from the stage end his artistic career. But to continue his career as he wished to, he needed the support and assistance of a number of key people. This chapter is devoted to those who worked with Gould as he explored the world of electronic media.

Some, like Andrew Kazdin of Columbia Records, Lorne Tulk of the Canadian Broadcasting Corporation and the filmmaker John McGreevy were skilled technicians, and also artists in their own right. Their relationships with Gould differed: Kazdin sometimes felt a lack of personal connection to Gould, whereas McGreevy became a friend and Tulk was almost a brother. Yet whatever their personal feelings, they recognized his genius, and were all prepared to go to great lengths to work with him.

John Roberts and Vincent Tovell were two key figures in Gould's work with the Canadian Broadcasting Corporation: decision-makers who facilitated Gould's access to the airwaves. No matter what Gould's ambitions were – whether he wanted to explain Bach fugues on television or create contrapuntal radio documentaries – their doors were always open. As Roberts's substantial testimonial here reveals, his professional relationship with Gould blossomed into a close friendship.

My conversation with CBC announcer Margaret Pacsu is also included in this chapter. Her collaboration on *A Glenn Gould Fantasy*, a radio-play created by Gould, owed much to a fondness for quirky voice characterizations they both shared. After creating the roles of Sir Nigel Twitt-Thornwaite, Dr. Karlheinz Klopweisser, and Theodore Slutz for himself, Gould entrusted the reading of Márta Hortaványi to Pacsu.

CE

Andrew Kazdin: Behind the Microphone

Andrew Kazdin was born in the Bronx in 1934, and grew up in Larchmont, New York. As a boy, he developed interests in both music and science. He pursued both these interests at Boston's New England Conservatory and the Massachusetts Institute of Technology. In 1964 he started working for Columbia (or CBS) Records as a producer, and stayed until 1979, at which point he embarked upon a freelance career.

At Columbia, Kazdin recorded many of the leading artists of the day, including the New York Philharmonic and the Philadelphia Orchestra, the pianists Murray Perahia and Ruth Laredo, the violinist Isaac Stern, and the organist E. Power Biggs.

Of several employees at Columbia who produced Glenn Gould's recordings, Kazdin worked with him the most, over a fifteen-year span – beginning with Gould's recording of Schoenberg piano pieces (released in 1966 on M2L 336), and ending in 1979.

This interview was conducted via a Skype connection between Toronto and Long Island, on August 24, 2011.

CE: What can you tell me about your musical background?

AK: My degree from the New England Conservatory was in composition. When I played in orchestras I was a percussionist – but my mental image of music was more connected to the fact that I was a composer. I wasn't much of a pianist: I seem to recall that in order to pass my piano requirements at the conservatory, I had to invite my piano teacher over for dinner!

CE: Do you recall the first time you met Glenn Gould?

AK: No, not exactly – although it was probably some time in 1964. As a young novice in the Masterworks department at Columbia, my first job was as the assistant of Thomas Frost, who was a producer there. Glenn was working with Frost at the time, so it was only natural that he would run into Frost's assistant: me.

When I started working with Glenn, there were some projects in the works that some others had already started. So at first I picked up a few uncompleted projects, until these were finished. The first LP I was the sole producer for may have been his *Emperor Concerto* with Stokowski.[1] That was certainly one of the earliest ones.

CE: *At Columbia Records, did you work with Gould more than other artists?*

AK: I think that's true. Our work together started in New York at the 30th Street Studio, and eventually we moved the operation to Canada. So instead of him taking a train to New York – by that time he had long given up flying – I went to him, in Toronto.

CE: *So how much of your time was taken up by Gould?*

AK: A lot! Nobody else would pick up the phone and call me at midnight, and speak to me for an hour. He would call any time he wanted, and I was automatically on the hook.

CE: *What was it like working for him as a producer? What was your role?*

AK: I learned very quickly that you didn't suggest anything to Gould about the way to interpret a piece. That would be a quick way to find yourself ending your collaboration with him. Yet I think I did more for him than he realized – I supported him in any way I could.

As far as he was concerned, I kept out of his way, and performed the normal tasks of a producer. But this was almost not necessary in his case. One of the things a producer normally did during a recording was to mark in his score any errors, to be fixed in subsequent takes. But he would carefully listen to every take, and formulate his own plans to fix any problems.

The interesting thing is that sometimes these recordings would lie around for years, until Columbia decided they wanted to release something. Then Glenn would take out the session tapes and look at his notes to see what kind of plan he had originally sketched in, and change it completely! With the passage of time, he would like another way better.

CE: *Did he fuss over things that you didn't perceive as problems?*

AK: I soon realized that he was who he was and I was who I was. If he made a judgement about something that I couldn't hear, I just assumed it was because he could hear what I couldn't. You never knew how a particular take would affect him: he might have a reaction that nobody else in the world would have.

CE: Of course, he had a reputation as a perfectionist.

AK: Yes, that's a good word to use. But sometimes he would learn something incorrectly – maybe something like a chord in a wrong inversion. Then he would be loath to change it. So I guess you could say he was a perfectionist to his own vision.

CE: What did you think of Gould's decision to change his place of recording from New York to Eaton Auditorium in Toronto?

AK: It was his choice – and I was perfectly willing to set up recordings wherever he wanted. When Glenn told me of his decision, he said, "I'll buy any equipment necessary to get recordings of the same quality that we get in New York." And he did.

In Toronto, we did a lot of shopping around, trying out several venues. When we hit Eaton's, Glenn knew it was what he wanted. From a technical standpoint, it was fine. It had a decent natural sound: it took a little while to figure out where to place the mics, but once this was established, we were happy. And there weren't any obtrusive noises – especially working at night, as we did. I think the only people in the building were me, Glenn, the piano tuner and the night watchman.

CE: Was Gould's humming a serious problem when you were recording him?

AK: That, and the squeaking of his chair![2] We tried to ameliorate the problem of the humming by putting a screen near his face to create a barrier between him and the microphones.

CE: Did you ask Gould to simply stop humming?

AK: Oh, no – you couldn't do that! It came to him so naturally that if you were to request him to stop, he would have to take a piece of his mind to concentrate on it – and that was something he probably wasn't willing to do.

CE: There are two recordings, in particular, that I want to talk to you about. The first is Gould's four-handed forays into his Beethoven and Wagner transcriptions for piano.[3]

AK: Yes, he did use four hands in a few places. He would overdub an extra part when he felt that playing it with two hands was uncomfortable. He was the only one who could judge this, and this is how he solved the problem to his satisfaction. I can't think of any other pianist I ever worked with who did this kind of thing. But in the pop music field it's done all the time.

CE: *Were you prevailed upon to keep Gould's unusual technique a secret?*

AK: I don't believe it ever came up. I have no memory of being asked not to say anything. But I don't think we advertised it, either.

CE: *The other recording I wanted to ask you about is his "acoustic orchestration" of music by Sibelius, with multiple microphones.*[4]

AK: I don't know how Glenn got the idea. But what I can tell you is that, for this project, we worked with eight or nine mics, instead of a standard set-up of three. We positioned the mics farther and farther from the piano: one, two and three were quite close; four, five or six, were farther away, and so on. The farthest microphones were about twenty-five feet away from the piano.

After the recording was made, we sat in Glenn's studio, and he would literally conduct me, while I was mixing the recording. In the mixing, the various ranks were sometimes used in combination, so that one would be fading in while the other was fading out. The effect was as if the listener was moving closer to or farther away from the piano all the time.

He also recorded a Scriabin sonata the same way.[5] But it was never released during his lifetime – and Gould was the only person who could have directed how the microphones were to be mixed. So when Columbia wanted to release it, after his death, I mixed it in a conventional way.

CE: *Gould was pleased with the results of this "acoustic orchestration" experiment?*

AK: He was pleased enough that he allowed it to be released. And I think he was also pleased because nobody had ever done anything like that before. By creating this mechanical sense of moving in an out, Gould was saying that a classical artist need not always strive for recordings to be realistic – which this recording certainly was not.

CE: *Was Gould a big revenue earner for CBS?*

AK: The most honest answer I can give you is no. Outside of the obvious soloists and ensembles, like the New York Philharmonic or Vladimir Horowitz, I don't think there was a great profit to be made in manufacturing any kind of classical recordings. At the Masterworks department, we were constantly reminded that we only accounted for six percent of the total revenue of Columbia Records.

CE: Yet he seemed very indulged by CBS – as if the executives decided to let him do anything he wanted.

AK: That's probably not too far from the truth. People in a supervisory capacity in the Masterworks department knew what kind of animal they had in Glenn Gould. They knew they had to treat him correctly.

CE: In your experience, did anyone at CBS ever say no to him about anything?

AK: I don't think so.[6] When he wished to be, Glenn could also be an unbelievably convincing speaker: he could talk you into doing almost anything. I have a feeling that this ability to win his case verbally helped him. I think people like Goddard Lieberson[7] realized what they had in Gould, and just let him do his thing.

CE: How and why did your association with Gould come to an end?

AK: Looking back on it, I'm not entirely sure. It may be that, deep inside, Glenn's real goal was to be his own producer. When that unfortunate incident took place concerning my recording with the New York Philharmonic – and Glenn sensed that there was something very unpleasant going on[8] – maybe he thought it was time to spring free and produce his own recordings.

After I was let go from Columbia, I could have continued to do recordings for Gould in Toronto as an independent contractor, supplying Columbia with finished tapes. But Glenn didn't support me at that time. He used the incident as a way of severing our relationship.

CE: Did Gould's idea of being his own producer make sense?

AK: I can't think of any other pianists who were their own producers. But let's face it – he was virtually his own producer, anyway. When I worked with Gould, he was calling all the shots. Most artists chose to exercise less control.

CE: In your years of working with classical artists, was there anyone else as eccentric as Gould?

AK: Does the name Antonia Brico mean anything to you?[9] She was a conductor who was catapulted to public recognition by a film about her, produced by the singer Judy Collins. This made enough of a splash in the press that Columbia decided to make a recording with her. I drew the short straw and had to produce it. She arrived at the recording session about ten minutes late – and the first thing she said was, "Does anybody have a baton?"

She may have rivaled the eccentricity of Gould. But if we're talking about an artist of Gould's stature and position in the musical world – then no, I can't think of anyone.

CE: *Why did you decide to write a book about Gould?*

AK: No one else was in the same position that I was to observe Gould. There was only me and the piano tuner, in session after session. Nobody else was allowed. So I felt that put me in a unique position – and if I didn't do it, who would?

CE: *Has the passage of time, since you wrote your book, changed your views about Gould?*

AK: No. I was there, and I witnessed what was going on. That doesn't change with time.

CE: *The world is still very interested in Gould. But has he been sensationalized?*

AK: I don't know of any other pianist I dealt with who had a technique that matched his, or that had such a wealth of ideas. As for whether his image has been sensationalized – he didn't do much to prevent it from happening!

Postscript

I made it my policy, when I began work on this project, to conduct all of my interviews in person. However, when I contacted Andrew Kazdin, and suggested meeting with him in New York, he proposed the idea of an interview via a Skype connection. Our subsequent conversation was the first time I used Skype for an interview – and I don't believe it was less effective than an in-person meeting.

Before I interviewed Kazdin, I read his 1989 book, *Glenn Gould at Work*, which is a very readable memoir of his years working with Gould. As I read it, I thought I detected a tone of bitterness – possibly even a touch of spite – underlying the narrative: a sense that Kazdin felt used and discarded by Gould. However, that's not the impression I received in my interview with Kazdin. Despite his disappointment with the termination of his working relationship with Gould, he was predominantly grateful to Gould for many of the most rewarding experiences in his career.

I was shocked to learn of Kazdin's death, following a battle with cancer, on November 28, 2011, just three months after our interview. I am grateful that I had the chance to meet him (electronically, at least) before he passed away.

CE

NOTES

1 This recording (ML 6288) was released by Columbia in 1966.

2 Gould insisted on using a special piano chair that his father had built for him, even after it became worn and decrepit. For more about this chair, see Chapter 1: Walter Homburger (p. 5).

3 Gould's recording of Liszt's arrangement of Beethoven's *Symphony No. 5* (MS 7095) was released in 1968. His Wagner recording (M 32351) was released in 1973. It consisted of Gould playing his own arrangements of the *Prelude to Die Meistersinger, Dawn and Siegfried's Rhine Journey,* and the *Siegfried Idyll.*

4 This recording (M 34555) was released in 1977, containing Sibelius's *Sonatines Nos. 1, 2 and 3, Op.67,* and his *Kyllikki Op. 41*. To record it, Gould devised an unusual technique of microphone placement that would allow him to change the listener's perspective – in effect moving his listener closer to or farther away from the piano – during the performance.

5 Gould's recordings of Scriabin's *Sonatas Nos. 3 and 5* were released in 1986 on *The Glenn Gould Legacy Vol. 4* (CBS M3 42150).

6 In his book, *Glenn Gould at Work*, Kazdin does suggest that Columbia declined Gould's offer to create an album that would be a humorous takeoff on the pianist Vladimir Horowitz's return to the concert stage following a twelve-year absence. However, Gould later revived the idea, in a modified form, as *The Glenn Gould Silver Jubilee Album* (CBS M2X 35914), released in 1980. Andrew Kazdin: *Glenn Gould at Work* (New York: E.P. Dutton, 1989), pp. 157-158.

7 Goddard Lieberson was president of Columbia Records from 1956 to 1971, and also from 1973 to 1975.

8 In his book, Kazdin describes an incident in 1979 in which he was severely criticized and ultimately fired at CBS for his decision to record the NYPO using analogue, rather than digital, equipment. *Ibid.* p. 160.

9 Antonia Brico was a Dutch conductor who came to the USA in 1908. During her career, she appeared before the Berlin Philharmonic, the Hamburg Philharmonic and the San Francisco Symphony – and was the first woman to conduct the New York Philharmonic. The documentary film *Antonia: A Portrait of a Woman* was released in 1974. She died in Denver, Colorado in 1989, at the age of eighty-seven.

John McGreevy: Documenting Gould's Toronto

John McGreevy was born in Ireland, in 1942. Raised and educated in England, he immigrated to Canada in the early 1960s, where he found employment at the Canadian Broadcasting Corporation in Toronto. He worked at the CBC until 1976, when he left to work independently. Since then, he has made more than 130 films around the world.

His first major independent film project was the thirteen-part *Cities* series, in which he invited famous people to give on-camera tours and offer their insights into cities they knew. For the episode on Toronto, McGreevy chose Gould as the film's guide, and produced *Glenn Gould's Toronto* in 1979. In 1983 (one year after Gould's death), McGreevy edited *Glenn Gould by Himself and His Friends*, a commemorative book of essays. In 2007 McGreevy created a theatrical piece called *An Evening With Glenn Gould* for Toronto's Luminato arts festival.

This interview took place at McGreevy's home in midtown Toronto on July 12, 2011.

CE: How did you come to create the Cities series?

JM: In the mid-1970s, some people began to embark on independent careers outside the CBC. It was the beginning of independent film production in Canada. Having spent ten very successful years at the CBC learning my craft, I decided I'd throw my hat in the ring – not because I had any reservations about my time at the CBC, but because I wanted to operate in a wider sphere.

I thought about how I could launch my own company and draw the attention of television networks around the world. In 1976 I came up with a very simple idea: thirteen films on cities around the world, hosted by remarkable individuals who were highly articulate and well known in the places I hoped the series would reach.[1] In a way, it was my calling card, announcing the creation of John McGreevy Productions. And while I was planning *Cities*, I always had Glenn Gould in mind for Toronto.

CE: Do you recall when you first met Gould?

JM: I had the good fortune to know Glenn through my work at the CBC. In the 1960s and 70s he was certainly the most extraordinary person haunting the hallways of the CBC.

The first time I had a conversation with him, we spoke over the telephone. I got a call from him late at night – it must have been about one or two o'clock in the morning. He introduced himself and said he hoped he wasn't disturbing me. Earlier that evening he had seen a program I'd made for the CBC, and wanted to congratulate me on it. He was particularly fascinated by my choice of music for the program. He said, "The risks you've taken clearly identify you as a non-musician – but I thought it was a work of genius. Congratulations." I then became one of the network of people he would call in the wee small hours of the morning.

CE: *How did Gould become involved in your Cities series?*

JM: By 1978 I knew Glenn well enough to know that I had to be very careful about how I made the invitation. Glenn had a very strong sense of his own direction, and liked to have control over everything. I knew that I didn't want to make a "performance" film, with Gould at the keyboard all the time, and I sensed that this would be key to attracting him.

What fueled our dialogue over the years was that he was very interested in my world: film. And I was very interested in the architecture of his projects. I thought that his radio documentary *The Idea of North* was a remarkable, pioneering piece of work. His ideas about structure had a big impact on my own work and thought-processes – and he remains an influence to this day, four decades later.

So what I did was embark on a few *Cities* episodes before I approached Glenn. I had already done Peter Ustinov in Leningrad, R.D. Laing in Glasgow, Mai Zetterling in Stockolm and Elie Wiesel in Jerusalem – before I introduced Glenn to the idea of the series.

He took my call late one night, and he said, "Where have you been?" I said, "I've been making films about cities around the world. And there's one that I'd love you to see. Why don't you come downtown and I'll screen my latest effort for you." I didn't tell him what it was – but I knew that he had a particular affinity for Leningrad.[2]

So he came downtown for a private screening, and up came Peter Ustinov in Leningrad. Glenn leapt up and said, "I know what you want me to do – you want me to do Glenn Gould's Orillia!"[3] I said, "Close, but not quite. Enjoy the film, and we'll talk afterwards." After the screening he said, "You want me to do Glenn Gould's Toronto. But I don't know Toronto – I've lived here all my life, but I don't know it. I certainly couldn't do what Peter Ustinov has done in Leningrad." I explained that wasn't what I wanted. I said, "In the film, I would love you to discover the Toronto that has changed since you grew up here." So the seed was planted: he was delighted to be in the company of Peter Ustinov and the others. Glenn had a very healthy ego, and was not shy about associating himself with them. He said, "What we should do is have dinner together at the Inn on the Park,4 and talk about it."

The plan was that he would pick me up at my house in Chinatown, and we'd drive up the Don Valley Parkway. When we got to the Inn on the Park, we went to Glenn's suite, which he had converted into an editing workshop. There, I was exposed to one of the most remarkable evenings of my life. Gould talked all through the night and played bits of music from his vast recording collection: I heard for the first time Richard Strauss's *Metamorphosen* and the *Four Last Songs*, and also Barbara Streisand and Petula Clark.5 At about one o'clock in the morning he saw me wilting a bit and asked if I would like something to eat. I said, "Yes – I thought we were coming here for dinner." So he ordered room service. His own diet was typically horrendous: watery scrambled eggs, white bread and weak tea. I had some Dover sole and a carafe of white wine.

I didn't leave the hotel until seven o'clock in the morning. By then, we had discussed Toronto, and how to go about making the film. He said that it would have to be scripted rather than improvised. The other episodes were not scripted, and all the people I was working with – Germaine Greer, Jonathan Miller, Studs Terkel and all the others – were immensely articulate and could improvise on camera. Glenn could also improvise, but he wasn't willing to do it. He asked me to supply him with a researcher who would feed him material on the locations in Toronto we selected for the film, so he could prepare a script. He assured me that it wouldn't sound scripted – it would all feel very spontaneous.

Gould asked me how long the text should be. I said, "About 7,500 words – but if you come up with 9,000 words, we can trim it back." I went off to film another couple of episodes in other cities, and he told me he'd have the script done when I got back. When I returned to Toronto I got in touch with Glenn. He said, "It's all done, and it's wonderful – but it's a tad long. I got carried away, and constructed it along the lines of a Mahler symphony. And I don't know where cuts could be made, because with Mahler, you can't take anything out without the whole structure falling apart." I asked, "How long is it?" He said, "45,000 words."

Of course, 45,000 words was impossible – and Gould understood that it was more than the series could accommodate. And he had indulged himself with all kinds of digressions into his philosophical concerns. So we had another long night at his studio. We hacked our way through his text, and the film that was made was almost exactly what we finally agreed to.

CE: Was the form of the film determined on that night at the Inn on the Park? And how much of the content was your idea, and how much was his?

JM: The plan was sketched out that night. He was relieved that I didn't want him to do a personal biography: his home in the Beaches, and the Royal Conservatory, and places like that. His starting position was, "Could we not do the whole thing in Don Mills?"[6] I said, "Glenn, I know you're fascinated with the anonymity of that part of town, but it won't really tell the story of Toronto." He replied, "Then you'll have to help me, because I don't know many of these places."

For example, he'd never been to the Eaton Centre.[7] He didn't often spend his time driving on the Yonge Street strip[8] on a Saturday night – and Yorkville[9] was a discovery to him. He knew about the old City Hall, but he had only seen the new City Hall from the outside.[10] He loved the harbour, but hadn't been to the Toronto Islands for years.[11] And he'd never been near the CN Tower.[12] So it was very much me suggesting what we might do – and Glenn putting his own accent on it.

CE: What was it like to work with Gould?

JM: It was a delight working with him. He was very professional – he went along with everything I asked – I never had a sticky moment. I remember at the very beginning I said to him, "We have to address the business of the hat and gloves, and the overcoat and galoshes. Some people have an impression of you as a Howard Hughes-like eccentric, and if we don't want that to be the impression we give in this film, you'll have to get rid of it. He agreed.

However, one thing Gould insisted upon was a very circumscribed shooting schedule. Glenn was available from six o'clock in the morning to eight, and then in the evening from seven o'clock – all through the night, if we wished. This was so Glenn could sleep during the day, as was his habit. So there wasn't much daytime filming. In total, it took us about ten days to shoot the film.

CE: What else do you remember about working with Gould on the film?

JM: He was delighted when we got access to film in the boardroom of the Royal Bank of Canada.[13] No other film crew, before or since, has ever had access to the boardroom of the Royal Bank – it was like the Vatican. Later, when we were shooting on the roof of the building, the chief of security approached me and said, "We have a firm rule that there can never be a film crew here. So I need to know how you cut through the layers of red tape to get up here." I said, "I'm sorry, my lips are sealed." He was very perplexed.

I also recall the scene with Glenn playing the organ. I had suggested to him that it would be perverse if he did no playing at all in the film. So he came up with a scene in the Church of the Holy Trinity, near the Eaton Centre. Glenn said, "I have a phobia about playing the organ – but I will appear to be playing. I will bring one of my recordings on tape, and the soundman can feed it to me in my off-camera ear, while my hands are on the keys. I promise you it will be impeccably in synch."

CE: Did he actually go up the CN Tower?

JM: No – but there was no reason for him to.

CE: Was the scene at the Zoo Gould's idea?

JM: I suggested the Toronto Zoo, because of Gould's professed affinity for animals, and his belief that he had a special communication with them. He loved the idea – although he'd never been to the zoo – and he came up with the idea of singing Mahler to the elephants. Who else could get away with that? That scene is probably the most widely remembered in the whole film.

CE: Did any scenes end up on the cutting room floor?

JM: The film opens with Gould playing the piano part of Strauss's *Enoch Arden*, for piano and narrator. Glenn wanted to perform both parts, so we filmed him playing the piano part, and then with him in a different costume doing the narration. It was awful! I never told him so – I just said we ran out of time. But I could not resist using the piano part at the beginning of the film.

And when he was driving on Yonge Street, we filmed a sequence where he collides with a black-leather type on a motorcycle. And the biker is Gould – who then has a row with the Gould in the car. That scene didn't find a place in the final film, either. There were times when Glenn had to be protected from himself.

CE: *What did he think of the final results?*

JM: I didn't let him near the cutting of the film. I took the footage to London to edit, because I'd done a number of episodes over there. And I brought back what was in effect a finished product. When he saw it, he was over the moon! Over the next two or three years, he burned through several copies showing it to people.

CE: *When and where was the premiere of Glenn Gould's Toronto?*

JM: It was towards the end of September, in the council chambers of the new City Hall.[14] We invited a few hundred people. Glenn said, "You know of course I can't be there for the screening – I'd be terrified of all those people. But may I come for the rehearsal screening, the previous evening?" I said of course. On the evening of the rehearsal, we were setting up the chambers as a theatre, and a security guard came in. He said, "There's a character outside who looks like a bum who says he's Glenn Gould!" I brought Glenn in, and he was thrilled to see himself up on the big screen. A week later it was broadcast by CBC Television.

CE: *So what did Gould really think of Toronto?*

JM: He loved Toronto. But what he loved most about the city was that he could live an anonymous life here: Toronto left him alone. His closing statement – that if Toronto ever changed to the point that he could no longer abide it, he would move to Leningrad – was his truly expressed view.

CE: *After the premiere of Glenn Gould's Toronto, did you and Gould ever talk about further collaborations?*

JM: He wanted to go way up north, to the Arctic. He was very interested in doing something up there – but of course he was gone before we could do anything about it.

CE: *How do you remember Gould in the last few years of his life?*

JM: *Glenn Gould's Toronto* cemented our relationship – after that we were in constant contact on the phone. We talked about whatever was on his mind, and what was on my mind. On the day of his fiftieth birthday,[15] I left messages on his phone service, congratulating him, and he called back at about 11:30 that evening. The suddenness of his death, just a few days later, was shattering.

I didn't realize the extent to which he'd gotten under my skin, until the memorial service, which I helped to organize.[16] Gould's second recording of the *Goldberg Variations* hadn't yet been released, but John Roberts managed to get a copy of it from Sony. He fed the closing aria into the sound-system in the church – and it was an intensely poignant experience. For two years afterwards, I couldn't bear to listen to the *Goldbergs* – I'd just erupt in tears. To me, that aria is Glenn's way of saying goodbye. I experienced Glenn Gould not just as a great artist, but as a tender, vulnerable human being.

Postscript

In *Glenn Gould's Toronto*, Gould comes across as rather alienated from the city he's presenting to the world. He didn't go up the CN Tower, he seems unimpressed by the Bay Street financial district, and he dismisses the iconic Yonge Street as a "grotesque distortion." Yet Glenn Gould could have lived anywhere in the world he wanted to – and he chose to remain in the city of his birth. His reason for doing so is unequivocally expressed at the film's conclusion. He calls Toronto "a truly peaceful city," and remarks, "The best thing I can say about Toronto is that it doesn't seem to intrude." Coming from Gould, that is high praise.

McGreevy's willingness to incorporate Gould's ambivalence into *Glenn Gould's Toronto* makes the film unique. And (although McGreevy couldn't have known it at the time), the film's appearance just three years before Gould's death makes it an invaluable record of Gould's later-life opinions about Toronto, the world, and life itself.

CE

NOTES

1. When complete, McGreevy's thirteen part *Cities* series featured Peter Ustinov in Leningrad, Elie Wiesel in Jerusalem, George Plimpton in New York, R.D. Laing in Glasgow, Glenn Gould in Toronto, Jonathan Miller in London, Hildegard Knef in Berlin, Germaine Greer in Sydney, Studs Terkel in Chicago, Mai Zetterling in Stockholm, John Houston in Dublin, Anthony Burgess in Rome and Melina Mercouri in Athens.

2. Gould formed his favourable impression of Leningrad on his concert tour of the USSR in 1957. For more information see Chapter 1: Walter Homburger (p. 8).

3. Orillia, Ontario, is a town located between Lakes Simcoe and Couchiching, about seventy miles north of Toronto. The Gould family had a summer cottage near

Orillia, at the village of Uptergrove. For more information see Chapter 2: Stuart Hamilton (p. 40).

4   The Inn on the Park was a luxury hotel at 1075 Leslie St. in Toronto. Gould kept a suite there where he sometimes stayed and which he used as a sound-editing studio.

5   Gould enjoyed some popular music, and was fascinated by both Streisand and Clark. In 1976, in *High Fidelity* magazine, he described Streisand's voice as "one of the natural wonders of the age." ("Streisand as Schwarzkopf," *High Fidelity*, Vol.25 No. 5, p. 74). And he devoted a CBC Radio program to Clark in 1967, whom he cryptically termed "pop music's most persuasive embodiment of the Gidget Syndrome."

6   Don Mills is a suburb in northern Toronto that was developed as a residential, light-industry and commercial zone following World War II. In *Glenn Gould's Toronto*, Gould describes Don Mills as his favourite part of the city, due to its "improbable Brasilia-like quality."

7   When the Eaton Centre opened in 1979, it was the largest shopping mall in Canada. It occupies the area of several city blocks, and is bounded by Dundas, Yonge, Queen and James streets.

8   Yonge St. runs the entire length of Toronto, from south to north, and is lined with retail and commercial businesses for most of its length.

9   Yorkville was Toronto's hippie enclave in the 1960s, but by the 1970s it had become one of the city's most expensive shopping areas.

10 Toronto's "old" City Hall, at 60 Queen St. W., was built in 1899. The "new" City Hall, one block west at 100 Queen St. W., was completed in 1965.

11 The Toronto Islands form the boundary between Toronto Harbour and Lake Ontario. Mostly, the islands are parkland, but a residential community and a small airport have been built there.

12 Completed in 1976, Toronto's CN Tower is 553 metres in height – the tallest freestanding structure in the world, until the Burj Khalifa was built in Dubai in 2010.

13 Royal Bank Plaza is bounded by Bay, Front, York and Wellington streets. The plaza is dominated by two towers with distinctive gold-tinted windows (real gold is mixed into the glass). The RBC's boardroom is located on the top floor of the South Tower.

14 *Glenn Gould's Toronto* was premiered at Toronto City Hall on September 20, 1979. On September 27, the film was broadcast nationally by CBC Television.

15 Gould turned fifty on September 25, 1982, and died of a stroke on October 4. For more information on Gould's death see Chapter 1: Ray Roberts (pp. 32-33).

16 Gould's memorial service took place on October 15, 1982, at St Paul's Anglican Church on Bloor St. For more information see Vincent Tovell (p. 108) and Chapter 3: John Roberts (p. 139).

Vincent Tovell: Gould on TV

Vincent Massey Tovell was born in Toronto in 1922. As a boy, he spent time in Europe, and became well acquainted with modern developments in the arts. In the early 1940s he was a student at the University of Toronto, where he involved himself in theatre productions. Also at this time he began to write for the Canadian Broadcasting Corporation. In 1948 he moved to New York, where he worked in broadcasting, and from 1953 to 1957 served as the CBC's correspondent at the United Nations.

In 1957 he returned to Toronto, where he worked at the CBC as a radio and television producer until his retirement in 1987. He interviewed Glenn Gould for the CBC on two occasions, in 1957 (for radio) and in 1962 (for television), and produced a television documentary on Gould in 1985, three years after the pianist's death.

Tovell is an Officer of the Order of Canada and a Senior Fellow of Massey College at the University of Toronto. As well, he was an original member of the Glenn Gould Foundation.

This transcription is a composite of interviews conducted on May 10, July 1 and August 16, 2010, at Tovell's apartment in a downtown Toronto retirement home.

CE: What can you tell me about your own cultural education?

VT: I had a privileged upbringing in Toronto – back and forth to Belgium and France, and also England – and parents who had lived in Germany before the First World War, and who had a very wide view of the world. We had a collection of contemporary European art, we had some historical prints, and we also had a lot of music in our home. My parents had many musical friends, and the Hart House Quartet rehearsed at our house. But I knew I was not going to be a musician – although it wasn't clear to me what I would become. I certainly had a stimulating childhood.

CE: And how would you describe the musical life of Toronto in the 1930s and 1940s?

VT: Toronto already had an advanced musical culture, with much more going on than people generally assume today. There was a great deal of good music available, with more becoming available all the time through recordings and radio. Then there was the great fortune of the presence in Toronto of Alberto

Guerrero, who became Gould's teacher. And of course there was Sir Ernest MacMillan, who was a big cultural force across the country, preaching the gospel of music. Somehow he managed to make a career for himself as conductor of the Toronto Symphony Orchestra. The orchestra never had much money behind it, but it had loyal money. People thought MacMillan was conservative, but he also strove for new things – and he deserves more credit for that.

CE: When did you first become aware of Glenn Gould?

VT: Effectively, after I came back from living in New York for ten years – which involved working in communications at Columbia University and the United Nations, and also for the CBC. In 1957 I returned to Toronto, to go into television full time at the CBC. I moved into a department called Public Affairs, which covered a very wide range, including the arts. Because of my background I had many interests, music among them. I was not formally trained as a journalist – my background was in literature and theatre, with a strong interest in the visual arts.

Along the way, Gould had surfaced in a spectacular way, and had become internationally famous. He'd already played in the USA and had gone to Russia. I never heard him play till I came back to Toronto. I didn't get to the famous debut in New York at Town Hall – no one in Toronto called to tell me it was happening, although I'm sure I must have read about it afterwards.[1]

When I came back, I'd already heard a lot about him, so I made a point of going to Massey Hall to see and hear him play. I didn't pretend to any critical abilities; I went as an avid and sympathetic listener. He was startling to watch and to listen to – and I don't mean his mannerisms, although that's what everybody was writing about.

CE: And how did you first come to conduct the At Home with Glenn Gould radio interview in 1959?

VT: I knew John Roberts, who worked as a CBC producer in Winnipeg, and was a friend of Glenn's. When I came back to Canada, John and I discovered that we had a lot of common musical interests. Also at the CBC, Harry Boyle had started a series of hour-long radio documentaries – radio was competing with TV in a new way, and was trying to do substantive material. The series covered very widely music and other arts. Somebody suggested to Harry that something should be done on Glenn, who had just gone on a tour to Russia.

Harry asked me to do the interview. I said, "I don't know what would come of sitting down with the great Glenn Gould, but I'm willing to try." I thought we'd better tread carefully, because I'd heard already that you couldn't shake hands with Glenn, and all that sort of thing.

It was John Roberts who introduced me to Glenn. He cunningly arranged an evening with about four or five radio producers, and I just happened to be part of the group. Glenn was invited, and when he arrived, we barely spoke – he was chatting with other people. But as a result of that first meeting, I arranged a lunch with Glenn and Harry. We agreed that we'd do an interview at the CBC. *At Home with Glenn Gould* was recorded in the CBC's studios on Parliament Street.

The plan was for Glenn to bring some music: it was agreed in advance that he'd play a little bit, and we'd just talk about whatever we wanted to. When he came to the studio, he arrived with the score of the string quartet that he was writing. He had some other scores as well, and he started to play the piano. I said to the operator, "Just get the tapes rolling, and keep them going." I had no idea if the interview would last for one hour or two hours, or what would happen.

Glenn started to play Bruckner,[2] and that gave me a clue as to how to begin the conversation: I asked if he was expanding his repertoire into the Romantics. We talked about Strauss and Mahler, and also his touring schedule. And before long, we got into the Russian tour. It was never hard to get Glenn going, if he was comfortable. He knew it was his show, and he wasn't worried about me because I was a nobody in his world. I was no competitor, nor was I someone who wanted to "use" him in any way. And so he said many lovely things.

The broadcast was about fifty-five minutes long. We had to do some editing, because I ended up with an extra fifteen minutes. It came together fairly quickly in production, and then it went on the air.[3] It got a great deal of attention, because nobody had ever really heard Glenn speaking, except for little news clips here and there.[4] What came across was a sense of improvisation, which was exactly what I wanted to get. I didn't want an interview, I wanted a conversation – and it worked.

CE: Do you remember the circumstances of the second interview, Ten Minutes with Glenn Gould, for CBC Television, in 1962?

VT: It was a CBC school broadcast. It was done in a studio, with Glenn sitting at the piano. I don't think we recorded much more than what got onto the air. By that time Glenn knew who I was, and was comfortable with me. I often had dinner with him when he was staying at the Windsor Arms Hotel. With John Roberts, we would sometimes spend the evening at Glenn's apartment, or sometimes at my apartment. We had endless conversations because I'd been working at the United Nations, and I could talk about things that gave him a bigger sense of the world. He was interested in international affairs – he wanted to know what was going on.

CE: How would you describe your approach to your television production Glenn Gould: A Portrait, which you made in 1985, after Gould's death? What were you trying to achieve?

VT: Having spent time with Glenn, I had insights into his development: I knew the culture that he had grown up in, and the Toronto that he knew as a child – and he had the same kind of United Church background that I had, so I understood that too. I felt that if anyone was going to do anything on television, I was the one to do it. It ended up as a big two-hour project.

I wanted to draw the line of Glenn's journey. I didn't want to do a journalistic hack-job, or to try to dig things up: I'd heard rumours about Glenn and Lukas Foss's wife, and I knew she was here in Toronto for a time, but I decided to leave all that alone.[5] I was interested in developing something that would build a sense of the kind of person, and the kind of artist, he was.

There wasn't much of Glenn on film, but there was lots of audio tape, and also video tape. I worked on the project with Eric Till, and we divided the work between us: one of the things I looked after was setting up all the interviews. We had very little time, and we both knew if we'd had a little more time, and more money, we would have done things a little differently. But the result was, on the whole, something that is still an important document. I'm not apologizing for a moment.

CE: Today, what would you say that Glenn Gould was like, as a man and an artist?

VT: Glenn had always known that he wanted to be important and famous. And he knew he was meant to become something – although it wasn't altogether clear how it would happen in a place like Toronto. Glenn had a powerful sense of the drama of his own life.

What I saw first in Glenn was a young man being himself, and this was central to Glenn's career. If I met him at an intimate gathering, Glenn would come in and throw himself on the sofa, and lounge around. He was awkward, and he had a mischievous boyish quality about him. He was not a dark person – he wasn't melancholy – but he was Byronic, in a certain sense. When he walked into a room, you couldn't help looking at him. Sometimes he could be difficult. But he wasn't trying to be difficult – he was trying very hard *not* to be difficult! And you couldn't know Glenn without wondering what would become of him. I worried about him.

He was a product, temperamentally, socially, and one might say philosophically, of the confusion of his musical times, which made him the radical conservative that he was. He's remembered as a radical, because of his interest in Schoenberg, whom he tried to persuade people to view more sympathetically. But he came back, over and over again, to the solid structure of Bach. His heart and mind were tuned to baroque music, in which form and structure were so important: he was interested in musical architecture, and in composers who echoed his own temperament. And he had a Wagnerian yearning for redemption: he loved *Parsifal* when not many people did. Some part of Glenn was searching for continuity, and for a way that the great musical traditions could be transformed into something new.

In some deep way, he knew he had to discover what his journey was, and he discovered that his journey was to the North. He never actually travelled very far north – rarely beyond his family's cottage on Lake Simcoe – but the North is a very apt metaphor for Glenn: a vast open space without physical or human limits.[6] This, I think, is the central idea of his life. There's a natural connection between Gould and Sibelius, who unfortunately didn't write enough piano music. Sibelius was the kind of composer who had a romantic and tempestuous side, but was also comfortable in a northern country, not unlike Canada. Glenn didn't care much for Spanish, French or Italian music – he was not a Latin!

CE: You've mentioned Gould's upbringing in Toronto. How do you think the city influenced him?

VT: Toronto shaped Gould, and it was in Toronto that he became what he became. I've always thought that he chose the right parents, the right time and the right place to be born. He grew up during the Depression and the Second World War in a safe, protected environment, sheltered from the terrible things that were going on in the world. His father had a solid business, so there was stability in the family. The only darkness was the fear of poverty beyond where they personally lived. But they were aware of it – everyone in Toronto was aware of it.

And Glenn grew up with Bach and Handel – particularly the great religious works, which were often done in Toronto at the time. Of course, it was Glenn's mother who was his first teacher and who got him into music professionally, but his father was also very musical. And Glenn was also influenced by all the people around him at the Conservatory.

Later on, Toronto was his refuge and his sanctuary. He knew its geography well, from driving around the city at night – and he was a wild driver! Once he became well known, there were people who wanted him to move to New York, or somewhere that "mattered." But he soon abandoned the idea of going to New York and working in an uncomfortable environment: in Toronto he could work comfortably in his own environment. Much of his radio work couldn't have been done anywhere else but at the CBC in Toronto.

CE: *Do you think that too much has been made of Gould's eccentricities?*

VT: Yes, definitely too much. He had vulnerabilities: he didn't want to catch colds – but who does? If you had Glenn Gould's marvellous hands and fingers, wouldn't you want to be protective of that mechanism? People constructed Glenn according to needs of their own. They imagined him a certain way.

CE: *What did you think of Glenn's decision to withdraw from the concert stage?*

VT: It was inevitable. There was plenty of warning, like the "Steinway episode," when he thought he'd been injured.[7] That was a clear signal – he was looking for a way to get out of doing live concerts. I don't think he ever enjoyed playing in public. Another factor was that he came to feel so very much at home at the CBC in Toronto, in that crummy old building on Jarvis Street. He loved the microphones and audio tape, and the CBC allowed him to become the kind of artist that he wanted to be. Apart from his music performances, radio was his art form. Through radio, he invented his own way to become a "composer," a "dramatist" and an "essayist."

CE: *You're talking about the radio documentaries?*[8]

VT: Yes. John Roberts secretly gave Glenn a key to the CBC's facilities, and some of this work was done quietly at the CBC. Then he got his own equipment, and worked in a studio on Front Street. He learned a lot from CBC technicians, but he also developed his own ways of doing things: technicians who worked with him knew he could edit tape better than they could! He was not a visual person, and television was not his natural medium – although on television he could be a good performer. What was most important to him was sound, and ideas that could be expressed through sound.

CE: *How did your association with Gould come to an end?*

VT: Like many who knew Glenn, I was close to him socially for a while. Things went along beautifully for five or six years. And then at one point, the connection was broken. That happened with a lot of people. But I don't think I was prepared for it, and I missed him.

He had a written script for one of his solo television shows – it was *An Anthology of Variation*.[9] I looked at the script, and I knew it was much too long. Because I was the producer, it was my job to tell him that his script had to be edited, and I knew that this could be the end of what had been a very easy, conversational, relationship. So I suggested to Glenn that there was too much material, and I asked him how it could be trimmed. He stiffened: he didn't like this at all, and I knew I had stepped over the line.

I'd never had to deal with him in this way before. Glenn was a real pro in many ways, and he wasn't inconsiderate – but he didn't like having to rethink what he'd planned to do in a specific way, and he didn't like the idea that his verbal expression was being criticized. After the show went on the air, about a week later, he phoned me a week or so later, to briefly thank me. But that was it: he informed me that our friendship was over by not responding to me further. If I saw him in a corridor, I made a point of avoiding any kind of confrontational meeting.

I was sad, because there was something truly loveable about Glenn. But I don't think I was ever a special favourite. And by that time, I'd seen enough of him and his career that I wasn't surprised. Different people filled his needs at different stages of his life. At one stage, I filled a need: he was fascinated with my work at the United Nations, and we would have long conversations about international affairs.

CE: *You knew Glenn's father, Bert, didn't you?*[10]

VT: I first met him at Glenn's funeral. Glenn was blessed to have a father like that. He was wise man, and he loved music. He knew that his son was a genius, and in some deep way, he had a deep sympathy for Glenn's struggles. And Bert was very supportive of my work on my *Portrait* documentary in 1985, he said, "Come over to the house and have a cup of tea. I have lots of photographs to show you." He was awfully kind and generous.

CE: *And you also knew his stepmother, Vera Dobson?*

VT: She was perfectly lovely. I sensed that the relationship between Vera and Glenn was just what it was: formal and correct. Glenn didn't speak about her very much.

CE: *What are your memories of Gould's memorial service?*

VT: It was an unforgettable event. The memorial service was held at St Paul's Anglican, on Bloor Street – which was the biggest space that could be made available – and the church was packed. But no exact date could be set until we could find the appropriate soloists to participate.[11] It was a group of wonderful Toronto musicians, including Maureen Forrester, who sang "Have Mercy from the Lord" from the *St Matthew Passion*. Afterwards she said to me, "I had a hard time getting through it – and that usually doesn't happen to me."

When we first started talking about the service, I was listening to the second *Goldberg Variations* recording, which had just been released. I said to John Roberts, "Glenn has to have the last word – it has to be Glenn performing." So after everything else was said and done, we played the Aria from the *Goldbergs* over a sound system that the CBC had brought in – and that's when tears began to flow. It was exactly the right moment.

CE: *Why do you think the world remains so fascinated with Glenn Gould?*

VT: There's a human, emotional tension in the story of his life: the unfinished journey and the abrupt ending. He required a certain kind of courage to become the artist he became, and that's certainly admirable. Also, part of it is that he was so forward looking. In a certain way, Glenn anticipated many of the developments that have happened since his death. He welcomed new technologies in media, and what they meant for him as an artist. They gave him the freedom and control to do what he wanted, when he wanted – and he succeeded brilliantly in this. In that sense, he was ahead of his time. But he was also *before* his time, reaching back to a simpler world, before the modern age, in a search for serenity.

Postscript

This interview transcription is the product of three separate interviews. This unusual approach was undertaken at Tovell's request: following the first interview, he thought of more things he wanted to say; and after the second interview he once again asked to refine and expand on his comments. As a result, this transcription is a composite: a "layered" amalgamation of material from all three interviews. (As with all other interviews in this book, the final draft of the transcription was approved by the interviewee.)

Tovell's wish to get things just right was, I suspect, a value he acquired at the CBC, where he spent four decades preparing radio and television programs for broadcast. Presenting his ideas on Gould exactly as he wished them to be presented was clearly very important to him. Editorial processes – cutting, inserting, correcting, polishing – are deeply ingrained in his way of thinking.

CE

NOTES

1. Glenn Gould made his New York debut in a recital at Town Hall on January 11, 1955.

2. *At Home with Glenn Gould* begins with Gould playing several measures of a piano transcription of the "Adagio" movement from Anton Bruckner's *String Quintet in F Major*.

3. *At Home with Glenn Gould* was broadcast on CBC Radio on December 4, 1959.

4. Gould was the subject of several short CBC interviews before Tovell's extended conversation in 1959. In 1956 he was interviewed for CBC Radio. The following year he appeared on television, in a CBC interview. In 1958 Gould was once again interviewed for CBC Radio.

5. Gould carried on a relationship for five years with Cornelia Foss, a painter and the wife of American composer, conductor and pianist Lukas Foss. In 1967 she left her husband, who was the conductor of the Buffalo Philharmonic Orchestra, and moved to Toronto to be near Gould. However, in 1972 she ended the relationship with Gould and returned to her husband. For more information, see Chapter 4: Cornelia Foss.

6. Gould also made several car-trips to the north shore of Lake Superior. The northernmost place in Canada that Gould visited was Churchill, Manitoba, on Hudson Bay, in 1965.

7. In 1960 Gould alleged that a piano technician at Steinway & Sons' New York showroom injured him with a friendly slap on the back. Gould underwent orthopedic and

chiropractic treatments, and cancelled some (but not all) of his engagements, including a tour to Australia. See Chapter 1: Walter Homburger (p. 9)

8 Central to Gould's *oeuvre* as a radio documentarian is the *Solitude Trilogy: The Idea of North*, an exploration of Canadian attitudes towards the nation's hinterland; *The Latecomers*, which is about Newfoundland; and *Quiet in the Land*, which examines a Mennonite community in Manitoba. As well, Gould produced radio documentaries about the cellist Pablo Casals and the conductor Leopold Stokowski.

9 This program was broadcast by CBC Television on June 3, 1964.

10 For more information on Gould's father, see Chapter 2: Stuart Hamilton (p. 40), and Chapter 4: Robert Fulford (p. 146).

11 Gould's memorial service took place on October 15, 1982. Performers included the Orford Quartet, flautist Robert Aitken and contralto Maureen Forrester. John Roberts delivered a eulogy. For more information see Chapter 3: John Roberts (p. 139).

Margaret Pacsu: a Kindred Spirit

Broadcaster Margaret Pacsu's parents were Hungarians who arrived in the United States in the 1920s: her father was invited to teach organic chemistry at Princeton University, and her mother was a concert pianist. Margaret was born in Princeton, and following university studies in the USA and France, she began her broadcasting career at WGBH in Boston. In 1970 she moved to Toronto, where she soon found work as an announcer at the Canadian Broadcasting Corporation. She worked for the CBC for the next twenty-two years.

In the 1970s, in the CBC's Jarvis Street studios, Pacsu met Glenn Gould, who had been provided with a small office next to the one she worked in. The two became friends, and in 1980 their friendship culminated in her contribution to *A Glenn Gould Fantasy*, which subsequently appeared on *The Glenn Gould Silver Jubilee Album* (CBS M2X 35914). In this satirical radio play, Gould portrayed himself and also four fictional characters of his own invention: the English conductor and music-critic Sir Nigel Twitt-Thornwaite, the German musicologist Dr. Karlheinz Klopweisser, the New York cabdriver/poet/journalist Theodore Slutz, and a Scottish recording engineer named Duncan Haig-Guinness. Pacsu alternated between playing herself as a radio announcer and portraying the Hungarian Marxist music theorist Márta Hortaványi.

This interview was conducted at Pacsu's home in central Toronto, on August 10, 2011.

CE: What can you tell me about your musical education? Did your mother teach you piano?

MP: I knew a psychiatrist who once told me, "In a family like yours, there's usually one concert pianist, and everyone else just plays the piano." That's pretty well the way it was: there was no "room" in my family for anyone else to have a musical career. My sister was more gifted at piano than I was, but I played the piano too. I could also sing, and I had ballet lessons, at the American School of Ballet.

CE: How and when did you first meet Gould?

MP: I first came to know him through his recordings, as a Bach specialist whom my mother absolutely adored. But I didn't actually meet him until 1976. Glenn had an office at the CBC, and he usually came in to work between seven and eight in the evening. Whatever he did in his messy little office – which was more like a closet – I don't know. The office was right next to ours, where Fredd Radigan and I were working on our radio program, *Listen to the Music*. We were on the air five days a week from 5:30 to 7:30 in the Maritimes; here in Toronto it was heard 6:30 to 8:30.[1] After the show was over, we would go back to our office to start to plan the next day's program.

So I met Gould at the CBC on one of those evenings, with Freddy. He didn't introduce himself, and we didn't introduce ourselves, either – everyone knew who everyone else was. And it soon became apparent that he was a regular listener to our program. He began to hang around for us, to talk, after our program was finished. He liked to chat with people around the CBC, once he felt safe with them.

CE: *What did you think of Gould, when you first met him?*

MP: I found him to be very warm and entertaining, and obviously an eccentric person. Soon he started playing tricks on us. He would leave us quizzes – things like, "Who were the great sopranos of 1894?" – for Freddy and me, and leave them on our desks, with hints as to the answers. Freddy, bless his heart, knew who all these people were, and he would write down the answers and leave them on Glenn's desk. Glenn realized that Freddy knew an enormous amount about music – much more than I did – and this kept things going.

Once, we played a recording of songs by Schoenberg on our show, and we said we'd give away some records to people who had called in and who could identify the pieces. We waited for the phone to ring, but for a long while there were no responses. Then the phone rang, and Freddy answered it. It was Glenn, and he said he could identify the pieces. Freddy said, "But Glenn, this is your own recording!" Glenn replied, "I know, but I want my free record, because I've identified it correctly."

CE: *When did you first work with him professionally?*

MP: In 1977 he was doing a week of programs on the CBC, filling in for some other announcer, Monday through Friday. He asked the department head if he could do what he wanted on the Friday, and the answer was yes. So he got me into the studio to do the Maude Harbour interview.[2] I played the interviewer, with my Smith College voice. And Glenn did all the other characters.

It was done in Studio D, and there was a men's room just around the corner. Just before we were ready to record, he said excuse me, and he left. A few minutes later, he came back and his hands were all red. He said that he always soaked his hands under hot water before a performance. I said, "Glenn, this isn't a piano performance." He replied, "I guess it's a little neurotic of me."

CE: Where did the idea for A Glenn Gould Fantasy[3] come from? And how did you get involved with it?

MP: That was entirely Glenn's idea – and he wrote the script in about three days. I'm sure that Columbia said he could do whatever he wanted, but I don't think many people understood what the final product would be like.

He called me, in June of 1980, around midnight, and asked if I would be interested in being involved. I said, "Of course!" But I also pointed out that I was a member of ACTRA,[4] and asked if there would be any royalties from the recording. He said, "I'll pay you a fee, of course. There won't be any royalties, but you'll benefit from it for the rest of your life."

We recorded it in Glenn's studio at the Inn on the Park, over two nights, between nine o'clock and two in the morning. He made sure there was fresh orange juice, and he had his scrambled eggs – and he treated me like a princess. And Jean Sarrazin, the recording engineer, was there too.

Glenn had a hard time settling down to work – sometimes it would take him an hour. Once, he started talking about *The Idea of North*,[5] and I said, "Glenn, I don't know it – I didn't come to Canada until 1970." So out of nowhere he produced a recording, and he played it for me. After about twenty seconds I just burst into tears, because it was overwhelming – I'd never heard anything like it in my life. Of course, Glenn was very flattered.

At about ten o'clock we would get started. Gould would sit across from me and cue me while I was reading my lines. And while he was doing this, with his other hand, he was practising a Haydn sonata, or something, on the table. When we had some down time, he'd sing his Country and Western songs for me. He was very proud of them. He said he had written them, just for the heck of it, as a teenager.

When I went into Glenn's bathroom, I was surprised to see all his pills.[6] But I was under the impression that this was a "collection." I don't think he was taking all of those things. I didn't check the dates on them, but it seemed to me that many of them were medications he hadn't bothered to throw out.

CE: How was your character, Márta Hortaványi, created?

MP: Glenn said he had two characters in mind for me: myself as a CBC announcer, and a foreign pedagogue. So I sent him some audio tapes of myself doing a Hungarian accent. In a note to me, he wrote: "Many thanks for your tapes. Mrs. Hortaványi turned out be exactly as I imagined, and no problem to write for at all. My Mrs. H. has a strong sense of mission, a strong sense of self, but no sense of humour whatever."

As ideas for the character's appearance, Gould suggested Gertrude Kolisch, Lou Andreas-Salomé and Pauline de Ahna. When I read this, I couldn't believe it – who's ever heard of these women? He was being his naughty-little-boy self by finding these totally obscure people and dropping their names. I just recently looked them up: they're Schoenberg's wife, Freud's mistress, and a German singer who married Richard Strauss. In fact, they're all fascinating women.

CE: And he wrote you a little song?

MP: It wasn't a song, exactly. [Pacsu takes a framed page of manuscript paper, written in Gould's hand, down from her mantelpiece. On it are a few bars of "music," written in a kind of Sprechgesang style – with rhythms and inflections carefully notated, but with few pitches.] It's a guide to speaking. There was a line of text that I couldn't say quite right – although I tried about twenty times.[7]

CE: Did this help?

MP: No, it just embarrassed me!

CE: I've noticed that there are two schools of opinion on Gould's sense of humour. Some people thought he was terribly witty and clever, and others thought his humour was lame and contrived.[8] What do you think?

MP: There were the musicological "grown-ups" who were writing about Glenn – and they didn't always find him funny. But some of us found him hilarious! His humour was a little bit like Monty Python's: it's surrealistic, in a way. Glenn was surrounded by all kinds of famous, high-powered people – so to find someone like that who wanted to do this kind of thing was pretty special.

CE: Did he talk of further projects?

MP: Yes. He said he wanted to write "Nashville: Summer of 1914" – you know, like Samuel Barber's *Knoxville: Summer of 1915*. It was going to be a take-off on all the "symphony ladies" who went to lunch and raised money for orchestras. I thought it was an absolutely brilliant idea. But then he got involved in his conducting and other things, and it never happened.

CE: It seems that Gould didn't have many female friends. Did you ever get the feeling that he was insecure around women?

MP: No, not at all.

CE: Did you ever get the impression that Gould wanted to be more than your friend?

MP: The very first interview I did after Glenn died was with the BBC, and they asked me the same question. I said, "No, absolutely not." And my husband said, "Why did you say that? You should have said yes!"

CE: You knew Gould late in his life. And there are some people who would contend that he was falling apart, both mentally and physically, in his final years. Did you see any sign of deterioration?

MP: I knew him from 1976 to 1980, and in those years I didn't notice much of that sort of thing. I think he gained some weight, and he did look rather sallow, as if he didn't go out during the day. But I didn't see anything wrong with his mental capacities.

CE: Do you remember the last time you saw Gould?

MP: The last time I saw him was in his car, in front of the Art Gallery of Ontario. He had stopped, and I talked to him. We had a very nice conversation. This would have been in the fall of 1980. We just sort of peacefully signed off.

CE: Some people have said that they felt discarded by Gould. Did you?

MP: That's a very strong word to use. People like Gould need to move on because they've just discovered a new scientific theory, or need to write a new concerto, or they're doing something else that's terribly important. I grew up in Princeton, where just about everyone was an Einstein, or an Edward Teller or a John O'Hara.[9] It always seemed to me that very unusual minds are more focused and are entirely taken over by physics, or mathematics, or some artistic endeavour. You learn to walk around them – and you don't fool around with them! So I grew up around people like Gould, and I learned to treat them with tremendous respect. In the case of Glenn and me, we happened to get along, because we shared a certain sense of humour. And I think it helped that I didn't want anything from him.

CE: *Do you think the world has an accurate understanding of Gould today? Has he been distorted?*

MP: I think the world has a very accurate understanding of his performances – and how they stand up so well in relation to everybody else's. And people have some idea that he was an eccentric Canadian who wore a coat and gloves in the summertime. In the long run, it's his music. I don't think many people know, or need to know, more than that.

Postscript

Margaret Pacsu lives in a meticulously restored Victorian house in central Toronto. She is proud of her home and its contents – a feeling that extends to her small collection of personal Gould souvenirs. During our conversation about Gould, she showed me the script of *A Glenn Gould Fantasy*, as well as several letters, photographs, newspaper clippings, and the "song" Gould wrote for her. These mementos are, however, merely the outward symbols of a cherished friendship. And her opportunity to work with Gould was, for her, a highlight of her broadcasting career.

CE

NOTES

1. Canada is divided up into six time zones: Pacific, Mountain, Central, Eastern, Atlantic and Newfoundland.

2. In this scripted radio-play, written by Gould, Maude Harbour is identified as a town in Ontario with an annual summer flute and recorder festival. In fact, there is no such place in the Province of Ontario; but there is a hamlet called Maude Harbour in Canada's Nunavut Territory, on the Arctic Ocean. In Gould's "interview" with Pacsu, he developed the characters of the New York cabdriver/poet/journalist Theodore Slutz and the English music-critic Sir Nigel Twitt-Thornwaite. The sketch aired on CBC Radio on August 26, 1977.

3. *A Glenn Gould Fantasy* is the title given by Gould to his radio-play of 1980, which he created for the two-disc LP, *The Glenn Gould Silver Jubilee Album*, released by CBS Masterworks in celebration of Gould's twenty-five years of recording with the

company. The play is in the form of a radio interview, in which Gould discusses his ideas and career with several critics.

4 ACTRA is the Alliance of Cinema, Television and Radio Artists. It is a professional association for Canadian actors.

5 *The Idea of North* was Gould's first radio documentary. For more information on it, see Vincent Tovell (p. 106) and Chapter 3: Lorne Tulk (pp. 118-119).

6 Pacsu was interviewed about this event in the film *Thirty-Two Short Films About Glenn Gould*. She said, "I remember going in there and seeing lined up on the wall all of these different bottles. And I came out and said, 'Glenn, surely you're not taking all of this stuff, are you?' And he said, 'Well, no, not all at once,' and sort of laughed."

7 The text that Gould set to rhythmic notation was, "So if one of you gentlemen would like to lead off with a question for Mr. Gould, then. Oh, well, perhaps we should have a little music first to get the interrogatory juices going."

8 The music critic William Littler, who reviewed *A Glenn Gould Fantasy* for the *Toronto Star*, suggested that a remark originally attributed to the conductor George Szell – "the nut's a genius!" – could be suitably rearranged as "the genius is a nut." However, Littler continued: "He has a wickedly witty if occasionally arcane sense of humour that delights in poking fun at sacred cows and covering truth with a sprinkling of laughter. Playing the clown, he comes as close as he has ever come in public to baring his artistic soul." William Littler, "Glenn Gould: The Musical Genius Is a Nut," *Toronto Star*, April 11, 1981, p. F1.

9 The physicists Albert Einstein and Edward Teller both worked at Princeton University. The novelist John O'Hara also lived and worked in Princeton.

Lorne Tulk: the Brother Gould Never Had

Lorne Tulk was born in Toronto in 1939. He began his professional career in radio at Toronto's CKFH station in 1954, broadcasting hockey games from Maple Leaf Gardens. In 1959 he went to work as a technician for the Canadian Broadcasting Corporation, and stayed there until his retirement in 1996. Much of his time at the CBC was devoted to *Ideas*, a spoken-word radio program that he worked on for thirty-three years. In his capacity as a studio technician, he was involved in the production of several radio documentaries created by Glenn Gould. The two men's professional association grew into a personal friendship, and Tulk remained close to Gould throughout the rest of his life.

This interview took place on December 8, 2010, in a coffee-shop on Toronto's Danforth Ave.

CE: When did you first meet Glenn Gould?

LT: We first met briefly in 1950 at Canadian Transcription Services, a small recording studio in downtown Toronto that was owned by my father. We connected again some fourteen years later at the Canadian Broadcast Centre on Jarvis Street.

The first project I worked on with Glenn at the CBC was a program about Petula Clark, who at that time was a big sensation in pop music.[1] Janet Somerville, a producer with *Ideas* asked me if I would be interested in working with Gould – so of course I didn't say no. Glenn and I spent a Saturday afternoon putting together that program. I can remember having to tell Glenn that he was talking way too fast – nobody would be able to understand him. But the show came together very well, and this established the relationship between us that lasted until he died.

CE: Did it strike you as odd that a concert pianist would be interested in a pop singer like Petula Clark?

LT: It's about more than just Clark – and it was amazing![2] It was aimed at teenagers, for a Saturday morning radio show.

CE: The second project you worked on with Gould was The Idea of North, which makes use of some unusual techniques: simultaneous voices fading in and out between the background and the foreground.[3] Didn't this seem to you like a strange way to make a radio documentary?

LT: No, I thought it was very interesting. It was an entirely different way of presenting radio.

CE: *How long did it take you to make it?*

LT: It seemed endless – a good month or two, working on it almost daily. It was Gould's mind at work, and for me it was amazing to get inside his head. It was like a musical composition – and it made me see that there was more than one way to do radio. My job was to find out what he was thinking, and putting it into some form that the public could hear.

CE: *And you were completely involved in the nuts-and-bolts creation of the documentary?*

LT: All of the interviews used in the documentary had already been done – I didn't record any of them. But I was the technician on the project. It was my job to put it together.

CE: *Did you ever find yourself having to tell Gould that something he wanted couldn't be done?*

LT: No. He asked for a lot of things that were technically difficult, but they weren't impossible. Between us we would figure out how things could be done – and he was determined to get it right.

CE: *How did people react to The Idea of North when it was broadcast?*

LT: "Confused" would be a good way to describe it. Every CBC master control in Canada issued what they called a Fault Report. Across the country, from St John's to Vancouver, they all had the same comment on their Fault Report: "Continuous cross-talk throughout." They thought we had two or three different programs running at once. And externally, we found that a lot of listeners had the same view.

CE: *What other Gould radio projects did you work on?*

LT: Glenn completed nine documentaries, altogether. I think my favourites were the documentaries on Stokowski[4] and Casals.[5] But I didn't work on all nine: after the fourth or fifth, I played more of a consulting role. Glenn had become familiar with most of the technical staff at the CBC by then – and he very much appreciated working with the different technicians as it gave him the opportunity to discuss his ideas and gain more insight into broadcasting.

CE: *You and Gould went on to become good friends, and you remained friends all his life. Why did your friendship with him endure so long?*

LT: Friendship with Glenn was based on the idea that you'll bring something to the table, and he'll bring something to the table – and you both eat at the same table because you like the same sorts of things. Glenn believed that friendship should be based on this kind of agreement. That didn't mean that you couldn't disagree with him, but it meant that you had to disagree constructively, as opposed to destructively. It could be a very simple incident that changed things: when Glenn felt someone was being destructive, that was the end of the relationship.

I'm not sure I knew all this at the time, but it explains why he thought a particular friendship was a good or a bad thing. And when he made a decision, it was final; he rarely recanted on any decision he made. So I guess I contributed to him in a positive way, as he did to me.

CE: *How did you socialize with him? What did you and he do together outside the studio?*

LT: Glenn probably spent as much time at our house as he did at his own apartment. And we frequently had coffee, went to dinner, and occasionally took in a movie together. He liked films that had an intellectual content: he wouldn't have gone to see the latest Sam Spade movie, but he loved Japanese films. And he once told me that the movie *Ship of Fools* was the basis for his *Idea of North*. Most of this was interspersed with a game we played that Glenn invented. It's called Identifications, and it's a twenty-questions kind of game: he would think of someone I knew, or knew of, and I would have to ask him indirect questions to find out the correct answer. If I successfully guessed the person, he was thrilled out of his mind.

CE: *What else can you say about Gould's personality?*

LT: He was the easiest person to talk to – you didn't have to be a musician or an intellectual to have a conversation with him. He was a highly intellectual human being, but he had a mind that could work on any level. He was eccentric, yes, but at the time I wasn't conscious of it. Now that so many years have passed, I realize that there was some eccentricity there.

I think he was also sensitive, and afraid of being hurt. And at times that caused him to make certain decisions about his friends. And he was certainly sensitive about being touched – especially on the shoulders. When we finished *The Idea of North*, I patted him on the shoulder, and he went berserk! He told me to never do that – and then he apologized for his reaction.[6]

If there is a negative thing I can say about Glenn – and I don't think I would have said it when he was alive – it's that he was a complete and total control freak. He had to control everything – there was no in-between for him. He was so utterly and consciously convinced that what he was doing was right.

CE: I understand that Gould was very much upset about his mother's death. What do you recall about that event?

LT: One of the things that terrified Glenn throughout his life was germs. He would not shake hands with you if he didn't think your hands were clean. The result was that he didn't go to hospitals, because they were germ factories. When his mother was sick, he didn't go to see her in the hospital – not realizing how ill she was, and that her life was in danger. It was only after she died that he came to the realization how silly it was for him to have this problem with germs that prevented him from saying goodbye to his mother in the way he would have liked to do. He was devastated that he didn't do that. The effects of his loss resulted in some permanent changes to his character. For a period afterwards he became withdrawn and didn't say much.

CE: Was Gould serious about legally naming you as his brother?

LT: He probably first suggested it when we were working on *The Idea of North* – and at first I thought it was a joke. But he persisted for a couple of years, and made it very clear to me that he was serious. He wanted to go to a lawyer and have a contract drawn up. I said to him, "Glenn, I have four brothers and a sister, and I think they should have some say in this." He never asked me again. What I had done was point out the reality of the situation to him. Of course, Glenn had no brothers or sisters of his own. His cousin Jessie was like the sister he never had, and I was like the brother he never had. That's how close we were.

CE: And what do you recall about his dealings with the opposite sex?

LT: Some people have thought he was gay – but he wasn't. I would say he was asexual.

CE: He did have a few lady friends, didn't he?

LT: Yes, he did. But I think for Glenn a relationship with a woman was like two kids in primary school. Is that a relationship or a friendship? I wasn't with him twenty-four hours a day – and I don't know what he did when I wasn't there – but I find it hard to believe that he would have any kind of sexual encounter. That would have meant touching, and he was too afraid of germs.

CE: Did you know about his relationship with Cornelia Foss, while it was happening?[7]

LT: I knew that she was living in Toronto with her two children, somewhere off Yonge Street. But I never really thought of her as Glenn's "girlfriend." In the film *Genius Within*, she says that she was going to marry Glenn – but if she was, she never made me aware of that.[8] In retrospect, there was some kind of relationship there – but again, I would find it really hard to imagine him having a sexual relationship, because Glenn didn't like touching or being touched.

CE: Did he grow more eccentric and idiosyncratic towards the end of his life?

LT: People had been saying that sort of thing throughout his life – and many more joined in after his death. There are many myths around Glenn, and there's a certain amount of truth to some of them. But to say that these things dominated his life isn't true at all.

First of all, he was not afraid to shake hands – he shook hands with most people I know – but when he did, he was very careful about it. His hands were his source of income, and he was afraid of meeting some "bone-crusher," as he put it. And in all the years I knew Glenn, I never knew him to wear gloves except when it was cold outside. I never saw him wearing gloves in the studio, and when we went to have dinner he didn't sit in the restaurant with his coat and gloves on.

Then there was his fear of flying. I think I understand now that this was about control: when you fly in an airplane, you have to sit there patiently for a few hours while someone else – the pilot – is in control of your life. As I said before, he liked to be in control all the time.

CE: What about his hypochondria and his fondness for prescription medications?

LT: Again, that's another myth. He did take some pills: when I first met him he was heavily into sleeping pills, and I think I was responsible for getting him off them. It was just after the death of Judy Garland, and I said to Glenn, "Do you know what killed her? She died of an overdose of sleeping pills."[9] I explained to him that it wasn't that she had taken a single overdose all at once, but had taken one or two pills every night for years. The chemicals built up in her body, and killed her.

I know that Glenn always carried a few Valium pills in his pocket, which were prescribed by his doctor. He'd take one if he even suspected that you were a person who was going to be confrontational: he would go to the bathroom and take a Valium, and then come back to you. And apparently he popped Valiums at home, which I wasn't aware of. Is that an addiction? I don't know. Was he a hypochondriac? I really don't think so. He was a normal person!

Also, if he was feeling unwell, or thought he might be coming down with something, he'd rely on an old family remedy and take some belladonna. Other than that, I'm not aware of any other medication that he took. There are stories that he took all kinds of pills, but I don't know about that.[10]

CE: *When did you last see or talk to Gould?*

LT: The last time I spoke to him was on the Sunday, the day after his birthday, on the phone. Then on Monday he had his stroke – and apparently he phoned me, but my wife said I was on my way to work. So he phoned his doctor, who told him to get to the hospital. He contacted Ray Roberts, who drove him to Toronto General Hospital. I didn't hear he was in the hospital until Thursday, and by then he was so deep in a coma that there wasn't any point in visiting him. So I never did get to say goodbye.[11]

CE: *What would Glenn have accomplished if he had lived for another twenty or thirty years?*

LT: Glenn had just renewed his contract with Columbia Masterworks. I know that he wanted to work with Herbert von Karajan, and I think he would have done more conducting himself. Beyond that, anything I might say would be pure speculation on my part. But whatever he did would have been just as interesting as the things he had already done. He would have kept on going – and he would have loved the digital age. Today you can do things in a studio in ten minutes that used to take us two weeks to do.

CE: *Today, does the world remember Glenn Gould in the right way, and for the right reasons?*

LT: I think so, yes. I think that all the myths and misunderstandings will die away, and ultimately the truth will be there. There are some people who will want to exaggerate his characteristics, but in the end, the man and his work will emerge. I think it's inevitable.

Postscript

Lorne Tulk does not figure as prominently as he might in Glenn Gould's biographies – but there are few people who knew and admired Gould more than Tulk did. And while many of Gould's relationships with other people proved ephemeral, his friendship with Tulk lasted until the end of his life.

Nearly three decades after Gould's passing, Tulk's devotion to his friend retains a warmth that is tinged with awe. And he retains a firm commitment to the idea that the Glenn Gould he knew was essentially a normal man – even if he did not always appear so to others. Yet the passing years have given Tulk time to reflect upon and re-evaluate Gould, to some extent. As a result, in this interview he expressed a willingness to offer some opinions about his friend that he probably wouldn't have voiced while Gould was still alive, or even shortly after his death.

CE

NOTES

1 Petula Clark is an English popular singer born in 1932. In the 1960s she rose to top-40 success with such hit songs as "Downtown," "My Love," "Colour My World" and "Don't Sleep in the Subway."

2 Gould's program *The Search for Petula Clark* was broadcast by the CBC on December 11, 1967. It begins with a lengthy preamble in which he describes the town of Marathon, Ontario, on the north shore of Lake Superior. This is where, he explains, he heard Clark on his car radio and developed an interest in her. Continuing his monologue, Gould summarizes the singer as "pop music's most persuasive embodiment of the Gidget syndrome," and describes her voice as "fiercely loyal to its one great octave."

3 *The Idea of North* was first broadcast by the CBC on December 28, 1967. The subject of this documentary was the varying feelings that Canadians who lived in remote northern communities had about their environment. In creating *The Idea of North*, Gould deviated from standard radio-documentary format, by deliberately mixing

together the voices of two or more speakers. Gould called this technique "contrapuntal radio."

4 Gould's *Stokowski: A Portrait for Radio* was first broadcast by the CBC on February 2, 1971. In it, he credits the conductor Leopold Stokowski as "the first great musician to realize that the future of music would be inextricably bound up with technological progress."

5 Gould's *Casals: A Portrait for Radio* was first broadcast on January 15, 1974, shortly after the death of the cellist, composer and conductor Pablo Casals.

6 In 1960, Gould's fear of being touched on the shoulder became the source of a lawsuit between Gould and the piano manufacturer Steinway & Sons. For more information on this incident, see Chapter 1: Walter Homburger (p. 9).

7 Gould carried on a relationship for five years with Cornelia Foss, a painter and the wife of American composer, conductor and pianist Lukas Foss. In 1967 she left her husband, who was then conductor of the Buffalo Philharmonic Orchestra, and moved to Toronto to be near Gould. However, in 1972 she ended the relationship with Gould and returned to her husband. For more information see Chapter 4: Cornelia Foss.

8 The documentary film *Genius Within: The Inner Life of Glenn Gould* was released by White Pine Pictures in 2009.

9 The actress and singer Judy Garland died on June 22, 1969. An autopsy revealed that she had died of "an incautious self-overdosage" of barbituates.

10 According to biographer Kevin Bazzana, Gould took Placidyl, Dalamene, Nembutal and Luminal, among other prescription drugs. Kevin Bazzana, *Wondrous Strange: The Life and Art of Glenn Gould* (Toronto: McClelland & Stewart, 2003), p. 355. For more information see Chapter 3: Margaret Pacsu (p. 113).

11 On September 27, 1982, Gould suffered a severe stroke, which paralyzed the left side of his body. He died in Toronto General Hospital on October 4, nine days after his fiftieth birthday.

John P.L. Roberts: Gould on the Radio and in Life

John Peter Lee Roberts was born in Sydney, Australia, in 1930, and after a sojourn in London, England, immigrated to Canada in 1955, where he became a CBC radio producer in Winnipeg and also worked in television. Two years later he was invited to go to Toronto, where in a reorganization of the CBC Music Department he became one of two national music program organizers. Eventually, he was appointed Head of Music for the English radio networks. Roberts moved to Alberta in 1987 to accept the position of Dean of the Faculty of Fine Arts at the University of Calgary, where among other things he was instrumental in the establishment of the Rozsa Centre for music performance.

Through his work at the CBC, Roberts came into contact with many extraordinary musicians – but none more extraordinary than Glenn Gould. The two men entered into an enduring friendship that lasted from their first meeting in 1955 to the end of the brilliant pianist's life. In 1992, with Ghyslaine Guertin, he published *Glenn Gould: Selected Letters* and later, independently, a critical edition of some of Gould's writings, *The Art of Glenn Gould*. He has lectured and published widely on Gould in Canada and abroad.

This interview took place on September 3, 2011 at John Roberts's home in Calgary.

CE: What can you tell me about your musical background?

JR: I grew up in Sydney, Australia, in a musical family. My father was an amazing man, and was both an organist and a pianist. The first piano recital I ever attended was given by him in our living room. I was a small boy in pyjamas, sitting on the floor. Among other things, he played the Bach *Italian Concerto* and also the *Chromatic Fantasia and Fugue*. He was absolutely obsessed with Bach – and in due course Glenn himself became interested in him, eventually sending him most of his recordings.

I gained a music performance diploma in Sydney and years later went to university in Canada. At the State Conservatorium of Music I studied for some years with a renowned teacher, Alexander Sverjensky. Before leaving Australia I auditioned for the Australian Broadcasting Corporation and was invited to give a national broadcast, which was well received. However, I finally felt that to have a performing career one has to have nothing short of staggering talent – and although I was not without musical gifts, I didn't have staggering talent, so I thought hard and long about developing another kind of music career.

CE: And how did you come to Canada?

JR: I went first to England, arriving in London in 1952, and to keep bread on the table I took a minor job at the Royal College of Music, then turned to music journalism and published my work in Australian newspapers. But when I learned that I would be drafted into the British army for two years of obligatory military service, on the advice of friends in London I took a ship for Canada to see if I could make my way in this country.

Music broadcasting had always interested me enormously, so I went knocking on the doors of the CBC in Toronto. After some weeks and several interviews I went to Winnipeg as a music producer. I spent two years in Winnipeg producing orchestral and other types of programs, and then was transferred to Toronto as a program organizer. Later I was made Supervisor of Music, and eventually Head of Music for the English radio networks.

CE: And where did you meet Glenn Gould?

JR: I met Glenn in Winnipeg, in December of 1955. My colleagues had told me about a young pianist in Toronto who was all the rage, and I was looking forward to hearing him. I was assigned to closely observe the production of his concert with the Winnipeg Symphony Orchestra, at the old Civic Auditorium.[1] I remember being backstage talking to one of my colleagues when I looked around and suddenly there was Glenn, just standing there. He introduced himself, and we had a brief but animated conversation.

Shortly afterwards, he walked on stage to perform the Beethoven *Piano Concerto No. 1* with his own cadenzas. They were not typical cadenzas – there was a vestige of Richard Strauss and possibly Max Reger, as well as a revelation of Glenn's passion for counterpoint – but I thought they were absolutely amazing: a fresh view of what a cadenza could be. And at the end of the concerto, which was absolutely masterfully performed, the audience went wild. There were a lot of young people there, and he was received like a pop star.

After the concert, as I was gathering up my things, Glenn walked in. I congratulated him on his performance, and he asked me if I was going to the reception. I replied, "No, I'm not invited – I'm just the new kid on the block." He then asked me if I would have breakfast with him at the Fort Garry Hotel the next morning. I was quite surprised and said I'd be delighted.

The next morning I got to the hotel early. Again we had an animated conversation, first about music. I remember asking him about what music he would like to record, and he said he would like to present Mozart piano concertos. So we talked about some of them – and it was obvious that he had highly individual realizations in mind. In retrospect, this is interesting, considering that he later expressed misgivings with much of this music and ended up recording all the Mozart piano sonatas rather than the concertos, in performances that shocked some people. He of course pushed back the frontiers of piano performance in many ways. He was a great "original," and certainly controversial.

CE: *What other things came up in conversation?*

JR: Glenn asked me about many aspects of Australia. He had been asked to tour there. Apart from music, he was fascinated with Australian animals and showed some interest in Australian history. And with a certain pride mentioned his own connection to Canadian history through the firebrand William Lyon Mackenzie, as well as a former prime minister, Mackenzie King.[2]

CE: *And how did you and Gould become such close friends?*

JR: Not too long after the CBC transferred me from Winnipeg to Toronto in 1957, I called Glenn, who was still living with his parents on Southwood Drive.[3] He said, "You must come and have supper at home," an invitation that I accepted, and I subsequently went to the house many times. Usually his parents disappeared after supper, leaving the two of us to talk or listen to recordings. But when talking he also liked to illustrate points at the piano.

CE: *What were those evenings at the Gould home like?*

JR: Glenn's dad Bert had organized the house so that beyond the living room there was an area for Glenn's piano and recording equipment and many scores. It was the three-quarter Steinway that's now in the residence of the Governor General in Ottawa. It looked a bit shabby because it was not infrequently shipped to the family cottage at Uptergrove on Lake Simcoe when Glenn was working up there.[4] Glenn also had another piano – an old American Chickering for which he had a great affection – with an easy action and somewhat twangy sound.[5] "This is a harpsichord that thinks it's a piano," he would say with a smile. It too looked rather down at the heel because it had been moved around so many times.

Glenn had whole operas in his memory – and he was a complete Wagner nut. I remember many evenings at the house in Toronto during which, if he started playing *Tristan und Isolde*, there was no stopping him. Relying on his prodigious memory, and looking a thousand miles away as if in a trance, he would be tilting with the impossible as he tried to accommodate the large forces at work, the big orchestra and all the singers, with only ten fingers. So he would play and sing, and if he was unhappy because he had left out something that was structurally important, he would sometimes go back and integrate it.

CE: So he was in effect improvising his own transcription of Tristan und Isolde?

JR: Yes, that's right. He had an extraordinary talent for coming forward with instant transcriptions. And if we weren't doing Wagner or other music at the piano, we were listening to records or tapes. And later on, when his own recordings were coming out more frequently, he would sometimes have acetate copies of records that hadn't been released yet. So we would put these on and listen together. Sometimes – particularly if it was something that had been made a year or two before and it had fallen out of mind – Glenn would say, "I don't know why he plays it like that." The "he" was of course him!

CE: What were your impressions of Gould's parents?

JR: They were fine, upright people – very conservative, products of their generation, and certainly very kind to me. He once told me that they were delighted we were friends. They probably thought that I was some kind of good influence – not too far out!

Glenn was very precious to his parents: they had tried to have a child for years, but each time his mother Florence had had a miscarriage. So after Glenn's birth his parents centred their lives around their amazing child. From the time he was very small, his mother had him on her knee, on the piano stool, with his little fingers on the keys. And when he was old enough she began to teach him the piano. But she was the very opposite of a "stage mother." She wanted him to be what she described as "normal." Certainly she wanted him to be immersed in music, but she didn't want him to be a child prodigy – she bristled if anyone mentioned the word "prodigy" around him.

His mother was the right teacher for him in the early days. But as Glenn grew – with his perfect pitch and developing photographic musical memory, combined with his probing mind and ever increasing independence – she knew that in the foreseeable future a real mentor would have to be found for him. This turned out to be Alberto Guerrero, an extraordinary musician who had come from Chile in 1918 and who also taught other remarkable Canadians.[6]

CE: And it was in these years that Gould's technique developed?

JR: There can be no doubt that Glenn had absolutely marvellous hands for the piano. I know that on several occasions I talked to him about his hands and other aspects of his performing mechanism, and quickly understood that during his teenage years he went through a period when he devoted a lot of time and attention to his technical development. Later, Glenn downplayed this and told me that he considered himself self-taught. I believe that he was thinking of the many works he performed in his maturity which he analyzed and realized himself. He also felt that, generally speaking, teachers should spend more time on teaching students how to analyze scores and come to terms with the structure of music.

CE: *What else did you do with Gould?*

JR: We did different things. At the cottage he introduced me to snowshoeing after I noticed some little huts in the distance on the ice of frozen Lake Simcoe, and we walked out to them to observe the people inside patiently fishing. It was a little later that I learned of his abhorrence of fishing as a sport. Glenn also liked to go for drives in his car. We went to the scenically beautiful Caledon Hills and the Forks of the Credit River quite often – I remember going there in the winter with him. We got out of the car and went for a good long walk in the snow. In the course of this he talked about music: what he was doing at the moment, projects he was considering, and future projects which were on the drawing board.

CE: *Of course, you were involved with some of those projects.*

JR: Glenn was contracted to do a certain number of CBC radio projects in the form of recitals and documentaries each year, for which I was responsible. I remember one occasion when I was in Europe for the CBC at a meeting of the music committee of the European Broadcasting Union, which had the task of putting together their main music series. The rule was that music projects had to be broadcast "live." My European colleagues always had their own ideas about stellar events they could present. When I said, off the top of my head, that we were suggesting a recital by Glenn Gould, there was a guarded response. I then said that because Glenn believed so strongly in the intercession of technology in the presentation of music, his program would have to be recorded, which of course was against the rules. I asked if they would be prepared to accept that. After a rather long discussion, in which the fear of establishing an unwise precedent was overcome, they were brought around to allowing the project to go ahead. That broadcast was recorded in Toronto and heard all over Europe, North America and other places by countless millions of people.

CE: What was the family cottage in Uptergrove like – and what was its significance?

JR: It was set on the shores of Lake Simcoe, and in some ways it was really a very modest place. The living room had been turned into a studio with large windows and a high ceiling. There was one bedroom downstairs and the others were upstairs. The significance of the cottage was that it provided Glenn with an escape. His fame and the public interest in him became so great that he was constantly pursued by the media and also individuals, including numerous women. Finally, in order not to be recognized, he sometimes ate at Voyageur Restaurants on the Trans-Canada Highway. I always felt very privileged to know what was going on in his mind, and he often talked about the big decisions in his career.

CE: I've read of you and Gould reciting Shakespeare's plays for fun.

JR: In the course of one of our dinner-time discussions, I told him that one of my great passions is Shakespeare. Glenn said, "I love Shakespeare too," so I then said, "Why don't we invite a few other people, and have Shakespeare readings?" His eyes lit up – he thought this was a marvellous idea. We met in my apartment in Rosedale[7] and Glenn would bring his super tape-recorder so that we could tape ourselves. We did various plays: *King Richard the Second, Macbeth, Hamlet, Twelfth Night, The Merchant of Venice, As You Like It* and others. We got great enjoyment from this. We also read plays by Oscar Wilde and other playwrights, and we did improvisations. There were times when things got a bit out of control, and it would turn into a hilarious evening. After a while, we had readings in his penthouse on St Clair Avenue.

CE: I understand that Glenn was a witness at your wedding.

JR: He was very excited about that; he wanted to know about the plans for the wedding. And he wanted a role in it. I wondered if he wanted to play the organ at the ceremony in St James Cathedral,[8] but he said no because switching between instruments presented him with problems of keyboard adjustment. He then agreed to be a witness. I remember that he asked me what I was going to wear, which was a strange question from someone who had no interest in clothes. I told him that I was hiring a morning suit and he laughed, saying, "I have one at home which I rarely wear. I'll give it a last appearance before consigning it to the moths!"

CE: When you discussed music, what subjects did he talk about with you?

JR: This happened so often it's hard to know where to begin. Originally he was going to record all the Beethoven piano sonatas. It was a project that interested him, but after about a year he said to me that he was not going to record them all. He said that he would never record the "Waldstein," which was "too pianistic," and he thought that he might not record the "Appassionata" either. He also had doubts about the "Hammerklavier." It stayed in the back of his head as a challenge – and like the "Appassionata" he did record it, but he was particularly unhappy with the results.

CE: Did Gould talk about his travels in his concert-giving days? For instance, did he have anything to say about his 1959 visit to London to perform the Beethoven piano concertos with Josef Krips and the London Symphony Orchestra?

JR: Oh yes, he was a great fan of Krips, and felt that he was undervalued by some musicians who should have known better. The great Greek pianist Gina Bachauer related to me some years later that a "who's who" of the leading pianists in Europe were present in the hall for those concerts, and she generously said, "We have all learned a great deal from him." She added that Glenn was a once-in-a-century phenomenon.

Glenn also talked to me about some other aspects of being in London at that time. Just to mention one thing, he discovered that William Walton's much anticipated opera *Troilus and Cressida* was on at Covent Garden. He didn't attend a performance but made a point of buying a score, knowing that he couldn't even look at it until he was on the plane taking him back to Toronto. Shortly after his arrival home there was a knock at my front door and when I opened it there was Glenn. After greeting me he said, "I have brought you a present," and he handed me a package inside which was the score of *Troilus and Cressida*. He went on to say how impressed he was with it. I was astonished when he sat down at the piano without the score and played a large part of it from memory.

CE: Did he talk to you about his performance of Brahms's Piano Concerto in D Minor with the New York Philharmonic, under Bernstein, in 1962?[9]

JR: Initially, he did this as we were walking along the banks of the Credit River. He said, "I've got a completely different conception of this work." I heard him practising at the cottage playing both the solo part and the orchestral part as best he could. He said, "I have been playing this piece much too fast in the past.

It's got to be slower. Let me sing it for you." First he sang it rather slowly, and then he sang it even slower – finally he sang it so slowly that I said, " Oh come on, Glenn, it would be very difficult for any conductor to sustain it at such a slow tempo." He just smiled and said, "That will be the challenge."

I heard the broadcast from New York. He played it very slowly, but there was a sort of tautness to it that held it together. But he had created a scandal: the orchestra was incredulous when Bernstein explained the way it was going to be. At the first performance, Bernstein made his famous speech: that he did not agree with Glenn, but because Glenn was such a fantastic musician, he should be given the chance to do it his way.[10]

At the last performance, when Glenn and Bernstein were backstage, Glenn leaned over and said, "Lenny, we're going to do it your way tonight." Of course it was a very big change. The tempo was quite brisk, and Bernstein and the orchestra were staggered by this. By all accounts it was an absolutely phenomenal performance. There had been terrible reviews after the first performance, but not a word was written after the last one.

I remember asking him years later, "If you were going to perform the Brahms *D Minor Concerto* now, would you do it the same as in New York?" and he replied as I expected, "No, I'd do it completely differently."

CE: It's said that Gould was in fact a distant cousin of Edvard Grieg. Did he ever show any interest in the Grieg Piano Concerto?

JR: He was rather tickled with the family relationship to Edvard Grieg through his mother – so when his recording company thought it would be a smart move for him to record the Grieg *Piano Concerto*, he agreed. With a certain glee he mentioned what fun it would be to catch up with "Cousin Edvard" this way. But by the time the orchestra was booked he hadn't even acquired the score. I dropped in to see him at home, and found him having a challenging time. He was obliged to tell his record company by the end of the day whether or not he was going ahead with the Grieg project.

Shortly after my arrival, the score was delivered by messenger. It turned out that Glenn had never set eyes on the music before and needed to play it through from beginning to end. So he roped me in as page-turner. He played the solo part and fitted in the orchestral part whenever he could. Glenn was a remarkable sight-reader, so after the pages had been smoothed down he set to work.

What happened then was certainly memorable. With his eyes glued to the score he delivered an astounding rendition. At the moment of the cadenza I was intrigued to know what he would do with it, because it is necessary to have a good idea of how to handle certain technical challenges in order to land on the right notes, and I wondered how he would make out. However, he undauntedly sailed right through it. The second movement was lyrical, dramatic and highly individual; the third was taken at a breakneck speed, and he brought it to a dramatic close. I must say that I was overawed with his stunning performance and the security he showed in facing all the challenges.

However, he shut the score and quite simply said, "It's delightful, of course, but not for me." To which I responded, "What on earth do you mean? You have just given a remarkable performance!" Glenn's response was "There are so many pianists who have really got something to say with this music, and I am afraid I have not. I think I must leave Cousin Edvard safely in their hands."

CE: *Two pianists who are often cited as influences on Gould are Artur Schnabel and Rosalyn Tureck. What impact did they have on him?*[11]

JR: Schnabel was his god in his childhood and adolescence because "He doesn't play the piano like a pianist, he plays like a great artist and to count for anything in music, that is what one must be." When Glenn was young he imitated the interpretations of Schnabel so much that his teacher, Alberto Guerrero, confiscated his Schnabel recording of Beethoven's *Fourth Piano Concerto*. However, it has to be admitted that for very many people there is an inherent authenticity in much of what Glenn touches. Some years ago the great American composer Aaron Copland said to me, "When Glenn Gould plays Bach it sounds so authoritative and genuine I feel as though I am actually listening to Bach himself."

As for Tureck, Glenn admired her enormously. I invited her to give a recital in Toronto for the CBC. She was a formidable woman – very impressive, and a great artist. She had a kind of integrity and uprightness in her playing that appealed to Glenn very much. She had a certain precision in her articulation, but Glenn's way of playing was less clinical. He never met her, but he admitted that he had learned a lot from her. And Tureck said to me, "He's an excellent artist and I think he's learned quite a bit from me."

CE: *Another woman closely associated with Bach's keyboard music was Wanda Landowska. What did Gould think about her?*

JR: I think he admired her in a certain way, but he did not feel warmly about her in the same way he did about Schnabel and Tureck. Landowska was deeply committed to the harpsichord. Glenn also loved the harpsichord, but his preference was for the piano. For him it was an orchestra. He always thought orchestrally about his piano performances. There are so many nuances that you can get from a piano that you can't get from a harpsichord.

CE: How did Gould feel about the early music movement?

JR: He respected it, but didn't take much interest in it as such. However, he was always interested in the musicology which was a part of this movement, and grateful to those musicologists who had contributed to it so richly.

CE: A few years after his famous Brahms D Minor Concerto with the New York Philharmonic, Gould stopped giving concerts. What did you think of this decision?

JR: Almost from the very first time I met him, he told me that he wasn't enjoying giving concerts. And every year he would say, "This is the year I'm going to stop," but he always had engagements booked into the future. Finally, around 1963 he said to me, "I've got to call a halt, otherwise it just keeps going on and on – one year leads to another, I have to find a way out." So in 1964 he decided he was not going to play concerts any more. He told Walter Homburger,[12] his agent, not to take any more engagements.

I can remember John McClure[13] at Columbia Records saying to me, "You've got to get to Glenn and talk him out of this – it will be fatal. His whole career will be ruined if he doesn't give concerts." I had talked to Glenn for a long time before this whole matter came to a head, and he said that a lot of people believed that playing concerts and making records were inextricably bound up together but that he did not. In any case, I knew that Glenn was listening to an inner voice which he had to pay attention to. He smiled and said, "I guess we'll see who is right." Glenn was breaking new ground. No other major artist had ever done anything quite like this before.

CE: What role did the CBC play in Gould's life and career? And why did the CBC take such an interest in him, allowing him to do anything he wanted?

JR: Glenn was a star. The people at the CBC, beginning in 1950,[14] recognized what he was, and they have been very good at projecting him to a large audience. And while producers there have come and gone, the newer people are just as devoted to him as their colleagues of the past. They see it as their duty to keep his name and art before the public. Of course, they are making use of newer technologies. There's now a Gould website and other developments.

If Glenn were here he would be delighted. He never felt more at home than when he was in a studio and working with technology. The performances he gave were riveting – and the producers and other CBC people were convinced that Glenn was an absolute genius. If he wanted to do certain things that the CBC hadn't thought of, they made it possible for him to do them. So the CBC was vitally important to his career.

He also loved the milieu: he would sit in the cafeteria and talk to people. To be honest, the CBC cafeteria was an awful place – but it was like a second home to him. He'd meet producers, technicians, writers and others, and sometimes engage in very long conversations with them.

CE: I believe that it was thanks to the CBC that Glenn had lunch with Igor Stravinsky in Toronto – and that you were there.

JR: I was always a great admirer of Stravinsky and I proposed to the then Head of Music, Geoffrey Waddington, that the CBC should bring him to Canada to undertake a cluster of major projects in honour of his eightieth birthday.[15]

In order to obtain access to him I tried to reach his New York agent numerous times, without success. In my frustration I mentioned this to Glenn who was shortly due to record the Schoenberg *Piano Concerto* with Robert Craft and the CBC Symphony. Craft was Stravinsky's assistant and also lived in his house. Glenn immediately said that when Craft came to Toronto for the recording sessions he would invite me to supper with him, so that the idea of a giant project, which would include a television component, could be brought forward without further delays.

The irony was that Glenn admired only a very few Stravinsky works. I told him he had a blind spot concerning Stravinsky and he answered, "I certainly don't think so, but I probably hold a minority opinion." He detested *The Rite of Spring*, but enjoyed the *Firebird* and *Movements for Piano and Orchestra* and a very few other things.

It's interesting to note that Stravinsky felt the opposite toward Glenn. He heard him perform late Beethoven in Los Angeles and probably had heard Glenn's recording of the last three Beehoven sonatas at some point, because he wrote Glenn a generous note saying he admired his playing of late Beethoven. Glenn didn't talk at all adversely about Stravinsky – he could see that our plans would provide a means of bringing important music as yet unknown in Canada to the public, while at the same time creating a coup for the CBC.

The project had another dimension that interested Glenn a great deal. A series of works by Schoenberg – a composer Glenn enormously admired and continually brought forward through his own performances – would be presented. All these works were virtually unknown in Canada. The conductor was to be Robert Craft, a musician for whom Glenn had the greatest admiration, and who was preparing all the works by Stravinsky for already-scheduled recording sessions. Earlier, I had paid a visit to CBS Records in New York, and it was agreed that this additional music would become part of the giant project – provided the CBC would initially present the unknown works by Stravinsky and Schoenberg in radio broadcasts, so they would be ready for subsequent recording sessions.

One day while we were waiting for the start of a rehearsal, Stravinsky turned to me and asked if it would be possible to invite Glenn to lunch. I said I knew that he was in town and promised to investigate and get back to him. When I called Glenn to invite him he was not very enthusiastic about the proposed luncheon and said, "Do I have to go?" I replied, "Yes, you absolutely have to go." When the day arrived Glenn turned up at the dining room on time.

It had been whispered to me that the composer's *Capriccio for Piano and Orchestra* was due to be re-recorded, and that among the names suggested as soloist Glenn's had figured prominently. The question was would he even be interested? In the course of the lunch when the conversation was veering in the direction of the *Capriccio*, Glenn very deftly deflected the topic. About dessert-time, Glenn stood up and said, "I am very sorry but unfortunately I must go now." As I followed him to the door he said, "I think I handled that rather well don't you?" I replied, "I'm sorry, but I don't agree. You don't know the *Capriccio*. I believe you don't know the score." "But I don't want to know it," was Glenn's comment. I said, "I have a score that I can lend you." "Thanks, but I don't want your score," and Glenn was almost out the door of the hotel. Later I was annoyed with myself for not keeping in mind that Glenn only played music that he could make totally his own, and this would be very hard to achieve if the composer was present.

CE: Until recently, few people knew about Glenn's relationship with Cornelia Foss.[16] *But surely you must have known about it all along?*

JR: Glenn and Cornelia came to our place for supper and we went to hers quite a few times. She is a lovely woman and was wonderful for him. Glenn was also very fond of her two children.

CE: Why did you and others keep the relationship such a closely guarded secret for so many years?

JR: I've always felt very protective toward Glenn. And I didn't want to blab about it to people who were looking for a good story. Several people tried to get me to talk but I just couldn't do it. And I didn't know how Cornelia would feel about it.

CE: Was Gould's health declining, late in his life?

JR: He was a hypochondriac, and always had health problems and anxieties about them. Generally, his health was up and down, and he didn't exercise or eat the right food. He was cruel to his own body without realizing it. He saw different doctors who didn't know about each other, or about all the medications he was taking.[17] Away back, I thought one of the few good things he was doing was to go to a chiropractor, and he insisted that I go too. In fact we often had back-to-back appointments. He was trying to fight off his problems, and they were certainly real.

It's true that there were changes toward the end of his life. He had high blood pressure, gained weight and became quite heavy, was rapidly losing his hair, often had a pale and drawn complexion, and he always looked tired. He always tried to sleep in the day and work at night, which very often meant that he was sleep-deprived and exhausted. However, he firmly believed that all his health problems could be solved by the right doctors and pills. It was difficult to talk to him about his medical problems because he often felt that he could diagnose himself. I felt something had to be done and suggested going to a major clinic in the USA. Nevertheless, he was absolutely convinced that he could arrive at medical solutions himself.

CE: When he had his stroke were you able to see him in the hospital?[18]

JR: Just after the stroke Bert Gould tried to phone me at home in Ottawa, but I wasn't there. I had in fact gone to Toronto, but our younger daughter, who spoke to him, didn't know exactly where I was. Two hours later, at a reception I attended, I discovered that there were rumours flying around that Glenn was seriously ill. I immediately phoned Bert who said that Glenn was in intensive care and not expected to live, and he asked me to meet him at the hospital right away. So I immediately went to the hospital, and there was Glenn.

It was the saddest thing I've ever seen: his head was enlarged and he was on total life support. The next day, I was included in a family telephone conference with the doctor who said: "He's already brain dead. Somebody might be brought in who could be saved, if we have the space in intensive care." We knew what Glenn would want, so it was agreed he would be taken off life support – but not until the next day, so that all the necessary arrangements could be made and an announcement prepared for the international media who were besieging the hospital night and day for information. I think we were all feeling very much for Bert, who was losing his only child.

CE: What was the funeral like?

JR: The funeral itself was private, at Mount Pleasant Cemetery – under a slate grey sky – with pouring rain. Only the family and a very few others were there. We were escorted to the gravesite under huge umbrellas. It was an incredibly sad moment, but the weather made me think that Glenn would have approved. He loved grey skies and grey was his favourite colour.

CE: And I believe you organized the memorial service, a week later?[19]

JR: Yes, Bert asked me to. At first we were going to have it in St James Cathedral – but it soon became apparent that a great number of people would be coming from across Canada and overseas, so I moved it to St Paul's Anglican Church, which is much larger.[20]

Bert asked me to deliver the eulogy. Among other remarks I said that Glenn had "blazed like a meteor across the horizon of the twentieth century." I was particularly concerned that the music be thoroughly appropriate. The Toronto Symphony sent brass players; the Festival Singers[21] and their conductor, Elmer Iseler, were in the gallery; John Tuttle was the organist; and Maureen Forrester also sang. I thought we should choose some German hymns, and allow the congregation to sing also. I felt that Glenn had to have the last word – so we played the "Da Capo Aria" from the *Goldberg Variations* by Bach, which he had recently re-recorded, through the excellent sound system lent by the CBC. In the recording you can hear Glenn quietly singing, and a lot of people broke down in tears.

CE: And you were also very much involved in the establishment of the Glenn Gould Foundation?[22]

JR: Yes, I was the founding President, but I had enormous help from many wonderful and very talented people. I couldn't imagine that Glenn would be forgotten. However, I thought there should be an organization concerned with his "afterlife," and I wanted to do something that would help safeguard his future. I think the Foundation – thanks to successive high-calibre presidents and devoted board members, as well as extremely committed administrators and a lot of outside support – has done a great deal to boost musical life. The Glenn Gould Prize has honoured the people who have received it, but it has also supported important music projects and kept the flame burning for Glenn.

CE: During all the years that you knew Gould, you must have been aware of his many eccentricities. What do you think of them?

JR: Glenn wasn't like anybody else. He lived in a rich inner world and wasn't concerned with outer appearances: sometimes he'd have an odd pair of socks on, and I once saw him wearing an odd pair of shoes. But he would just laugh about it. I had some idea of the workings of his mind: one must remember that he almost always had music playing in his head, and also that he had an amazing ability to focus on different things simultaneously.

I don't believe that Glenn had Asperger's syndrome, as some people do.[23] I'm not a medical man. But Peter Ostwald, who was an eminent psychiatrist and knew Glenn personally, found that he showed symptoms of other possible conditions as well, so his opinion remains inconclusive.

I always found Glenn to be very kind, very thoughtful, extremely loyal – and he was the best friend I ever had. I loved Glenn like a brother. He was wonderful and impossible at the same time, and being his friend was a whole career in itself.

Postscript

John Roberts lives in a suburban house in Calgary that's full of photos and other mementos of a life spent with musicians – including a photo of Igor Stravinsky signed "Strawhisky." But no musician in his collection is more prominent than Glenn Gould, and photos of him are found throughout the house. (Some were taken by Roberts himself.) It's clear from his collection of Gouldiana that the pianist made a deep impression and left Roberts with memories that he is proud to cherish.

In Gould's "inner circle," Roberts is an exceptional figure: he was both a professional associate and a close friend. No other person knew Gould better, artistically, professionally and personally. And, unlike some other relationships with Gould, this friendship lasted from the day they first met to the end of Gould's life. Athough I asserted in the Introduction to this book that there's no "one-stop shopping source" for understanding Gould, Roberts came very close to knowing the whole man.

CE

NOTES

1 This concert took place on December 12, 1955. The conductor was Walter Kaufman.

2 William Lyon MacKenzie (1795-1861) was a Canadian journalist, politician, and a leader of the Rebellion of 1837. William Lyon MacKenzie King (1874-1950) was Canada's tenth prime minister. Gould claimed to be related to both men.

3 Glenn Gould was born at his family's home at 32 Southwood Dr., in Toronto's Beaches neighbourhood. He lived there, with his parents, until 1959.

4 The Gould family had a cottage near the village of Uptergrove, about sixty miles north of Toronto.

5 For more information on this instrument, see Chapter 1: Verne Edquist (p. 13).

6 For more on Alberto Guerrero, see Stuart Hamilton (pp. 38-39), and Chapter 2: John Beckwith (pp. 46-49).

7 Rosedale is a prosperous mid-Toronto neighbourhood known for its tree-lined streets and stately homes.

8 The Cathedral Church of St James (Anglican), built in 1853, stands at the corners of King and Jarvis streets.

9 Gould performed Brahms's *Piano Concerto No. 1* with the New York Philharmonic on April 6, 1962. For more information see Chapter 1: Walter Homburger (p. 9), Stuart Hamilton (p. 41), and Chapter 2: Anton Kuerti (p. 61).

10 Before the performance, Bernstein made a public statement in which he carefully hedged his bets. On one hand, he gave full credit to Gould for the "unorthodox" musical interpretation that the audience was about to hear. On the other, he made it clear that he did not agree with Gould. Bernstein cryptically concluded, "I can assure you that it has been an adventure this week collaborating with Mr. Gould on this Brahms concerto."

11 The pianist Artur Schnabel was born in Bielitz, Silesia, in the Austro-Hungarian Empire (now in Poland), in 1882, and died in Axenstein, Switzerland, in 1951. He recorded prolifically, and was best known for his Beethoven and Schubert interpretations. The American pianist and harpsichordist Rosalyn Tureck was born

in Chicago in 1913, and died in New York in 2003. She was renowned for her Bach interpretations.

12   For more information on Gould's relationship with his concert manager, see Chapter 1: Walter Homburger.

13   John McClure was appointed Director of Artists and Repertoire for Columbia Masterworks in 1959.

14   Gould's first recital performed and recorded expressly for radio was broadcast nationally on the CBC on December 24, 1950.

15   Igor and Vera Stravinsky first visited Toronto in April 1962, where he conducted Toronto's Festival Singers and the CBC Toronto Orchestra.

16   From 1967 to 1972, Gould carried on an affair with Cornelia Foss, a painter and the wife of the American composer, pianist and conductor Lukas Foss. For more information, see Chapter 4: Cornelia Foss.

17   For more information on Gould's medications, see Chapter 1: Ray Roberts (p. 34), and Chapter 3: Margaret Pacsu (p. 113).

18   Gould suffered a stroke on September 27, 1982, two days after his fiftieth birthday, and died at Toronto General Hospital on October 4. For more information about Gould's stroke and hospitalization, see Chapter 1: Ray Roberts (pp. 32-33).

19   Gould's memorial service took place on October 15, 1982.

20   St Paul's Church is located at 227 Bloor St. E. It is the largest Anglican church in Toronto.

21   The Festival Singers were a professional chamber choir, based in Toronto.

22   For more information on the establishment of the Glenn Gould Foundation, see Chapter 1: Stephen Posen (p. 25).

23   For more information on the theory that Gould suffered from Asperger's syndrome, see Chapter 2: Timothy Maloney (pp. 76-78), and Chapter 5: Tim Page (p. 175).

Chapter 4: Two Personal Relationships

Introduction

Glenn Gould was so wrapped up in music and his other artistic pursuits that it's sometimes easy to forget that he associated with people who were not part of the classical music world. Unfortunately, many of the people who were a part of his life outside his professional circles – his parents, other relatives and some friends – are no longer available for interview.

However, I was able to interview two people who were close to Gould, for personal rather than artistic reasons. Robert Fulford and Cornelia Foss both knew Gould very well, albeit at different times in his life. Neither was a musician, although both had a deep admiration for Gould's artistry.

Fulford knew Gould as he grew from a boy to a young man. They lived on the same street, went to the same school and shared some of the same interests. Yet although Fulford portrays himself as an essentially normal kid, it was apparent to him that Gould was also something special. He firmly believed that his next-door neighbour was destined for greatness – and his conviction led him to assist Gould in the creation of his short-lived concert series, New Music Associates.

When Foss first met Gould she was already well ensconced in the world of classical music, as the wife of the American conductor, composer and pianist Lukas Foss. She and Gould grew close – and in 1967, she left her husband to move to Toronto. While she never lived *with* Gould, she lived near him, for five years, until she came to the conclusion that marrying him would not be a good idea.

In her description of her time in Toronto, she portrays Gould as warm, funny, brilliant, hard working and good with children. But the Gould she knew was also fragile: deeply adverse to performing in public, and even a little afraid of some of his stranger fans.

Both Fulford and Foss had the unhappy experience of seeing their friendships with Gould end. In Fulford's case, he and Gould simply grew apart. In Foss's case, she chose to terminate the relationship.

CE

Robert Fulford: the Boy Next Door

Born in 1932, Robert Fulford became a well-known Toronto journalist, writing for the *Toronto Star* and *Globe and Mail* newspapers, and editing Toronto's *Saturday Night* magazine from 1968 to 1987. However, it was not as a journalist that he came to know Glenn Gould, but as a boyhood friend. In 1941, the Fulford family moved into the house at 34 Southwood Dr., in Toronto's "Beach" neighbourhood, next door to the Gould family. Both Gould and Fulford were nine years old at the time – and remained close friends throughout their years at Williamson Road Public School and Malvern Collegiate Institute.

This interview took place July 14, 2010, at Fulford's home in downtown Toronto.

CE: *What were Southwood Drive and the surrounding Beach neighbourhood like in the 1940s?*

RF: It was a quiet part of Toronto. In the 1940s, the neighbourhood was about ninety-eight percent white, and mostly Protestant. People living in the area weren't against impropriety because they had never heard of it – and vulgarity simply didn't exist. People habitually voted Conservative: even when the government in Ottawa was Liberal, we had a Conservative MP.

The Beach was not chic, like it is nowadays. Ten blocks away there were some poorer areas, and there were also houses that were much grander than the ones Glenn and I grew up in, only three or four blocks away. So there was some variety, but most of it was solidly middle-class.

CE: *Did you like growing up there?*

RF: I now realize that I liked it a lot. It's still the best part of Toronto for parks, and it's close to Lake Ontario. For a child it was wonderful, but for an adolescent it was pretty boring. By the time I was a teenager, I knew that anything happening in the world was happening somewhere else.

CE: *Do you feel that Gould was strongly influenced by his upbringing in Toronto?*

RF: Toronto had its Conservatory, which was a well-established institution.[1] The Mendelssohn Choir was also well established, and there was the Toronto Symphony, although it was still quite young.[2] As well, the Kiwanis Music Festival was very important for Glenn, and CBC radio was ambitiously broadcasting lots of music.[3]

Anyone in Toronto who was going to be as fine an artist as Glenn became would, almost of necessity, have been a musician. To become a painter would have been much harder, and the same is true for literature, dance or film: you'd have to somehow get way beyond what the city had to offer. But there was a solid tradition of music in Toronto that was available to Glenn.

CE: *Can you remember the first time you met Glenn?*

RF: We were in the same classroom, and he turned around and we introduced ourselves. It took a few days for us to figure out that my family had moved into the house next door to his. At that stage he was just an interesting kid, but I soon discovered that he was extraordinary.

CE: *What did you think of Gould's mother?*[4]

RF: Florence Gould was forty – old, by the standards of her generation, when Glenn was born. It was very unusual. And she was Glenn's first piano teacher. He was very attached to her, and there was no chance of him revolting against her.

But I didn't like Mrs. Gould at all. She was very censorious and very particular in her attitude towards things. She believed in things without giving them a lot of thought: of course she was Christian, of course she was Protestant, of course she was United Church – what else would she be?[5] That was the entire extent of her religious beliefs, as far as I know.

If you wanted to make a child into a hypochondriac, Mrs. Gould would be the best person for the job. She was always concerned about whether Glenn should or should not put on a sweater when he left the house: it was a big issue. She was constantly worried about whether he was eating enough, or too much. And she kept asking Glenn to sit up straight, which he found impossible.

Above all else, Glenn's mother insisted that he was not to practise the piano beyond a certain number of hours. Here, I could see her point: if left to his own devices, he would play all day. He had found this wonderful thing that he could do, with great pleasure. It was something that he loved, and there was no end to how much there was to learn. But his mother wanted some balance in his life. I think she approved of my friendship with him because she thought I was normal, and thought I'd be a good influence on Glenn. I could be relied upon *not* to practise the piano all day.

CE: *And what about his father?*[6]

RF: Russell Gould was a good man, and much more relaxed than Florence. He was a businessman, and made a good living. At some point, he mentioned to my father that he was spending $3,000 annually on Glenn's musical studies – and that was as much as my father was earning in a year. Mr. Gould was enthusiastic about Glenn, without overdoing it and telling him he was a genius.

CE: *As a boy, did Gould always want to be a professional musician?*

RF: I can't imagine there was one moment when he didn't think he was going to become a pianist. When he was a teenager, the great musicians of the world had never heard of him – he hadn't yet played in New York and Washington – but he considered himself on a par with them. Many people in Toronto felt the same way. I can remember him playing a recording of Bach by Rosalyn Tureck – the great interpreter of the era – and then performing the same piece on the piano, and explaining why his interpretation was better.

CE: *I can imagine some people finding a young man like that rather pretentious.*

RF: I didn't, and I don't know of anyone who did. High-school students at Malvern Collegiate had no real ability to judge, but we thought we had a world-class pianist in our school – and we were right! Yet there must have been other good pianists at other high schools in Toronto, and people in those schools must have also thought they had the best.

There was a girl who lived on the opposite side of Southwood who played the piano. She was six years older than Glenn: she was a prodigy, and had won a number of prizes, and considered herself on the way to becoming a wonderful pianist. Then one day she heard Glenn, who was younger and better than she was. The girl had a very hard time with this – for years she would recite to all her friends a list of his faults. She ended up in Paris, teaching at the Sorbonne – English literature, not music.

CE: *Was there any resistance, on the part of either of Gould's parents, to the idea of him becoming a professional musician? Or were they entirely supportive of this goal?*

RF: At some point, they understood that he was going to be a concert pianist. He was never told he had to go out and get a job, or anything like that. I don't believe there was ever any pressure of that kind.

CE: Gould also played the organ as a boy. Did he ever think about becoming a professional organist rather than a pianist?

RF: No, I don't think so. He thought he could be a concert pianist, and he didn't have a fallback plan. He wasn't going to settle for anything he didn't want.

CE: Why did you and Gould become such good friends? What sort of things did you do together?

RF: One common interest was politics. I can remember that we were both very interested in the 1948 Republican convention: American politicians were more interesting to us than Canadians. We would listen for a while, and then Glenn would play something, and then we would go back to the radio. Of course we also gossiped about friends, parents and teachers. There was always lots to talk about.

CE: Did you see signs of his eccentricities as a boy?

RF: I only knew one musician, and it was Glenn, so I had no basis for comparison. He would walk home from school conducting a piece – some concerto that he had mastered in his head – as he walked along. And you couldn't throw a ball to him: he would turn away rather than try to catch it. He didn't want to hurt his hands.

CE: I believe you turned pages for him on at least one occasion?

RF: Glenn asked me to turn pages when he gave a concert on the organ at Eaton Auditorium.[7] I couldn't read music, but he indicated when it was time to turn each page. It was a notable event in my life, although I may not have realized it at the time.

CE: What did people think of Gould leaving high school to pursue music?

RF: By the time Glenn was at Malvern, he was already spending so much time at the Conservatory that he made an arrangement to only attend school at certain times during the week. And if he had been at Malvern all week, he would have died of boredom. I can remember in Grade 10 we all got our geometry books, and we were all slowly working through the lessons, but after a couple of weeks Glenn had read the book and absorbed it all.

At a certain point, Glenn felt he didn't want to go to high school any more. He had his Associate diploma from the Conservatory, and he decided that was enough, as far as formal credentials were concerned.

CE: And this didn't strike anyone as ill advised?

RF: No. Even if he wanted to be a music teacher, his diploma from the Conservatory would be all that he needed – although I never heard him express any interest in teaching.

CE: One side of the music business Gould did pursue, a little bit, was concert presenting: he presented the New Music Associates series in the 1950s.[8] And you were involved in this venture, too. What made you want to run a concert series with Gould?

RF: It was Glenn's idea. I wanted to get involved because I liked him so much: we were just into our twenties, and it seemed like an exciting thing to do. I was there to do the office work, and I had nothing to do with choosing the music.

CE: What was the purpose of the venture?

RF: Glenn wanted to spread his wings. He would say, "We should be playing these great musicians – Schoenberg, Berg and Webern – and nobody is playing them in the whole country." People in Toronto heard this music for the first time, and even if they hated it, it was still good for them to hear it.

CE: Would you say the concerts were successful?

RF: In some ways the concerts were successful, but sometimes they were colossal failures. One concert took place the day after Hurricane Hazel: it rained all night, morning and afternoon, and we had a tiny audience.[9] But in the audience was Sir Ernest MacMillan, and that was the first time he heard Maureen Forrester.[10] He had her singing with the TSO in no time at all.

CE: As Gould became known nationally, and then internationally, did the extent of his fame surprise you?

RF: No, not at all. By then I was a believer. And he had solid support from musicians I knew and respected.

CE: In your memoirs, you say that Gould would sometimes tell you stories about his touring. Are any particularly memorable?

RF: The tour to Russia in 1957 was a big deal for Glenn, and for everyone.[11] One thing I recall is that he was very interested in the paintings of Kandinsky, because Schoenberg liked Kandinsky. Glenn was excited because he was going to meet with an art collector in Moscow: George Costakis, a Greek man who worked for the Canadian Embassy.[12] By this point in time, the art from the great period in Soviet history, up to about 1930, had vanished from public view. But Costakis had bought up many of these works for ten or twenty dollars, and had a whole apartment full of them. Glenn had heard that he owned some Kandinskys, and he offered to buy one. Costakis said no – he wasn't an art dealer – and Glenn realized that if he had done things differently, he might have been given one.

Glenn also talked about people in Russia guiding him around, trying to control every step he took. Once, he remarked to his guide on how many prostitutes there were outside his hotel, and was told, "There are no prostitutes in the Soviet Union." He realized that in many ways Soviet culture was a façade.

CE: Did Gould ever say anything to you about his desire to stop giving live performances?[13]

RF: He never talked to me about it. But on the other hand, I was not at all surprised: I knew that his passion was much more for electronic media. His decision seemed to make sense, and as the years went on, it made more sense.

CE: At what point did you sense that your friendship with Gould was fading? Why did this happen?

RF: It's hard to know. When we were both about thirty, we saw less and less of each other. By then I had two children, and two or three jobs, and was very busy. And he was pretty busy, too. I followed his career with great interest, but I didn't see much of him. The last time we talked on the phone was about 1969 or 1970.

CE: What are your thoughts today on Gould's posthumous reputation?

RF: Do you mean musically or psychologically?

CE: Both.

RF: First of all, as a career strategy, I think he made a brilliant move when he gave up live performance. For one thing, he didn't want to do it any more, and that was a good reason. In addition, he could see the future: there was a world opening up in which people would have huge musical libraries, and would want everything that was recorded. But when he said he wasn't going to play any more live concerts, Goddard Lieberson, the head of CBS records, thought Glenn was throwing his career away. No one had done it before.

Glenn left the world twice as many recordings as he would have been able to do if he had continued to do live performances. And his posthumous reputation rests on his recorded catalogue. It was almost as if he invented recording – or, rather, invented a new way of thinking about recording.

As for Glenn's mental condition, Peter Ostwald's book hints at the idea that Glenn might have had Asperger's syndrome, and I've given a lot of thought to this.[14] Many people had an intimate relationship with Glenn, which at some point suddenly stopped. So I take Ostwald's point of view seriously – but nothing I experienced in Glenn's life would point to Asperger's. The young fellow I knew had a very good sense of humour about himself, and people with Asperger's can't laugh at themselves.

Postscript

Of all the people interviewed here, none knew Gould from a younger age than Robert Fulford. As was often the case with Gould, however, the friendship built up over childhood, adolescence and into adult life withered away in later years. The demands of divergent careers and responsibilities took their toll, as Fulford himself points out. No doubt, Gould's tendency to distance himself from established relationships when new interests beckoned was also a factor.

Fulford clearly regretted this loss. Yet in my interview with him, I detected no trace of bitterness or anger towards Gould – only a sense of gratitude that he had the good fortune to grow up next door to one of the twentieth century's greatest musical geniuses.

CE

NOTES

1 The Toronto Conservatory of Music (later Royal Conservatory of Music) was founded in 1886. Gould studied there from 1940 to 1946.

2 The Toronto Mendelssohn Choir, a large amateur choral society, was founded in

1894, and the Toronto Symphony Orchestra was established in 1922. Gould began attending TSO concerts at the age of seven.

3. Toronto's annual Kiwanis Music Festival was first presented in 1944. Gould won prizes in the festival's first year, and also in 1945 and 1946. The Canadian Broadcasting Corporation's national radio network was founded in 1932.

4. Florence Emma "Flora" Gould (née Greig), was born in the town of Mount Forest, Ontario, and moved to Toronto when she married Russell Gould in 1925. She was an amateur pianist and singer, and began to give Glenn piano lessons when he was four years old.

5. The United Church of Canada, to which the Gould family belonged, is the largest Protestant church in Canada.

6. Russell Herbert "Bert" Gould (originally Gold), was born in the town of Uxbridge, north of Toronto. He was a furrier and owned a fur shop on Spadina Ave. in Toronto.

7. Gould made his professional debut as an organist on December 12, 1945, at Eaton Auditorium in Toronto, playing works by Bach, Mendelssohn and Dupuis.

8. Three concerts were presented by New Music Associates. The first, on October 4, 1952, featured Schoenberg's *Ode to Napoleon*, as well as songs and solo piano works. The second, on January 9, 1954, consisted of Schoenberg's *Book of the Hanging Gardens*, Berg's *Piano Sonata*, and Webern's *Five Movements for String Quartet*, *Saxophone Quartet* and *Variations for Piano*. The third program, on October 16, 1954, deviated from the series's modernist agenda and was entirely devoted to Bach: excerpts from the *Musical Offering*, the *Violin Sonata in C Minor*, and Gould's first public performance of the *Goldberg Variations*.

9. Hurricane Hazel struck the Toronto area on October 15, 1954, with winds of eighty mph and eleven inches of rain. The storm left eighty-one people dead in southern Ontario and several thousand homeless.

10. Sir Ernest MacMillan was the music director of the Toronto Symphony Orchestra from 1931 to 1956. Contralto Maureen Forrester first sang with the TSO on January 14, 1955.

11. Gould's first tour outside North America was to the Soviet Union, in 1957. He gave recitals and lectures in Moscow and Leningrad. For more information on Gould in Russia, see Chapter 1: Walter Homburger (pp. 7-8).

12. George Costakis was born in Moscow, to Greek parents, in 1913, and served as Head of Personnel at the Canadian Embassy from 1942 to 1979. In 1946 he began acquiring suprematist and constructivist art, amassing a collection of over 1,000 works. For more information see: Peter Roberts, *George Costakis: A Russian Life in Art* (Ottawa: Carleton University Press, 1994).

13. Gould's last public appearance as a pianist was on April 10, 1964, in a recital at the Wilshire Ebell Theatre in Los Angeles.

14. Peter Ostwald writes: "... some of the behaviour he [Gould] manifested later in childhood and during his adolescence – a marked fear of certain physical objects,

disturbances in empathy, social withdrawal, self-isolation, and obsessive attention to ritualized behaviour – does resemble a condition called Asperger disease, which is a variant of autism." Peter F. Ostwald, *Glenn Gould: The Ecstasy and Tragedy of Genius* (New York: W.W. Norton, 1977), p. 42. For more information on the theory that Gould suffered from Asperger's see Chapter 2: Timothy Maloney (pp. 76-78).

Cornelia Foss: a Woman in Gould's Life

Cornelia Foss (née Brendel) is a painter who was born in Rome, and married the American composer, conductor and pianist Lukas Foss in 1951. Cornelia Foss first met Gould through her husband – and her friendship with him grew into a romance. She left her husband in 1967, and moved from Buffalo (where Lukas was the conductor of the Buffalo Philharmonic Orchestra) to New York. A year later, she moved to Toronto with her two children, Christopher and Eliza, to be with Gould. However, she ended the relationship with Gould in 1972, and returned to her husband, living with him until his death in 2009.

Today, she continues to paint and teach painting in New York. This interview took place on March 21, 2011, in Foss's apartment on Manhattan's Upper East Side.

CE: Do you remember when and where you first met Gould?

CF: I can never remember dates – but it was when he first came to Los Angeles, in the 1950s.[1] He was playing a concert there. We met because he invited us to a party which was being given for him after the concert. He didn't know me at the time.

CE: What was your initial reaction to him?

CF: I thought that he played beautifully, and was very handsome.

CE: How did you come to know him better?

CF: As you know, he had a penchant for calling people and having lengthy conversations on the phone. He had lots of conversations with my husband, and little by little he started to have conversations me, when I answered the phone. This went on for quite a long time. My husband never really had the time or the inclination for this sort of thing – but he found a willing listener in me, because I thought his ideas were fascinating. And he was so much fun to talk to – he had such a wonderful sense of humour!

My husband and I were beginning to have some serious problems, and I was rather unhappy in the marriage. While I was in New York, Glenn and I were having long conversations about all sorts of things – and at one point he asked me to come to Toronto and marry him. This was four or five years after I first met him. By then, he had come to Buffalo and to New York to see me several times, and we had become very close. So I finally decided that I would move to Toronto, with my two children and my cat.

CE: Had you ever been to Toronto before you moved there in 1967?

CF: It had never occurred to me to go there. But at Glenn's urging, I did go once or twice, shortly before I moved there.

CE: Did you live with Gould in Toronto?

CF: Glenn and I decided we wouldn't live together until we were married, which was the correct thing to do, vis-à-vis the children. We were very careful about the children.

CE: I understand that Glenn was very good with your children.

CF: He loved the children! And very soon after we arrived, Glenn got us a dog.

CE: Gould himself was sometimes described as child-like, in certain ways.

CF: That depends on what you call child-like. Children are pretty serious.

CE: So how would you describe his personality?

CF: Let me talk about something a little bit different. Many people, when they think of a genius, or someone who does something extraordinarily well, think this is a person who has sprung full-blown like Athena from Zeus's head – and who can compose or perform or paint like a god. That's total nonsense. What happens is that the person is born with an extraordinary talent, perhaps – but even when you have talent, it's absolutely meaningless unless you work very, very hard. I've known quite a few people who have done extraordinary things, whether writers, poets, composers or pianists – and Glenn was one of them – and the kind of disciplined, focused and exhausting hard work that people like that are accustomed to is beyond most people's imagination. Their concentration is laser-like. It's not a question of being a genius, it's a question of working like a genius.

CE: What else would you say about his personality?

CF: He wasn't someone who was serious or glum. People who are hard workers are usually people who have the greatest sense of humour.

CE: What incidents stand out as particularly revealing of his character?

CF: Day-to-day life was wonderful. I was working pretty hard myself as a painter. I remember that he made up wonderful plays for my children and the children in the neighbourhood. We had a little gaggle of children around, much of the time.

CE: Your children called him "Uncle Glenn"?

CF: That's what we decided would be the best way of getting around all kinds of difficulties.

CE: Did he seek your advice on musical matters?

CF: No, nor would I ever have given any advice – I'm not a musician. I had some opinions, but I don't think I ever discussed those with him. I would have been much too respectful.

CE: And what were your opinions?

CF: I couldn't stand his Bach, and I loved his Beethoven.

CE: Some people would put it the other way around.

CF: I know. But I grew up with Bach: my father was the son of a Lutheran minister, and Bach was very much in the household. We would go to hear the *St Matthew Passion*, and my father played Bach on the piano. The thing that informs Bach's music is religion – and if one decides to take that component out of the music, what you have left has very little to do with the intentions of the composer.

CE: Or perhaps you could say that Bach's music is amenable to a wide variety of interpretations.

CF: I'm sorry to disagree, but I believe the best interpretations are those closest to the composer's intentions and ideas. But Bach's music is so strong that it takes a great deal to destroy it.

CE: Did Gould talk about his artistic plans and ambitions with you?

CF: He talked about the fact that he didn't want to do live concerts any more, at great length. He very much meant what he said.

CE: *Did you and Glenn socialize much in Toronto?*

CF: John Roberts and his wife were his closest friends. And Lorne Tulk was around sometimes.² Otherwise, we really didn't see many other people. We didn't have time: when people are very much in love, they tend to stick to one another pretty much. The social part comes later on.

CE: *Did you meet Gould's parents?*

CF: Never. But he didn't have anything to do with them at that time, which was sad.

CE: *Did many people in Toronto know that you and he were in a relationship? Was it a secret?*

CF: No, it wasn't a secret: that's making something out of it that it really wasn't. We just didn't bother to tell people. Obviously, all my friends knew it, and most of Lukas's friends knew it. Some thought it was scandalous, other didn't. People's reactions ran the gamut.³

CE: *Did you produce much art in Toronto?*

CF: To some extent, but not much – I didn't have a studio. But I helped Glenn with his documentaries. I was two of the people in *The Idea of North*.⁴ And then I produced television documentaries of my own. One, *The History of Book Illustration*, had been broadcast eleven times on Canadian television by the time I left Toronto. At least that's what Glenn told me – he was very proud of me. And Glenn chose all the music for my shows.

CE: *Did you ever paint or draw Gould?*

CF: Not when I was living in Toronto.

CE: *What happened to your idea of marrying Gould?*

CF: After a while, I realized that it was not a good idea. My husband was very eager to have me come back, and little by little I changed my mind. Glenn very much wanted to marry me, but I came to believe I was making a mistake: I was more in love with my husband than I realized I was. Affairs of the heart are very hard to take apart and figure out.

CE: What did your husband think of Gould?

CF: Lukas admired him. They both had extremely strong egos, but they certainly didn't dislike each other – they had great mutual respect. Glenn thought my husband was the greatest pianist, as well as the greatest composer, of our time. And my husband did not share my thought about Glenn's Bach at all, and admired Glenn's playing tremendously.

And they loved playing tricks on each other. When I was with my husband, he would pretend to be the housekeeper when Glenn called. He'd say, "Missy no here! Missy go out!"

CE: You had further contact with Gould after you left Toronto, didn't you?

CF: Very much so, yes. He tried to convince me to come back. He would phone, and he came to see me on Long Island. I finally ended it – I stopped returning his calls.

CE: I first read about your connection with Gould in the Toronto Star newspaper, in 2007.[5] What did you think of that article?

CF: That was a dreadful article! The journalist called me up out of the blue, and began asking me all these questions. I answered as truthfully as I could. Later on, a friend of mine sent me the article. To my horror, there were quotation marks around things that I had never said. And not only that, the intentions expressed were things I never would have dreamt of saying! It was shocking to see that kind of inaccuracy, or dishonesty, in a major newspaper. But I was told that there was nothing I could do: there was no way of suing, or anything like that.

CE: In the Toronto Star article, there's mention of you witnessing Gould experiencing a "serious paranoid episode." Is this true?

CF: No. You must remember that when you're famous you get hate-letters as well as love-letters. He got some terrible letters and phone calls. He was terrified of parking his car in the underground garage: if you've just had a threatening letter, it's not crazy to think there's someone lurking down there. So any kind of paranoia was partially justified – but all of this has been exaggerated so much!

CE: What did you make of his eccentricities?

CF: When you're very busy, working extremely hard – and you're not a social person – you begin to develop certain habits that you otherwise might not. Also, you realize that there's a certain kind of adulation people have for you, and you might start to think about how far you can go with things. It becomes a kind of game you play with your public.

He thought it was incredibly funny that at the University of Toronto they were giving a course called "The Mind of Glenn Gould."[6] He told me about it, and was doubled over with laughter: he thought this was the silliest thing he had ever heard! He said, "We've got to go! Maybe we could go in disguise so they won't recognize us. I'm dying to know what on earth they could possibly be saying!"

CE: Some people have even suggested that Gould may have suffered from Asperger's syndrome.[7] Do you agree with this theory?

CF: No – but then, who cares? Maybe Picasso had Asperger's too. Does it make any difference?

CE: Do you think Gould is well understood today, as a man and an artist?

CF: Yes and no. Certainly he is appreciated for his extraordinary playing and for his beautiful radio plays, like *The Idea of North*. But the strange stories that have been woven around his life serve more to obscure than elucidate what an interesting and astonishing person he was.

Postscript

Gould regarded his love life as a very private matter – and this led some people to suspect that he was either gay or asexual. Yet in the years following his death, rumours surfaced of various girlfriends and love interests, including the soprano Roxolana Roslak, the pianist Monica Gaylord and Cornelia Foss, who is briefly mentioned in James Ostwald's 1997 book, *Glenn Gould: The Ecstasy and Tragedy of Genius*. In 2007, Foss agreed to be interviewed by the *Toronto Star* newspaper, putting an end to speculation about Gould's sexuality.

Yet when I first spoke to Cornelia Foss – in the summer of 2010, by telephone – she expressed a strong reluctance to grant an interview for this book. "I'm not doing any more Gould interviews," she said, flatly. When I asked why, she replied that she wasn't pleased with how her words had been used (or misused) by others in the past.

When I explained that I would allow her to make any alterations to the transcribed interview that she wished, she relented slightly, and said she would consider my request. However, it was not until February 2011 that I spoke to Foss again, and she offered me one hour of her time for the purpose of an interview.

I arrived at her home on New York's Upper East Side at the agreed-upon day and hour – which, despite our plans, turned out to be an inconvenient time, as her cat was unwell and had been taken to a veterinarian. This emergency upset both her schedule and her emotional equilibrium. Nevertheless, I was duly admitted to her apartment, and ushered into a sitting room, where several of her canvasses hung on the walls – including a striking portrait of her late husband, Lukas Foss.

At first, she seemed impatient with my questions. But as the interview progressed, she relaxed, and spoke with fondness of her memories of Gould.

CE

NOTES

1 Gould's first performance in the Los Angeles area was in Pasadena on March 8, 1957. He returned to Pasadena for another recital on January 9, 1959.

2 John Roberts was Head of Radio Music for the Canadian Broadcasting Corporation in Toronto, and Lorne Tulk was a studio technician at the CBC. Interviews with Roberts and Tulk appear in Chapter 3.

3 One person who noticed Gould's relationship with Cornelia Foss was Gould's producer at CBS Records, Andrew Kazdin. In his book, *Glenn Gould at Work*, he notes that the two "had developed a close friendship," adding that "it was impossible to tell whether the relationship could be categorized as 'romantic'." Andrew Kazdin, *Glenn Gould at Work* (New York: E.P. Dutton, 1989), pp. 59-60.

4 For more information on Gould's radio documentaries, see Chapter 3: Vincent Tovell (p. 106), and Lorne Tulk (pp. 118-119).

5 A newspaper article entitled "The Secret Life of Glenn Gould," written by Michael Clarkson, appeared on the front page of the *Toronto Star* on August 25, 2007.

6 It seems likely that Cornelia Foss is recalling one or more public lectures by the Gould scholar Geoffrey Payzant, a professor of philosophy at the University of Toronto, and the author of *Glenn Gould, Music and Mind*, the only book on Gould published during his lifetime.

7 The theory that Gould may have had Asperger's syndrome was first put forward by Peter Ostwald in his book *Glenn Gould: The Ecstasy and Tragedy of Genius*. The idea

was further developed by Timothy Maloney in his article "Glenn Gould, Autistic Savant," published in *Sounding Off: Theorizing Disability in Music*. For more information see Chapter 2: Timothy Maloney (pp. 76-78) and Chapter 5: Tim Page (p.175).

Chapter 5: Writing About Gould

Introduction

From the outset of Glenn Gould's career, the press was fascinated with the young pianist from Toronto. He was articulate, witty, engaging (when he wanted to be) – and at least as interested in seeing his picture in the newspapers as the newspapers were in printing it. His views were novel, unconventional and sometimes iconoclastic, and his personal eccentricities were page-turning material. He was a breath of fresh air in the staid and proper world of classical music, and newspaper editors must have loved him for it.

To the music critics of the day, the task fell to write about his performances, and try to account for what made him such a remarkable artist. Of course, most of the critics who wrote about his performances – both his live recitals and his recordings, after he gave up playing in public – had little or no personal contact with Gould. They wrote about what they heard, vied with one another for superlatives, and interpreted his unique personality and career as best they could.

However, two critics did come to know Gould on a more personal basis: William Littler, in Toronto, and Timothy Page, based in New York. Both men were allowed a measure of access to Gould the man, and this helped them to formulate their views on the relationship between his character and his art.

Littler was the classical music (and also dance) critic for Toronto's largest daily newspaper, the *Toronto Star*, from 1966 to 2005. Inevitably, Canada's foremost pianist was very much a "person of interest" to Littler. But when he co-incidentally found himself living in the same apartment building as Gould – even as his post-concert career took new and fascinating directions – Littler had direct access to Gould's ideas, concerns and intentions.

Page didn't get to know Gould until relatively late in Gould's life. He first spoke to Gould in 1980 – in an interview with the relatively obscure *SoHo Weekly News*, published in New York. The two hit it off – due, in part, to a commonly shared way of looking at the world – and by 1982, Page was in Toronto, working with Gould in a scripted interview about the pianist's second recording of Bach's *Goldberg Variations*.

Both Littler and Page were ardent admirers of Gould. And their contact with him served both to sharpen their critical perceptions and bring a depth of understanding to their admiration that few other critics were able to achieve.

CE

Willam Littler: the Critic Downstairs

William Littler was born in Vancouver in 1940. After studies at the University of British Columbia, he began to work as a freelance music critic at the *Vancouver Province* in 1963. In 1966 he moved to Toronto to become the music and dance critic for the *Toronto Star*, a position he held until his retirement in 2005. He also taught at several Canadian universities, and has served on the board of directors of the Music Critics Association of North America. In 1980 he received Canada's National Newspaper award for his writing.

In his professional capacities as a journalist and broadcaster, Littler took a keen interest in the "post-retirement" career of Glenn Gould. And a coincidence brought him into close contact with Gould in 1971, when he inadvertently moved into the same apartment building that Gould lived in.

Today, Littler is retired, but he still occasionally contributes articles to the *Toronto Star*. This interview was conducted at a mid-Toronto restaurant, on February 28, 2011.

CE: *When did you first hear Glenn Gould in a live performance?*

WL: I grew up in Vancouver, and while I was in high school in the late 1950s he came and played. With the Vancouver Symphony he played the first movement of the *Emperor Concerto* on a family pops concert. Another time I heard him play a recital with the *Goldberg Variations* in it. And another time I heard him do a Schoenberg program.[1]

CE: *What was it like to see and hear one of his performances?*

WL: Well, it was kind of funny. He had a kind of slouch in his walk, and he brought a glass of water with him, which he set down on the piano. But once he began to play, everything just flowed out, without any sense of effort. I was amazed at how low he sat, on that peculiar chair his father built, and the orang-utan-like spread of his arms over the keyboard. What I found especially surprising was how much sound he could reproduce without adopting the traditional higher position to give greater strength.

He made everything sound contrapuntal, even when it wasn't supposed to be. And he had what my own piano teacher called "independence of the fingers." There was no sense of one finger being weaker than another, so he loved to make all the small details and inner voices come out. It was a kind of playing I hadn't heard before. I was really quite struck with it.

CE: Did you review any of his live performances?

WL: No, I wasn't a critic at the time.

CE: But of course you later reviewed many of his recordings.[2] Did he ever respond to your criticisms in any way?

WL: Usually, he responded with laughter. I don't think he cared about criticism much, one way or the other. We got along surprisingly well, and I've never really understood why.

I once asked him if he had to hum on his recordings. He replied that he was aware of the criticism, and tried to stop, but found that he didn't play as well. And we had a bit of an argument about his Mozart recordings. I asked, "Why is it that you play Mozart as if he were Bach?" He laughed and said, "I didn't really want to record those Mozart sonatas, I wanted to record Haydn sonatas. But my record label said let's see how the Mozart sells, and maybe we can do Haydn later." Because he didn't really want to do the Mozart, he just had some fun with it, and his tempos were all over the place. Gould once famously said that Mozart's tragedy was not that he died too early, but that he died too late.

CE: Did you have a lot of personal contact with him?

WL: We lived in the same apartment building: the Park Lane Apartments, at 110 St Clair Avenue West.[3] I was on the third floor, and he was in the penthouse. It's a twin-towered building, a medium-rise, with two elevators. When I first moved into the building, I noticed the mailbox for the top floor said "Gould," and I later learned that it was Glenn Gould. But the name on the mailbox soon vanished. In one of my articles I jokingly referred to him as "the Hermit of St Clair" – and then I got one of his telephone calls late at night. He said, "Don't tell people where I live!" I replied, "Glenn, St Clair Avenue runs clear across the city." And he replied, "You don't know how persistent some people are."

He liked most of his contacts with other people to be on the telephone. But sometimes when we were at the CBC together, he would offer to drive me home. I always hated that, because I thought it would be my last day on Earth! He drove a big American sedan, and as he drove he would turn to you and talk, and not look forward. How he managed to avoid killing himself anytime someone else was in the car, I have no idea.

On one occasion, we came back to the apartment building, and he drove into the underground parking garage. We just sat there in the dark, and he kept talking, and I saw that he had no inclination to leave the car. I decided we were going to be there all night unless I got out. So we walked to the elevator, and came up to my floor – and he continued talking. The buzzer started to sound because people on other floors wanted to use the elevator, but he just filtered it all out. All he was interested in was talking. I thought perhaps I should invite him into my apartment, but I knew I had to go out that evening, and I was afraid he wouldn't leave. So I finally got out of the elevator, and he went up to the top floor.

He didn't want a dialogue – he wanted an audience. All you had to do was say, "uh-huh, uh-huh," and he would keep talking. When he got excited about an idea, he would go on and on – but always in perfectly formed sentences. If you read his program notes, they sound somewhat convoluted, with a lot of subordinate clauses. But that was the real Glenn Gould. That was the way he talked.

CE: I want to ask you about Gould's decision to stop performing in public. Why do you think he did this?

WL: He knew he wanted to do it. He made up his mind, and carefully invested his money, because he knew he wouldn't have the same income when he stopped performing. Apparently he was very astute in his stock-market investments.

When I asked him about his decision, he said that most pianists want to take their repertoire on the road, and play concert after concert before they go into the recording studio. But he discovered that when he was giving concerts, he would play to the audience, and get into all sorts of bad habits. He decided that performing for an audience wasn't making his playing better, it was making it worse. He felt he was much better off just recording.

In addition, he did have a kind of stage-fright. He did not like going out on the stage and performing: he called it a "blood sport." A lot of his theorizing was really a rationalization of what was comfortable for him.[4] He generalized his personal needs into universal truths for the rest of us.

CE: What did you think at the time, when Gould stopped playing in public?

WL: I think a lot of people weren't convinced that it would be permanent.[5] Horowitz withdrew on a couple of occasions for years, but then he came back. I don't think we understood the depths of Glenn's aversion to the concert-hall experience. We thought maybe he was burned out, or exhausted. But I think the truth was the explanation that he offered us: he wasn't at his best on stage, he was at his best in the studio.

CE: In what other ways can Gould and Horowitz be compared?

WL: Gould and Horowitz had different approaches to their instrument. Horowitz was about playing the piano. Gould would always say, "The piano is my instrument – it's what I use to make music. But it's only a tool to me." That's one of the reasons why composers like Chopin and Liszt didn't appeal to him, because they were largely about the piano, about making the instrument sound good. Of course, both Gould and Horowitz had extraordinary virtuosity. I once challenged Harold Schonberg on the famous review he wrote of Gould playing Brahms's *D Minor Piano Concerto* with the New York Philharmonic.[6] Harold said, "I think I did go too far." The accusation that Gould played slowly because he couldn't play it fast was ridiculous.

CE: What do you think of Gould's non-pianistic work in radio and television?

WL: As I mentioned before, he was obsessed with counterpoint, so he called his documentaries "contrapuntal radio."[7] I went through *The Idea of North* with him: he told me how he had interviewed all the people individually – not one of them had met any of the others – and then he constructed conversations that never existed, as though they were travelling on a train together. This is the creative instinct in him: it took hundreds of hours to do this. Most people would think this was a boring activity, but for him it was a reflection of his impulse to control things. Now, when you listen to them, the documentaries don't sound so remarkable, because we have the technology to easily do what once took many hours. But in their day, they were quite remarkable.

CE: And what about his characterizations, such as Karlheinz Klopweisser and Sir Nigel Twitt-Thornthwaite?[8]

WL: He used those voices on his late night telephone calls. I'd pick up the phone and I'd hear, "This is Theodore Slutz, of the *East Village Other*," in a New York accent. I once complimented him on his German accent when he was doing Klopweisser, and he said, "Yes, but I have no vocabulary." He couldn't speak German. Gould thought he was hilarious – even if the rest of us were not so convinced. He over-estimated his sense of humour: it was rich, but very peculiar.

CE: What do you think was so very special about Glenn Gould?

WL: There was a quality of originality in his playing that people could detect right away. He didn't sound like anyone else. You may or may not have agreed with his interpretation, but it always had a clarity of argument.

And there was an extraordinary focus – not just in his playing, but in everything he did. I remember I once visited him at his studio, and he pointed out a sequence of a few seconds which he had submitted to something like two hundred edits – and he was so proud of doing this. If genius is, as it's sometimes defined, the infinite capacity for taking pains, then Leonard Bernstein might have been right in calling Gould a genius. And even George Szell said, "That nut's a genius!" His ability to absorb himself completely in his interest of the moment, and to more or less shut out the rest of the world, was quite significant to understanding him.

Essentially, Gould was a creative artist trapped in the body of a performing artist. He wasn't interested in replicating anything: he regarded the musical score as a blueprint, not a building. He wanted to rethink it, and do it his way. And I sometimes think that if he had gone to university, it might have wrecked him. Education is a great way of destroying truly brilliant people, because formal education teaches conventional thought.

CE: Did Gould's Canadian-ness help or hinder him?

WL: Being Canadian didn't help his international career – it never does. It was unusual that he was from Canada, but "exotic" and "Canadian" are not words that are characteristically put together. As you know, he always claimed that he only felt at home in Canada, and he would never think of moving from Toronto. He took some ribbing in the United States for that attitude, because Toronto is regarded as relatively provincial, compared to New York and some other places. He once said that if he lived in another city, it would have to be St Petersburg, in Russia. He was a Northerner – but to my mind, he was more of a mythic than an actual Northerner. He idealized the North, and it's connection with the Canadian character. But he didn't go much north of Wawa.[9]

CE: What do you think of Gould's famous eccentricities?

WL: We have discovered that a lot of his behaviours were medically founded. In the National Library there's a suitcase that belonged to Gould, filled with pillboxes. He had some real maladies, but he made them worse. He'd go to one doctor and get a prescription, and he'd go to another doctor and get a different prescription. And he'd take them both, and compound his problems. And there's the theory developed by Timothy Maloney that he was autistic. The psychiatrist Peter Otswald also buys into the idea.

He was not a classic shrinking violet, and he knew how to get his picture in the paper. He understood the value of publicity. Like Princess Diana, he courted the photographers and he hated the photographers. He was reclusive, but he wanted it both ways.

CE: Did you know anything about his relationship with Cornelia Foss?

WL: I think very few people knew about that – and I was not one of them. Those of us who knew him quickly discovered that he compartmentalized his relationships. In this way, he retained complete control of the situation. That was very characteristic of his behaviour throughout his career.

CE: At a casual glance, one might think that everything Gould touched turned to gold. But were there also failures?

WL: Some things did elude him. I remember talking to him about a project he wanted to do with Herbert von Karajan.[10] Both men wanted it to happen, but each wanted it to happen on his own terms.

CE: I've always been impressed with how much Gould seemed to get away with: refusing to fly anywhere, cancelling recording sessions, and insisting on obscure repertoire. He did things that would be career-death for a musician today. Why was he so indulged?

WL: He pushed people to do what he wanted to do, as much as possible, and he didn't always know where the limits were. But people recognized that he was special – and people are sometimes willing to make extra efforts for people who are special. Also, he had a very engaging personality, and could use words very effectively. He lived in a sort of pre-Copernican universe, where everything revolved around him.

CE: Do you have any thoughts on what he might have done, if he had lived for another twenty or thirty years?

WL: He certainly had ideas. Whether he would have gone on as a conductor or not is uncertain. It would have only been in the studio, of course – he wouldn't have given live performances. Perhaps he would have written more, and he certainly would have followed new technologies closely. And he told me more than once that he felt he'd said pretty much all he cared to say with the piano: he had played and recorded what he wanted. But he might have changed his mind about that, too.

CE: *What were Gould's greatest achievements?*

WL: In terms of his recorded legacy, I think that the Bach is his most important contribution. But Gould's example, as an independent thinker, is very important. He was an artist who sought complete control of what he was doing – and he managed, to an extraordinary degree, to get what he wanted. It's almost like the nineteenth-century notion of the artist as hero, who dares to do what others will not venture to do. The most dramatic part of that was giving up the concert stage, where he was very popular, for the studio. That was a very brave move for a performer. He was the most important creative musician we have produced in this country – even though he was ostensibly a re-creative musician – because of the amount of originality he brought to everything he did. Of any Canadian musician, he's had the biggest impact on the world at large.

Postscript

During his years at the *Toronto Star*, William Littler was probably Toronto's most prominent classical music critic. Certainly he seemed more engaged with the city's musical life than John Kraglund, the critic at Toronto's other major daily newspaper, the *Globe and Mail*. As well, he was more interested in new developments than Kraglund – whether they were trends in contemporary music or the burgeoning early music movement.

It's not surprising, then, that Littler took a more open-minded approach to Gould's preference for electronic media over live performance. While Kraglund dismissed Gould's withdrawal from the concert stage as a self-indulgence and a peculiar kind of publicity stunt, Littler – while not exactly endorsing the decision – seemed to consider it a worthy and intriguing experiment, and was interested in where it might lead. And in my interview with Littler, he gave the impression that the passage of time has done nothing to blunt his fascination with Glenn Gould.

CE

NOTES

1 Gould first performed with the Vancouver Symphony on October 28, 1951, playing Beethoven's *Piano Concerto No. 4*; however, the VSO concert that Littler attended took place on December 9, 1956. Gould's Schoenberg recital was given at the Vancouver International Festival on August 2, 1960; and his Bach program was performed at the VIF on August 9, 1961.

2 Littler's reviews of Gould's recordings tended to be quite favourable. In one article for the *Toronto Star*, Littler reviewed five recordings by Gould: Bach's *French Suites*; Beethoven's *Op. 31 Piano Sonatas*; Hindemith's piano sonatas; Mozart's *Piano Sonatas K.331, K.545, K.533* and the *Fantasy in D Minor K.397*; and a transcription of Wagner's *Siegfried Idyll* with excerpts from *Die Meistersinger von Nürnberg* and *Götterdämmerung*. He wrote: "There isn't a dull note to be found on any of these discs, and the sheer range of their musical contents pays eloquent testimony to the pianist's musical scope." William Littler, "'Retired' Pianist Glenn Gould Is Busier Than Ever," *Toronto Star*, December 8, 1973, p. G3.

3 Gould moved into the Park Lane Apartments in 1960, and lived there for the rest of his life.

4 On several occasions, Gould articulated sophisticated theories that served to position his decision to withdraw from the concert stage in the context of cultural and technological developments. On June 1, 1964, he gave a convocation lecture at the University of Toronto, in which he said, "It is my firm conviction that the concert experience with which all of us have grown up will not likely outlive the twentieth century." He added, "In my mind, the relationship between music and the various media of electronic communication is the key to the future not only of the way in which music will appear or be consumed, but also the key to the manner in which it will be performed and composed." "An Argument for Music in the Electronic Age," *The Art of Glenn Gould*, John Roberts, ed. (Toronto: Malcolm Lester Books, 1999), p. 226.

5 Another Toronto music critic, John Kraglund, writing for the *Globe and Mail*, openly challenged Gould's decision to withdraw from the concert stage. "Toronto pianist Glenn Gould seems to be convinced that if he repeats the words, 'concerts are out, recordings are in,' frequently enough he will make it so. Judging by the reactions of the public, and those of his fellow recording artists who are still concert performers, Gould's theory is rapidly gaining no support whatsoever." "Scant Support for Gould's Anti-Concert Drive," *Globe and Mail*, November 26, 1966, p. 17.

6 On April 7, 1962, a review entitled "Inner Voices of Glenn Gould," by Harold C. Schonberg, appeared in the *New York Times*. In it, Schonberg criticized Gould's tempos, suggesting, "maybe his technique is not so good." For more information, see Chapter 2: Stuart Hamilton (p.41).

7 For more information on Gould's radio documentaries, see Chapter 3: Lorne Tulk (pp. 118-119).

8 The German musicologist Karlheinz Klopweisser, the English conductor Sir Nigel Twitt-Thornthwaite and the New York journalist Theodore Slutz were among the fictitious characters invented by Gould. He portrayed them on CBC radio and television programs.

9 Wawa, Ontario, is a town on the north shore of Lake Superior. On one occasion, Gould did venture further north: his 1965 train trip to Churchill, Manitoba, on Hudson Bay.

10 According to Ray Roberts, Gould devised a novel plan to record a piano concerto with the conductor Herbert von Karajan: Gould would record the piano part in Toronto, and von Karajan would record the orchestral portions with his Berlin Philharmonic Orchestra in Europe. The two recordings would then be mixed together in a studio. See Chapter 1: Ray Roberts (p. 34).

Tim Page: a Special Bond

Tim Page was born in San Diego, California, in 1954. The Pulitzer-prize winning music critic and broadcaster began his writing career at New York's *SoHo Weekly News*, but soon moved to positions at the *New York Times*, *Newsday* and the *Washington Post*. Today he is a professor of journalism and music at the University of Southern California.

Page first interviewed Gould in 1980, and the two men became "telephone friends." However, Page didn't meet Gould in person until 1982, a month before the pianist passed away. After Gould's death, Page edited *The Glenn Gould Reader*, a collection of Gould essays and interviews.

At the age of forty-five, Page was diagnosed with Asperger's syndrome, a mild form of autism that makes it difficult to interact with other people in social situations. Some people have suggested that Glenn Gould suffered from the same condition.[1]

This interview took place on September 26, 2011, at a hotel in downtown Toronto.

CE: Are you from a musical family?

TP: Not really. My mom loved music, though, and had a record collection. And I had a great aunt who studied at Juilliard.

CE: So how did you get involved in music?

TP: Music was a world where I always felt at home. I was obsessed, and strangely knowledgeable about it, from the age of one or two. As a little kid, it made sense to me when nothing else did. The way to calm me down was to get me to the record player: aside from that, I was frantic and a little hysterical.

About the age of seven, I developed my own system of composing, and at the age of nine I was given formal music lessons. And from the age of ten I spent a lot of time in the local library, where I took out books and listened to records. Later, I played in a rock band where I wrote most of the music. Then I studied music for two years at the Mannes School of Music in New York, where I studied piano and composition – but I transferred out, because I was an exceedingly slow composer.

CE: And how did you get involved in writing about music?

I found that writing words came to me much more naturally than writing music. So I transferred to Columbia University to study creative writing. Then I started writing music criticism, just out of the blue, and sent something to the *SoHo Weekly News*. They liked it, and I started writing for them. And within three years and three months, I was at the *New York Times*, as their lowest man on the totem pole, covering all the things that the staff critics didn't want to cover.

I was at the *New York Times* for five years, then I became the chief critic at *Newsday*, where I was for seven and a half years, and then I went to the *Washington Post*. I retired from the *Washington Post* about three years ago to help start the arts journalism program at USC.

CE: When and how did you first hear Glenn Gould?

TP: My dad was always fascinated with eccentric and brilliant people, and he showed me a magazine that did a big spread on Glenn. But my first real Glenn Gould memory was in 1969 in Caracas, Venezuela, where I spent a year. To lessen the pain on the first day of school, my mom would take us out and buy us a present. I chose Glenn's recording of the Liszt transcription of Beethoven's *Fifth*, which came with a conversation with John McClure. I listened to *Glenn Gould: Concert Dropout*[2] a lot. And I bought a couple more recordings in Venezuela, and liked them, although they seemed a little cold to me in some cases. I then saw the film *Slaughterhouse Five* and thought what Gould did with the music was wonderful.[3] I bought the soundtrack, and also the *Goldberg Variations*.

However, I didn't get fully interested in Glenn until I went to music school in New York. I had a friend, the composer and inventor Paul Alexander, who was a huge fanatic, who pressed Geoffrey Payzant's book, *Glenn Gould: Music and Mind*, on me.[4]

CE: How did you come to interview Gould in 1980?

TP: The word went out from CBS that Gould was going to give interviews for the twenty-fifth anniversary of his recording work with the label. People who wanted to interview him had to write a letter of introduction before he'd get on the phone. I wrote a letter that said I wasn't going to ask him when he was going to come back to the stage, or why he hums while he plays, or any of the typical

"Glenn Gould questions." I said I was interested in his ideas about contrapuntal radio, and that I shared his love of Richard Strauss. I wanted to ask him questions that would interest him intellectually, and wouldn't treat him like some kind of circus act.

Gould didn't care at all that I was writing for the *SoHo Weekly News*, which was a tiny newspaper. But I think CBS was not pleased with the idea: they wanted a big *New York Times* article, or a piece in *Time* magazine. Glenn promised me half an hour on the phone, and I spent at least two hours talking to him.

My editor put him on the front page, but she headlined the story, "Bach's Bad Boy: Glenn Gould, Pianist and Crank." I was horrified when I saw it! So I called Glenn and left a message saying I was so sorry that he was called a crank, and it was very embarrassing. He called back about ten minutes later and said that he understood the malignancies of editors – and with the exception of an interview early in his career, it was his favourite interview.[5] After that, we became friends, and he'd call me once or twice a week.

CE: What did you talk to him about?

TP: We got to the point where we would talk for four or five hours a week. He was kind, courteous and funny – and I don't think I flatter myself when I say that he was genuinely interested in my ideas. We talked about music, of course – but also about religion, philosophy, politics and even the stock market. He told me he was a socialist, which in the USA was a kind of dirty word at the time. And he hated Pierre Trudeau with a passion, because Trudeau had given the finger to some striking workers, which offended Glenn on many levels.[6]

Musically, we talked a lot about Strauss, and Sibelius, and Leopold Stokowski, who was a hero of mine, too. We also talked about the minimalists: Philip Glass, Steve Reich and Terry Riley.[7] He didn't really like them, but intellectually they fascinated him. He even wrote a song about minimalism, which he started to sing to my answering machine. Unfortunately, I picked up my phone before he finished, so I only have a fragment of it on tape.

CE: Did he talk about other pianists?

TP: Maybe a little bit – and if he did he was always very generous. But he preferred to talk about music. He once sang me the entire *G Minor Rhapsody* of Brahms over the phone, just to point out to me a few ideas he had about the tempo.

CE: *And there were more interviews?*

TP: I did a few more interviews with him over the next couple of years – including one I did for radio that didn't work at all. I wrote out five questions, and sent them to him, and he sent me a tape of his answers that he made in his Toronto studio. Glenn called this tape "The Unquestioned Answers." Then I played the tape live on WNYC, and read my questions in the right places. Of course we had no room-tone in common, and Glenn included lots of fake-sounding things like, "Hmm, that's an interesting question, Tim." It was a very Gouldian way of doing things.

CE: *Did you review his recordings?*

TP: Only once: it was for *Saturday Review*, and it was a review of his Haydn set.[8] I liked it, and I said so, but I had a couple of quibbles. And the next time I talked to him, he was a little defensive, but not super-defensive.

CE: *And how did you come to do your scripted interview with Gould about his second recording of the Goldbergs?*

TP: The whole project started about three weeks before I actually went to Toronto. I went to see the film of Glenn playing the *Goldbergs* in a Columbia Masterworks screening room.[9] Then he called me up and interviewed me fairly extensively about what I thought of it. After that, he sat down and wrote the radio script and asked me if I would come up to Toronto and record it with him. CBS wanted nothing to do with my expenses, and I had no money whatsoever. But I had a brand-new American Express card, and I agreed to do it. I arrived in Toronto in August 1982.

The script Glenn had written was a kind of play about Tim Page and Glenn Gould speaking – supposedly spontaneously. It was something I probably wouldn't have agreed to do once I became a professional journalist, but in those days I was more of a radio host. My expectation was that this "interview" would be aired only once. But then Glenn died just after the *Goldbergs* came out, and it became a kind of cult item. CBS originally released it on LP,[10] and re-released it on CD in 2002. I wish now that I'd been more awake when we recorded it, at about two o'clock in the morning.

CE: *Did this scripted interview contain many of your own views? For instance, did you actually time some of the movements with a stopwatch – as the interview suggests – or was the whole discussion of timings Gould's invention?*[11]

TP: Here's how I'd describe it: Glenn took my thoughts on the *Goldbergs* and worked them into a script, and then hired Tim Page to play a fictional Tim Page. None of the stopwatch stuff really happened: that was all faked. But the opinions were pretty much all mine. I'd say ninety percent of the interview was me – albeit a fictional me created by Glenn to say things I believed.

I should also say that Glenn also made a point of mentioning our recording engineer, Kevin Doyle, because he felt that Columbia would never credit him. At the very end of the interview, he scripted me to thank Kevin, in a way that couldn't be readily edited out. I thought it was a very collegial thing for Glenn to do.

CE: So what was it like to finally meet Gould face-to-face?

TP: I recall that Glenn came to my door at the Inn on the Park. He looked terrible, something like what we used to call a bag-man. He was very pasty, and it looked like whole chunks of his hair had fallen out of his head. He held out his hand, which I shook very gently. He was obviously nervous; eventually he made eye-contact, but it took a while. But when we got to his studio[12] he relaxed, and he played recordings by Barbara Streisand, and he showed me the film *The Wars*, which he was involved with.

CE: You yourself have been diagnosed with Asperger's syndrome. What's your opinion of the theory that Gould also suffered from a form of autism?

TP: When Glenn was alive, very few people knew anything about Asperger's syndrome. But now we're finding that some people with Asperger's have considerable gifts, because of their ability to shut out the world and do their own thing. Asperger's people tend to create their own movies in their heads, and live in them. When you look at Glenn's isolation and his perfectionism, and the fact that he didn't like being touched, it seems to me abundantly clear that he had a very Aspergian fear of losing control of situations.

And another thing you can say about autistics is that whatever else we may be, we're not well rounded. We may be very good at some things, and we may train ourselves to be nice to people and live in the world. We may learn how to act and how to present ourselves. But a lot of us have very serious problems: we can become alcoholics, and depressives and suicides. And we know that Glenn was pretty unhappy and lonely much of the time; although he never touched alcohol to the best of my knowledge, he was a legendary pill-taker: Valium and others.

CE: Gould withdrew from the concert stage in 1964 to concentrate on making records – and the Beatles did much the same thing, about two years later. Coincidence?

TP: It's not a direct influence, but it was the Zeitgeist. Like Gould, the Beatles were dealing with the ordeals of touring. Imaging how crazy it would be to be a Glenn Gould, or a Beatle! And like Gould, they realized they could do things in the studio that they couldn't do on stage.

CE: You once asked Gould what composers he would send into outer space to communicate with alien life forms.[13] So what Gould recording would you send into space to communicate with aliens?

TP: Can I boil it down to a couple? I'd choose the second of the *Goldberg* recordings – or maybe one of the Bach concerto recordings. And outside Bach, I might pick the Brahms *Intermezzi*. And I know which one Gould would choose: the Byrd and Gibbons record. He loved that music – it was his favourite recording.

CE: It's been almost thirty years since Gould passed away. What influence do you feel he's had on the musical world? Or was he too unusual to be an influence?

TP: To overtly imitate Gould is to misunderstand him. Certain things in his playing can be imitated – the detaché sound, the sparing use of the sustaining pedal – but if you hear that kind of Gould clone, you're hearing someone who's misunderstood him completely. The basic message of Glenn Gould is to come up with the most personal vision you can for whatever you're playing. His influence was the idea that you should look deeply into yourself and ask what you want to say about music – and you don't have to accept received wisdom from anyone.

He certainly didn't accept conventional wisdom: he wasn't interested in the idea that Bach led to Haydn who led to Beethoven, and the whole list of "begats." And he didn't try to be well rounded in his repertory. Although he played a lot of Bach, he wasn't a "Bach specialist," the way Rosalyn Tureck was. He believed he could take an interest in any composer he wanted to: he *might* be attracted to anything on the whole historical spectrum of classical music. So he had no problem admiring both Schoenberg and Strauss, two composers who seem to represent opposing values in the twentieth century. But, on the other hand, he felt no need to admire Stravinsky very much.

CE: And what about his predictions for the future of music?

TP: I think he was wrong about the concert dying away, because today concerts are doing better than record companies. But he was right when he predicted that it was through electronic media that people would come to know the repertoire. It's been estimated that the night Birgit Nilsson sang *Elektra* at the Met, in 1981, more people heard that opera than the sum total of everyone who'd heard it since it was composed in 1909. So the effect of electronic media has been huge.

It's a tragedy that Glenn never got to work with the Internet, because he would have loved it. He could have told the executives at Columbia Records to go to hell, and create his own podcasts, just the way he wanted to. He would have been in seventh heaven with the Internet.

Postscript

Knowing, as I did, that Tim Page had been diagnosed with Asperger's syndrome, I didn't quite know what to expect when meeting him. Yet from the moment when he opened the door of his hotel room, I felt I was in the company of a charming, friendly and perfectly normal person.

One of the most interesting things, I think, about Page's comments is the light he sheds on Gould's penchant for contrived "interviews." The idea of scripting an interview, so that the interviewee, and not the interviewer, is in effect driving the conversation – which is hardly a "conversation" at all, in the ordinary sense of the word – is pure Gould.

Page's description of Gould's preferred interview methods led me to revisit Gould's interview with John McClure from 1968, *Glenn Gould: Concert Dropout*. In this dialogue, sound-levels for Gould and McClure are strangely imbalanced, and McClure's questions are delivered in a flat, disconnected tone. This leads me to suspect that as early as 1968 Gould was experimenting with scripted interviews, with the questions and answers recorded in different places.

CE

NOTES

1 For more on the theory that Gould suffered from Asperger's syndrome, see Chapter 2: Timothy Maloney (pp. 76-79).

2 In *Glenn Gould: Concert Dropout*, Gould described the life of a concert pianist as "hideous," adding, "it has no relevance to the contemporary music scene."

3 This film, based on the novel of the same name by Kurt Vonegut, was released by Universal Studios in 1972. For it, Gould devised a soundtrack of excerpts from his Bach recordings.

4 Payzant's 1978 book – the first published about Gould, and the only book about him to appear while he was still alive – is an inquiry into the philosophical underpinnings of Gould's ideas about music and recording.

5 This interview was later republished (with some modifications) under the title "Glenn Gould in Conversation with Tim Page," in the Fall 1981 issue of *Piano Quarterly* magazine, and also in *The Glenn Gould Reader*, (pp. 451-461).

6 On August 8, 1982, while travelling through the town of Salmon Arm, British Columbia, Pierre Elliott Trudeau (then Canada's prime minister) raised his middle finger to a group of striking postal workers. The insulting gesture was Trudeau's response to the strikers' anti-Quebec taunts.

7 According to Gould biographer Kevin Bazzana, Gould's reaction to hearing Terry Riley's minimalist score *In C*, with its seemingly endless repetition of C-major sonorities, was to rhetorically ask, "And you thought Carl Orff had found an easy way to make a living?" Kevin Bazzana, *Wondrous Strange: the Life and Art of Glenn Gould* (Toronto: McClelland & Stewart Ltd., 2003), p. 271.

8 Gould's 1981 album *Haydn: the Six Last Sonatas* (CBS Masterworks M2K 36947) was a 2-LP release containing sonatas Hob. XVI Nos. 42 and 48-52.

9 Page saw Bruno Monsaingeon's 1981 film *Glenn Gould: The Goldberg Variations*.

10 The LP version was released as Columbia BS 15 in 1968.

11 In the interview, Page points out that some of the movements of the 1981 *Goldbergs* were considerably slower than Gould's 1955 recording. For example, the opening "Aria" was 1:51 in 1955 and 3:04 in 1981, and the closing "Da Capo Aria" was 2:07 in 1955 and 3:42 in 1981. For this, Gould jokingly declares Page a "stopwatch freak."

12 Gould maintained a recording studio at the Inn on the Park Hotel. For more information see Chapter 1: Ray Roberts (p. 31).

13 Tim Page, ed., *The Glenn Gould Reader* (Toronto: Lester & Orpen Dennys, 1984), p. 460.

Index

Aitken, Robert, 110 (n. 11)

Ancerl, Karl, 19 (n. 4)

An Anthology of Variation 107

Applebaum, Louis, 54, 58 (n. 6)

Arrau, Claudio, 47

The Art of Glenn Gould, 126

Ashkenazy, Vladmir, 62, 79

Asperger's syndrome, 27, 37, 76-78, 79, 80 (n. 11, 12 and 13), 140, 150, 152 (n. 14), 158, 159 (n. 7), 171, 175

At Home with Glenn Gould, 102-103, 109 (n. 2 and 3)

Bach, Johann Sebastian, xii, 11 (n. 8), 38, 48-49, 52 (n. 7), 62, 64, 69, 105, 106, 134, 151 (n. 7), 155, 168, 173
    Chromatic Fantasia and Fugue, 52 (n.7), 126
    French Suites, 169 (n. 2)
    Goldberg Variations, 7, 11 (n. 8), 21, 27 (n. 1), 43, 45 (n. 17), 64, 99, 108, 139, 151 (n. 8), 174-175
    Italian Concerto, 52 (n.7), 126
    Keyboard Concerto No. 3 in D, 27 (n. 1)
    Musical Offering, 151 (n. 8)
    Sinfonias, 40
    Sonatas for Viola da Gamba and Harpsichord, 68-69, 71 (n. 6)
    Sonatas for Violin and Harpsichord, 66-69, 151 (n. 8)
    St. Matthew Passion, 108, 155
    The Well-Tempered Clavier, 21, 48, 62

Bachauer, Gina, 132

Barber, Samuel
    Knoxville: Summer of 1915, 115

Bazzana, Kevin, 12 (n. 14), 59 (n. 10), 178 (n. 7)

Beatles, xiii, 176

Beckwith, John, 37, 46-52

Beethoven, Ludwig van, xii, 38, 87, 136, 155
    Piano Concerto No. 1, 127
    Piano Concerto No. 4, 3, 51 (n. 2), 169 (n. 1)
    Piano Concerto No. 5, "Emperor", 14, 19 (n. 4), 86, 162
    Sonatas Op. 31, 169 (n. 2)
    Sonata Op. 53, "Waldstein", 132
    Sonata Op. 57, "Appasionata", 132
    Sonata Op. 78, 62
    Sonata Op. 106, "Hammerklavier", 132
    Sonata Op. 109, 42
    Symphony No. 5, 91 (n. 3)

Berg, Alban, 8
    Lulu, 48
    Piano Sonata, 48

Berlin, Boris, 42, 45 (n. 15)

Bernstein, Leonard, 9, 11 (n. 12), 22, 61, 132-133, 141 (n. 10), 166

Böszörményi-Nagy, Béla, 42, 45 (n. 13)

Boyle, Harry, 102

Brahms, Johannes, xii
    Ballades, 22
    Intermezzi, 22, 176
    Piano Concerto No. 1 in D Minor, 9, 12 (n. 12), 22, 41, 44 (n. 7), 61, 65 (n. 3), 132-133, 141 (n. 9 and 10), 165
    Rhapsodies, 22, 173
    Sonatas for Clarinet and Piano, 53

Brendel, Alfred, 62

Brico, Antonia, 90

Brindle, Augustus, xi

Bruckner, Anton, 103
    String Quintet in F Major, 109 (n. 2)

Brussels, 54, 58 (n. 4)

Buffalo, 5, 11 (n. 3), 35 (n. 4), 153

Canadian Broadcasting Corporation (CBC), xi, xiii, 14, 19 (n. 4), 22, 44 (n. 9), 83, 93, 101-104, 111, 118, 135-136

Cassals, Pablo, 64, 110 (n. 8), 119, 125 (n. 5)

CBS: see Columbia Masterworks

Chalmers, Joan, 25

Chalmers, Floyd, 25, 28 (n. 3)

Chickering piano, 1, 13, 128

Chopin, Frédéric, xii, 32, 41, 43, 165
    Ballades, 41

Churchill, Manitoba, 109 (n. 6), 170 (n. 9)

Clark, Petula, 95, 100 (n .5), 118, 124 (n. 1)

Cleveland, 16, 63

Columbia Masterworks (CBS, later Sony Classical), 7, 21, 65 (n. 5), 83, 85-89, 91 (n. 6), 123, 135, 142 (n. 13)

Copenhagen, 8

Copland, Aaron, 134

Cortot, Alfred, xiii

Costakis, George, 149

Craft, Robert, 136

Czerny, Carl, 38

Debussy, Claude, xii, 39
    Claire de Lune, 38

Di Bello, Victor, 72, 75

Dobson, Vera, 35 (n. 5), 108

Dohnányi, Ernö von, 45 (n. 13)

Doyle, Kevin, 175

Dudley, Ray, 39, 44 (n. 3), 46

Dupuis, Albert, 151 (n. 7)

early music movement, xii, 43, 135, 169

Eaton Auditorium, xi, 14, 15-16, 19 (n. 7), 29, 30-31, 67-68, 87, 147, 151 (n. 7)

T. Eaton Co. (department store), 13-15, 17, 19 (n. 5), 20 (n. 10)

Edquist, Verne, 1, 13-20

European Broadcasting Union, 130

Faull, Ellen, 56

Fischer, Bobby, 79

Fleisher, Leon, 28 (n. 5)

focal dystonia, 27, 28 (n. 5)

Forrester, Maureen, 108, 139, 148, 151 (n. 10)

Foss, Cornelia, 9, 12 (n. 13), 32, 104, 122, 137, 143, 153-159, 159 (n. 3), 167

Foss, Lukas, 12 (n. 13), 153, 156-157

Franklin, Barbara, 41, 44 (n. 11)

Frost, Thomas, 85

Fulford, Robert, 48, 52 (n. 5), 143, 144-152

Garland, Judy, 123

Gaylord, Monica, 159

Gibbons, Orlando, xii, 11 (n. 5), 43, 176

Gilels, Emil, 8

Glass, Philip, 173

Glenn Gould: A Portrait, 104

Glenn Gould Estate, vii, 1, 26

A Glenn Gould Fantasy, 111, 113-114

Glenn Gould Foundation, 1, 25-26, 101, 139-140

The Glenn Gould Reader, 171

Glenn Gould Studio, 26, 40

Godden, Reginald, 42, 45 (n. 12)

Goldschmidt, Nicholas ("Nikki"), 25, 50

Gould, Florence ("Flora"), 4, 40-41, 106, 121, 129, 145, 151 (n. 4)

Gould, Glenn (compositions by)
    Five Pieces for Piano, 50, 52 (n. 10)
    So You Want to Write a Fugue?, 50, 52 (n. 12)
    String Quartet, 50, 56

Gould, Russsell Herbert ("Bert"), 3, 31, 35 (n. 5), 40, 106, 107, 129, 146

Greer, Germaine, 95

Greig, Jessie, 121

Grieg, Edvard
    Piano Concerto in A Minor, 133-134

Guerrero, Alberto, 3, 18, 37, 38-39, 46-49, 51 (n. 1 and 3), 52 (n. 7), 101, 129, 134

Hafner, Katie, 20

Hamilton, Stuart, 37, 38-45, 46

Haydn, Franz Joseph, xii, 6, 49, 113, 163, 174, 176
    Piano Sonatas, 178 (n. 8)

Hétu, Jacques, xii

Hindemith, Paul
    Piano Sonatas, 169 (n. 2)

Hofmann, Josef, xiii

Homburger, Walter, 1, 3-12, 21, 49, 52 (n. 9), 80

Horowitz, Vladimir, 63, 65 (n. 5), 68, 88, 91 (n. 6), 164-165

Hume, Paul, 4, 11 (n. 2)

Hupfer, William, 12 (n. 11)

The Idea of North: see *Solitude Triology*

Inn on the Park, 31, 34, 35 (n. 3), 95, 113, 175

International Bach Piano Competition, 52 (n. 14)

Kafka, Franz, 52 (n. 11)

Kallmann, Helmut, 76

Kandinsky, Wassily, 149

Karajan, Herbert von, 34, 123, 167, 170 (n. 10)

Kaufman, Walter, 141 (n. 1)

Kazdin, Andrew, xiv, 16, 17, 65 (n. 5), 68, 83, 85-92, 159 (n. 3)

Kernerman, Morry, 59 (n. 10)

Kilburn, Weldon, 42, 45 (n. 14)

King, William Lyon Mackenzie, 128

Kiwanis Music Festival, 144

Kraglund, John, xiii, 71 (n. 4), 168, 169 (n. 5)

Krips, Josef, 5

Kuerti, Anton, 37, 60-66

Landowska, Wanda, 7, 134-135

Laredo, Jaime, 37, 66-71

The Latecomers: see *Solitude Trilogy*

Leacock, Stephen, x

Leningrad (or St Petersburg), 8, 94, 98, 166

Leroux, Georges, xiv

Lieberson, Goddard, 89, 91 (n. 7), 150

Liszt, Franz, 43, 165, 172

Littler, William, 117 (n. 8), 161, 162-170

Los Angeles, 10, 15, 19 (n. 6), 136, 151 (n. 13), 153, 159 (n. 1)

Mackenzie, William Lyon, 128

MacMillan, Sir Ernest, 42, 102, 148, 151 (n. 10)

Mahler, Gustav, 95, 97, 103

Maloney, Timothy, 37, 72-81, 167

Malvern Collegiate, 144, 146

Marriner, Neville, 34

Marshall, Lois, 41, 44 (n. 9), 46

Massenet, Jules
    Manon, 40

Massey Hall, 42, 51 (n. 2), 102

Mazzoleni, Ettore, 51 (n. 2)

McClure, John, 135, 142 (n. 13), 172, 178

McGreevy, John, 83, 93-100

Mendelssohn, Felix, 151 (n. 7)
    Fingal's Cave (*The Hebrides*), 75

Menuhin, Yehudi, 12 (n. 15)

Mesaros, Helen, 80 (n. 13)

Messiaen, Olivier, 63

Michelangeli, Arturo Benedetti, 19 (n. 4)

Mohr, Franz, 17, 20 (n. 13)

Moiseiwitsch, Benno, xiii

Monsaingeon, Bruno, 178 (n. 9)

Moore, Barbara, 80 (n. 10)

Moscow, 8, 11 (n. 9), 12 (n. 10)

Mozart, Wolfgang Amadeus, xii, 49, 52 (n. 8), 128, 163
    Fantasy in D Minor K. 397, 169 (n. 2)
    Piano Concerto in C Minor, 48
    Piano Sonatas, 169 (n. 2)

Neel, (Louis) Boyd, 54, 58 (n. 3)

New Music Associates, 48, 52 (n. 5), 53, 143, 148, 151 (n. 8)

New York City, xi, 7, 17, 31, 47, 49, 86, 106, 165, 166

Nilsson, Birgit, 177

Oistrakh, David, 8

Oppenheim, David, 7, 11 (n. 7)

Orff, Carl, 178 (n. 7)

Orford Quartet, 110 (n. 11)

Orillia, Ontario, 94

Ostend, 54

Ostwald, Peter, 27, 74, 76-77, 80 (n. 7 and 11), 140, 150, 151 (n. 14), 158, 159

Pacsu, Margaret, 83-84, 111-117

Page, Tim, 161, 171-178

Payzant, Geoffrey, 159 (n. 6)

Pearson, Lester B., 7

Perkins, Faye, vii

Peterson, Oscar, 34

Pincoe, Ruth, 33-34

Posen, Stephen, 1, 21-28

Quiet in the Land: see *Solitude Trilogy*

Rachmaninoff, Sergei, 43

Radigan, Fredd, 112

Reger, Max, 127

Reich, Steve, 173

Richter, Sviatoslav, 8, 11 (n. 9)

Riley, Terry, 173

Roberts, John P.L., 25, 60, 83, 99, 102-103, 106, 108, 126-142, 156, 159 (n. 2)

Roberts, Ray, 1, 24, 29-35, 78, 123, 170 (n. 10)

Rose, Leonard, 55, 59 (n. 8)

Royal Conservatory of Music, xi, 11 (n. 1), 41, 44 (n. 10), 48, 53, 96

Rubinstein, Arthur, 64

Sabiston, Colin, xi

Salvation Army, 24

Sarrazin, Jean, 113

Scarlatti, Domenico, xii

Schabas, Ezra, 37, 53-65

Scheveningen, 54

Schnabel, Artur, 134-135, 141 (n. 11)

Schoenberg, Arnold, xii, 8, 12 (n. 10), 40, 50, 52 (n. 5 and 8), 58 (n. 2), 85, 105, 112, 137, 148, 151 (n. 8), 162, 169 (n. 1), 176
    Ode to Napoleon Op. 41, 41
    Piano Concerto Op. 42, 48, 136
    Sechs kleine Klavierstücke Op. 19, 48
    Suite for Piano Op. 25, 48

Schonberg, Harold C., 11 (n. 8), 41, 44 (n. 8), 165

Schuller, Gunther, 74, 80 (n. 6)

Schwarzkopf, Elisabeth, 12 (n. 15), 71 (n. 7), 100 (n. 5)

Scriabin, Alexander, 62, 88
    Sonatas Nos. 3 and 5, 91 (n. 5)

Shakespeare, William, 131

Shepard, Tom, 66

Shumsky, Oscar, 55, 59 (n. 8)

Sibelius, Jean, 88, 105, 173
    Sonatines Nos. 1, 2 and 3, 91 (n. 4), 105
    Kyllikki Op. 41, 91 (n. 4)

Slaughterhouse Five, 22

Solitude Trilogy, 42
    The Idea of North, 45 (n. 16), 52 (n.6), 64, 94, 110 (n. 8), 120-121
    The Latecomers, 52 (n. 6), 110 (n. 8)
    Quiet in the Land, 52 (n. 6), 110 (n. 8)

Somerville, Janet, 118

Steinway & Sons, 9, 12 (n. 11), 14-17, 106

Steuermann, Edward, 53, 58 (n. 2)

Stokowski, Leopold, 86, 110 (n. 8), 119, 125 (n. 4), 173

Stratford, Ontario, 51 (n. 4), 54-56, 58 (n. 5), 59

Strauss, Richard, xii, 41, 56, 63, 70, 103, 127, 173
    Cello Sonata, 70
    Enoch Arden, 97
    Four Last Songs, 44 (n. 9), 95
    Metamorphosen, 95
    Ophelia-Lieder, 44 (n. 9), 71 (n. 7)
    Vier Lieder Op. 27, 44 (n. 9)
    Violin Sonata, 7

Stravinsky, Igor, 136-137, 142 (n. 15), 176
    Capriccio for Piano and Orchestra, 137

Streisand, Barbara, 95, 175

Sweelinck, Jan Pieterszoon, 6, 11 (n. 5), 43

Szell, George, 63, 117 (n. 8), 166

Toronto Humane Society, 24

Toronto Mendelssohn Choir, 144, 150 (n. 2)

Toronto Symphony Orchestra, xi, 3, 8, 102, 144, 150 (n. 2)

Tovell, Vincent, 83, 101-110

Troup, Malcolm, 4

Trudeau, Pierre Elliott, 173

Tulk, Lorne, 29, 83, 118-125, 156

Tureck, Rosalyn, xii, 7, 134-135

Tuttle, John, 139

University of Toronto, 46, 158, 169 (n. 4)

Uptergrove cottage, 40, 44 (n. 5), 46, 131

Valdepeñas, Joaquin, 72

Vinci, Ernesto, 38, 44 (n. 1)

Wagner, Richard, xii, 68, 87-88, 128
    Die Meistersinger von Nürnberg, 16, 20 (n. 12), 91 (n. 3)
    Götterdämmerung, 20 (n. 12)
    Parsifal, 105
    Siegfried Idyll, 20 (n. 12), 37, 72-75, 80 (n. 7), 91 (n. 3)
    Tristan und Isolde, 128

Walton, William
    Troilus and Cressida, 132

The Wars, 175

Washington, 4

Wawa, Ontario, 166

Webern, Anton, 48, 52 (n. 5), 148
    Saxophone Quartet, 53

Wilde, Oscar, 131

Willis, Stephen, 76

Wilson, Chris, 33-34

Wilson, Frank, 27

Winnipeg, 102

Yamaha piano, 17, 20 (n. 14), 24

ABOUT THE AUTHOR

Colin Eatock is a composer, music critic, author, editor and educator. Born in Hamilton, Canada, in 1958, he has lived in Ontario all his life (except for one year in London, England), and has called the city of Toronto home for the last quarter-century.

Eatock frequently writes about music for Toronto's *Globe and Mail* newspaper, and has also written for the *New York Times* and the *Houston Chronicle*. As well, he has contributed to many periodicals, including *Queen's Quarterly*, the *Literary Review of Canada*, *Opera Canada*, *Opus* and the *WholeNote* in Canada; *American Record Guide*, *Early Music America*, *Listen* and *Strings* in the USA; and *BBC Music*, the *Strad*, *Opera*, *Musical Opinion* and *International Piano* in the UK. His first book, *Mendelssohn and Victorian England*, was published by Ashgate Press in 2009.

As a composer, Eatock has written songs, chamber music, choral works and orchestral compositions. His music has been performed and broadcast in Canada, the USA and the UK, and has been released on the Furiant, Echiquier and Toreador record labels. He is also an associate member of the Canadian Music Centre, where most of his scores are available. A CD wholly devoted to his music, *Colin Eatock: Chamber Music*, is a 2012 release of the Canadian Music Centre's record label, Centrediscs.

Eatock holds a PhD in musicology from the University of Toronto, and has also lectured at the U of T. As well, he holds masters degrees in music composition (U of T) and music criticism (McMaster University), and a bachelor of music degree (University of Western Ontario). Before he became a freelance writer, he worked for ten years within the administration of Toronto's Canadian Opera Company, as an editor, publicist and fundraiser.

A NOTE ON THE TYPE

The book you are reading is set in Laurentian, a typeface designed by Rod McDonald in 2003 for *MacLean's Magazine*. Laurentian was the first text typeface ever commissioned by a Canadian magazine, and its design took reference of the types designed by both Claude Garamond & William Caslon. McDonald blended these two influences together and gave his alphabet a strong vertical stress, high x-height, and narrow proportions to allow the font to function well in tight settings. Lurentian has been used as the text face in *Quill & Quire* and books in the *Champlain Society*.

Printed on Zephyr Antique Laid paper, which was manufactured, acid-free, in Saint-Jérôme, Quebec, from second-growth forests.
This book was designed by Stan Bevington.

A NOTE ON THE IMPRINT

Archives of Canadian Arts, Culture and Heritage is an imprint of Penumbra Press. John Flood is the founder (1979), editor, and publisher.
www.penumbrapress.com

Remembering Glenn Gould: Twenty Interviews With People Who Knew Him
First Edition / First Printing 2012

Penumbra Press
Archives of Canadian Arts, Culture and Heritage
The logos are designs by Carl Schaefer.